DUBLINERS

By James Joyce

With a Guide to the Craft of Fiction for Readers and Writers

By Nicholas Leither

Illustrated by Dede Leither

Copyright © 2012 by Heteroclite

All rights reserved. No part of this book may be reproduced in any form without the permission of the publisher and author.

ISBN-13:   978-0615679877 (Heteroclite)

ISBN-10:   0615679870

For more information:
www.NicholasLeither.com

SHORT CONTENTS

ABOUT THIS BOOK	10
THE SISTERS	18
CRAFT: THE SISTERS	27
AN ENCOUNTER	37
CRAFT: AN ENCOUNTER	47
ARABY	59
CRAFT: ARABY	67
EVELINE	71
CRAFT: EVELINE	77
AFTER THE RACE	83
CRAFT: AFTER THE RACE	90
TWO GALLANTS	94
CRAFT: TWO GALLANTS	105
THE BOARDING HOUSE	109
CRAFT: THE BOARDING HOUSE	117
A LITTLE CLOUD	123
CRAFT: A LITTLE CLOUD	137
COUNTERPARTS	143
CRAFT: COUNTERPARTS	155
CLAY	160
CRAFT: CLAY	167
A PAINFUL CASE	171
CRAFT: A PAINFUL CASE	181
IVY DAY IN THE COMMITTEE ROOM	187
CRAFT: IVY DAY IN THE COMMITTEE ROOM	205
A MOTHER	210
CRAFT: A MOTHER	222
GRACE	227
CRAFT: GRACE	249
THE DEAD	257
CRAFT: THE DEAD	298

LONG CONTENTS

ABOUT THIS BOOK — 10
   How to Read this Book — 11
   Why *Dubliners*? — 13
   What is Craft? — 13
   The Authors and the Illustrator — 15

THE SISTERS — 18
  CRAFT: THE SISTERS — 27
   Premise or *Donnée* — 27
      Theme, Contract
   Idea — 29
   Point of View — 31
      Narrative Mode
   Symbolism — 34
   Synthesis — 35

AN ENCOUNTER — 37
  CRAFT: AN ENCOUNTER — 47
   The Joycean Gnomon — 47
   Pun — 48
   Protagonist and Antagonist — 49
      Goal
   Story versus Plot — 50
      Action
   Narrative Structure — 52
      Setup, Conflict, Resolution, Exposition, Climax, Denouement, Tension
   Narrative Structure, Sequence, Story, and Plot — 54
   Foreshadowing — 56
      Dramatic Irony

ARABY — 59
  CRAFT: ARABY — 67
   Image and Imagery — 67
   Personification — 68
   Sentence Length — 68
      Dynamic, Static

EVELINE — 71
CRAFT: EVELINE — 77
- **Verbal Irony: Character Names** — 77
  - Pun
- **Close Third Person & Point of View Inflection** — 78
  - Limited Third Person, Omniscient Third Person, Subjective and Objective Third Person
- **Choice and Discourse** — 80

AFTER THE RACE — 83
CRAFT: AFTER THE RACE — 90
- **Trope: Metaphor and Simile** — 90
  - Chiasmus
- **Show versus Tell** — 92
  - Exposition

TWO GALLANTS — 94
CRAFT: TWO GALLANTS — 105
- **Foil and Epiphany** — 105
  - Protagonists and Antagonists
- **Idiom** — 107

THE BOARDING HOUSE — 109
CRAFT: THE BOARDING HOUSE — 117
- **Narrative Mode: Omniscience** — 117
  - Point of View, Narrative Structure, Premise, Discourse, Backstory
- **Rhetorical Motif** — 119
- **Details** — 120
  - Idea, Premise, Contract, Narrative Structure, Symbolism, Gnomon

A LITTLE CLOUD — 123
CRAFT: A LITTLE CLOUD — 137
- **Setting** — 137
- **Dialogue: Do and Undo** — 138
  - Epiphany, Show, Tell
- **Motif** — 140
  - Symbolism

COUNTERPARTS — 143
  CRAFT: COUNTERPARTS — 155
    Increasing Action, Tension, and Conflict — 155
      Climax
    Character versus Type — 156
      Details
    Character in Conflict with Setting — 157
      Protagonist and Antagonist, Tension

CLAY — 160
  CRAFT: CLAY — 167
    Tone: Dramatic Irony — 167
      Point of View Inflection, Action, Objectivity and Subjectivity, Foreshadowing

A PAINFUL CASE — 171
  CRAFT: A PAINFUL CASE — 181
    Metafiction — 181
      Distance, Trope
    Verisimilitude — 182
      Suspension of Disbelief, Details, Jargon
    Epiphany and Peripeteia — 184
      Point of View Inflection, Narrative Structure

IVY DAY IN THE COMMITTEE ROOM — 187
  CRAFT: IVY DAY IN THE COMMITTEE ROOM — 205
    The Objective Correlative — 205
      Peripeteia, Epiphany, Symbolism, Foreshadowing
    Allusion or Reference — 207

A MOTHER — 210
  CRAFT: A MOTHER — 222
    Satire — 222
      Caricature
    Dynamic versus Static & Round versus Flat — 225
      Exposition, Tension, Crisis

GRACE — 227
CRAFT: GRACE — 249
Parody versus Allegory — 249
Plot, Narrative Structure, Pathos, Objective Correlative, Tension, Irony
Understatement — 251
Sentimentality, Verbal Irony
Chiasmus — 252
Image and Imagery, Symbolism, Trope

THE DEAD — 257
CRAFT: THE DEAD — 298
Reading as a Writer and Writing as a Reader — 298
Characterization — 299
Telling, Showing, Observation, Exposition, Backstory, Inner Thoughts, Appearance, Action, Dialogue

ENDNOTE: Transcendence — 314

Bibliography — 315

Indexed Glossary — 317

Acknowledgements — 328

About this Book

When I was a carpenter in northern Minnesota, building cabins in the woods and on lakeshores, my boss would often complain about the blueprints from architects who had never picked up a hammer. "This is horseshit!" he said on one occasion, with clenched fists and a wrinkled brow. The blueprint in front of us was an idea—an incredible idea and a beautiful drawing—but it wasn't a house. "The foundation will crack and the roof will sag with one heavy snow," he told me. It was also full of outright mistakes—  things that looked possible on paper, but didn't translate to wood and nails. When we built that house, our crew had to exhaustively adapt and re-craft that drawing in order to make the house a reality.

Two months later, my boss unrolled a blueprint by an architect who had once been a builder, and a wave of delight washed over his face. "Yes," he said, his eyes darting from line to line. "Look at this, will you? Just take a goddamn look at this." That drawing had what my boss called "craft."

Often, when we're referring to writing, the word craft is a concept only writers seem concerned about. In English literature classes, the word craft rarely slips out of a student's mouth. In fact, many regard it as either hokey ("This is art!") or beyond their grasp because they are not writers. Just the idea of James Joyce's craft can intimidate those who know of his lofty literary reputation.

But readers *are* writers, even if all they write are emails. Unlike so many art forms out there, all of us can understand the craft of writing in a real and intimate way. Understanding the craft of painting or filmmaking or sculpture is more difficult because most of us don't paint, sculpt or make films every day. But all those master writers, they sat down and struggled to express themselves like all of us do—struggled to punctuate, to structure, to create ideas, and imbue their writing with a sense of deeper meaning. One of the biggest mistakes that readers make is to ignore the writer's craft or mistakenly believe that a writer like James Joyce, for example, was up to something entirely different when he penned his stories.

One of my colleagues who teaches architecture in San Francisco told me that he almost never brings in an architect's drawing when his students first study one of the city's buildings. He takes them to the building. He lets them walk around inside. He encourages them to look at it from a distance, from above, from the side. He asks them to get a sense of the building's dimension—to make measurements and draw their own plans. After they understand the experience of that building, engage in the crafting of it, then he shows them the architect's drawings.

That is what I hope you will be able to do here: Walk around, explore, and enjoy each of these stories before we discuss the crafting of them. Like those architecture students trained in the skills necessary to understand design, we can all understand and identify with the craft of writing whether we call ourselves writers or not. What critical readers and creative writers all want, of course, is often the same thing. We want to understand why, when we read stories like these from a master craftsman, our eyes dart from line to line and we say, "Look at this, will you? Just take a goddamn look at this."

How to Read this Book

As an **edition of James Joyce's *Dubliners*,** this contains all the stories in the intended order with brief annotations that define primarily outdated language. I have arranged this book with great care, observation, scholarship, and integrity to the ideas in the fiction. While I did insert quotation marks around dialogue where Joyce originally used dashes, I have kept all spellings and punctuation unchanged (for example, *Mr.* and *Mrs.* appear *Mr* and *Mrs*).

About this Book

As a **guide to the craft of fiction**, this edition leads readers through Joyce's fifteen stories, defining and exemplifying the fundamental techniques of the fiction writer's craft.

For readers this text illuminates the core elements that go into crafting fiction, and presents a text that has inspired a plethora of writers ever since its publication. It is the starting point for literary interpretation and criticism, and will, I hope, give readers a better idea of what goes into "building" a narrative.

For writers this text unpacks the literary craft Joyce employed to create *Dubliners,* and will aid in examining fictional texts and creating and assessing their own writing.

At the end of every story, readers will find explanations of several carefully chosen craft elements. By no means should readers understand this as a complete craft analysis of each story. Instead, over the course of all fifteen stories, I have defined and offered examples for the fundamental craft principles of fiction. These principles, for the most part, progress from basic to more complex, choosing elements like point of view and symbolism in early stories and chiasmus, verisimilitude and point of view inflection in later stories.

Following the analyses, several **discussion questions** build off the defined craft principles for further thought, investigation, and discussion. Therefore, this analysis starts the conversation about craft; it doesn't end it. It is meant to focus the microscope in an attempt to invite readers and writers to explore further.

The back pages of this book contain an **indexed glossary** that define all the craft terms I cover in this book and direct readers to the pages in which I discuss those craft elements. Craft terms that appear in bold can be found in the glossary.

Why *Dubliners*?

The first time I read the definition of the word "metaphor" I had no idea what it was until I saw an actual example. Then I was like, "Oh yeah. Those!" When I work through literary theory or philosophy without examples, I'm easily lost and often skeptical. I love examples, and I love them because they demonstrate and support ideas.

Because the examples about craft in this book come from the same source, I hope that readers will start to see the larger architecture of craft—see how one writer uses many of these craft techniques to build an aesthetic. What's the use of understanding a bunch of craft principles without seeing the way writers synthesize those craft elements to form a cohesive whole?

James S. Atherton, in his essay "The Joyce of *Dubliners*," writes that Joyce's stories "owe much of their strength and interest to the variety of techniques employed by them."[1] This variety makes *Dubliners* an ideal text to investigate under the lens of craft. It has both individual stories and an overarching cohesiveness, much like a novel, in which we can begin to synthesize those craft techniques.

What is Craft?

My favorite definition of craft is of the verb form: **to make by hand**. To me, that says it all, because it focuses on the process, the "making" of a narrative rather than the attempt to interpret its meaning or appraise its aesthetic value. The fiction writer's craft defines the skills and techniques a writer uses to "make" a narrative.

If you walk into a museum, look at a sculpture, and interpret its glossy patina as

---

[1] Thomas F. Staley, ed., *James Joyce Today: Essays on the Major Works* (Bloomington and London: Indiana University Press, 1966), 41.

suggestive of expensive jewelry and therefore a fine piece of art, you're not making an observation about craft, but an interpretation and evaluation of its aesthetic worth. However, if you analyze how the sculptor went about creating that patina—the brushes he used and the way he polished the surface with steel wool—you're analyzing craft. Likewise, when we discuss the psychoanalytical interpretation of Gabriel's self-doubt and sexual paralysis in Joyce's story "The Dead," we're not analyzing craft. However, when we discuss how Joyce either explicitly or implicitly created Gabriel's self-doubt, we are analyzing craft. If we see Joyce's blending of symbolism and realism through the lens of a Modernist collision of genre and aesthetics, we're not analyzing craft. If we investigate how Joyce believably inserted symbolism into a realistic narrative, we're analyzing craft.

That is not to say that when we're investigating craft we completely disregard any interpretation of the meanings or ideas in the narratives—both of which are a part of making a narrative. We cannot, for example, discuss the construction of a symbol in fiction if we don't first agree that it has meaning and suggest what the meaning might be.

In the very beginning of his book, *The Art of Fiction*, John Gardner writes, "What the beginning writer ordinarily wants is a set of rules on what to do and what not to do in writing fiction."[2] In my experience the exact opposite is true. When I teach writing, the one thing that can really raise the hackles of some of my students is the suggestion that there are rules to creating successful stories. Even worse are discussions about narrative structure or "formula." You can practically see little bombs exploding in corners of their souls when anyone speaks the words "rule" or "formula." For many—especially beginning writers—art doesn't have any rules or

---

[2] John Gardner, *The Art of Fiction: Notes on Craft for Young Writers* (New York: Alfred A. Knopf, 1984), 3.

formulas! Art is abstract and all about ideas and freedom and raw expression!

Nevertheless, if you were to give two writers the same idea for a story—the same setting, characters, and set of conflicts—one might craft an incredible piece of art out of that idea, inventing an effective plot and creating round and dynamic characters with evocative and beautiful prose. The other writer might craft something without details, without structure, without believable characters or descriptions or readable sentences. Simply put, ideas are easy. Even good ones. If you're a writer you know this because every person you know tells you constantly what you should be writing about. "I had an idea for a story" or "She should be a character in your novel!" While those ideas may be fabulous, they are only a small part of creating a piece of art. It's the crafting of those ideas that separate the amateurs from the masters.

Craft takes practice and investigation, and this book will help writers do both. For readers I hope this will liberate them. At readings, audience members seem to always ask writers: "How did you come up with the idea?" The audience members seem mystified, as though ideas alone are what separate published writers from unpublished writers. But everyone has ideas, and many of them are wonderful. Craft is what got those writers into print and behind those podiums. What they really should be asking writers is "How did you make this?"

The Authors and the Illustrator

James Joyce
Author

Born in 1882, James Joyce's parents raised him in a large family in Dublin, Ireland. After graduating from the University College Dublin (1903), Joyce travelled to Paris to study to be a doctor, but quickly became uninterested in the study of medicine and moved back to Ireland.

In 1904, he tried unsuccessfully to publish an early version of *A Portrait of the Artist as a Young Man*. In 1905 he sent an early version of *Dubliners* to a publisher named Grant Richards that started a long, nine-year struggle to get the book published. It faced harsh criticism from editors, censorship, accusations of libel, ridiculous revision requests, and many changes before its publication in 1914. In fact, James Joyce didn't even start writing what is now known as the collection's most successful story, "The Dead" until 1907, after he had moved away from Ireland to Rome and then Trieste.

James Joyce is best known for his novels *A Portrait of the Artist as a Young Man*, *Ulysses*, and *Finnegan's Wake*. He died in Zurich in 1941.

Nicholas Leither
Author and Editor

I have had a long history of experiences with James Joyce's *Dubliners*. I first read many of the stories in high school. I then read *Dubliners* as a struggling and anxious writer in a craft class in graduate school. Later, I taught many of the stories in *Dubliners* to my own students. Because I have read this book under a number of different concave and convex lenses, I have developed a versatile and nuanced appreciation of Joyce as a narrative craftsman that I hope to bring to readers and writers alike.

More information at:
www.NicholasLeither.com

Dede Leither
Illustrator

I came to oil painting in my mid-forties after an eclectic career as a teacher, floral designer, museum docent, antique dealer and my magnum opus: mother. Using a tablet computer as my medium, the intriguing challenge of the *Dubliners* project was to condense complex concepts, elaborate storylines, and a celebrated author into quickly-read single images.

More information at:
www.DedeLeither.com

The Sisters

There was no hope for him this time: it was the third stroke. Night after night I had passed the house (it was vacation time) and studied the lighted square of window: and night after night I had found it lighted in the same way, faintly and evenly. If he was dead, I thought, I would see the reflection of candles on the darkened blind for I knew that two candles must be set at the head of a corpse. He had often said to me: "I am not long for this world," and I had thought his words idle. Now I knew they were true. Every night as I gazed up at the window I said softly to myself the word *paralysis*. It had always sounded strangely in my ears, like the word *gnomon* in the Euclid and the word *simony* in the Catechism. But now it sounded to me like the name of some maleficent and sinful being. It filled me with fear, and yet I longed to be nearer to it and to look upon its deadly work.

Old Cotter was sitting at the fire, smoking, when I came downstairs to supper. While my aunt was ladling out my stirabout[1] he said, as if returning to some former remark of his:

"No, I wouldn't say he was exactly... but there was something queer... there was something uncanny about him. I'll tell you my opinion..."

He began to puff at his pipe, no doubt arranging his opinion in his mind. Tiresome old fool! When we knew him first he used to be rather interesting, talking of faints and worms;[2] but I soon grew tired of him and his endless stories about the distillery.

"I have my own theory about it," he said. "I think it was one of those... peculiar cases... But it's hard to say..."

He began to puff again at his pipe without giving us his theory. My uncle saw me staring and said to me:

"Well, so your old friend is gone, you'll be sorry to hear."

"Who?" said I.

"Father Flynn."

"Is he dead?"

---

[1] Porridge
[2] "Faints" are impurities and "worms" are the worm-shaped pipes of a distillery.

"Mr Cotter here has just told us. He was passing by the house."

I knew that I was under observation so I continued eating as if the news had not interested me. My uncle explained to old Cotter.

"The youngster and he were great friends. The old chap taught him a great deal, mind you; and they say he had a great wish for him."

"God have mercy on his soul," said my aunt piously.

Old Cotter looked at me for a while. I felt that his little beady black eyes were examining me but I would not satisfy him by looking up from my plate. He returned to his pipe and finally spat rudely into the grate.

"I wouldn't like children of mine," he said, "to have too much to say to a man like that."

"How do you mean, Mr Cotter?" asked my aunt.

"What I mean is," said old Cotter, "it's bad for children. My idea is: let a young lad run about and play with young lads of his own age and not be... Am I right, Jack?"

"That's my principle, too," said my uncle. "Let him learn to box his corner. That's what I'm always saying to that Rosicrucian there: take exercise. Why, when I was a nipper every morning of my life I had a cold bath, winter and summer. And that's what stands to me now. Education is all very fine and large... Mr Cotter might take a pick of that leg of mutton," he added to my aunt.

"No, no, not for me," said old Cotter.

My aunt brought the dish from the safe and put it on the table.

"But why do you think it's not good for children, Mr Cotter?" she asked.

"It's bad for children," said old Cotter, "because their minds are so impressionable. When children see things like that, you know, it has an effect..."

I crammed my mouth with stirabout for fear I might give utterance to my anger. Tiresome old red-nosed imbecile!

It was late when I fell asleep. Though I was angry with old Cotter for alluding to me as a child, I puzzled my head to extract meaning from his unfinished sentences. In the dark of my room I imagined that I saw again the heavy grey face of the paralytic. I drew the blankets over my head and tried to think of Christmas. But the grey face still followed me. It murmured, and I understood that it desired to confess something. I felt my soul receding into some pleasant and vicious region; and there again I found it waiting for me. It began to confess to me in a murmuring voice and I wondered why it smiled continually and why the lips were so moist with spittle. But then I remembered that it had died of paralysis and I felt that I too was smiling feebly as if to absolve the simoniac of his sin.

    The next morning after breakfast I went down to look at the little house in Great Britain Street. It was an unassuming shop, registered under the vague name of *Drapery*. The *Drapery* consisted mainly of children's bootees and umbrellas; and on ordinary days a notice used to hang in the window, saying: *Umbrellas Re-covered*. No notice was visible now for the shutters were up. A crape bouquet was tied to the doorknocker with ribbon. Two poor women and a telegram boy were reading the card pinned on the crape. I also approached and read:

July 1st, 1895
The Rev. James Flynn (formerly of S. Catherine's Church,
Meath Street), aged sixty-five years.
R. I. P.

    The reading of the card persuaded me that he was dead and I was disturbed to find myself at check. Had he not been dead I would have gone into the little dark room behind the shop to find him sitting in his arm-chair by the fire, nearly smothered in his great-coat. Perhaps my aunt would have given me a packet of High Toast[3] for him and this present would have roused him from his stupefied doze. It was always I who emptied the packet into his black snuff-box for his hands trembled too much to allow him to do this without spilling half the snuff about the floor. Even as he raised his large trembling hand to his nose little clouds of smoke dribbled through his fingers over the front of his coat. It may have been these constant showers of snuff which gave his ancient priestly garments their green faded look for the red handkerchief, blackened, as it always was, with the snuff-stains of a week, with which he tried to brush away the fallen grains, was quite inefficacious.

    I wished to go in and look at him but I had not the courage to knock. I walked away slowly along the sunny side of the street,

---

[3] Snuff brand.

reading all the theatrical advertisements in the shop-windows as I went. I found it strange that neither I nor the day seemed in a mourning mood and I felt even annoyed at discovering in myself a sensation of freedom as if I had been freed from something by his death. I wondered at this for, as my uncle had said the night before, he had taught me a great deal. He had studied in the Irish college in Rome and he had taught me to pronounce Latin properly. He had told me stories about the catacombs and about Napoleon Bonaparte, and he had explained to me the meaning of the different ceremonies of the Mass and of the different vestments worn by the priest. Sometimes he had amused himself by putting difficult questions to me, asking me what one should do in certain circumstances or whether such and such sins were mortal or venial or only imperfections. His questions showed me how complex and mysterious were certain institutions of the Church which I had always regarded as the simplest acts. The duties of the priest towards the Eucharist and towards the secrecy of the confessional seemed so grave to me that I wondered how anybody had ever found in himself the courage to undertake them; and I was not surprised when he told me that the fathers of the Church had written books as thick as the *Post Office Directory* and as closely printed as the law notices in the newspaper, elucidating all these intricate questions. Often when I thought of this I could make no answer or only a very foolish and halting one upon which he used to smile and nod his head twice or thrice. Sometimes he used to put me through the responses of the Mass which he had made me learn by heart; and, as I pattered, he used to smile pensively and nod his head, now and then pushing huge pinches of snuff up each nostril alternately. When he smiled he used to uncover his big discoloured teeth and let his tongue lie upon his lower lip—a habit which had made me feel uneasy in the beginning of our acquaintance before I knew him well.

As I walked along in the sun I remembered old Cotter's words and tried to remember what had happened afterwards in the dream. I remembered that I had noticed long velvet curtains and a swinging lamp of antique fashion. I felt that I had been very far away, in some land where the customs were strange—in Persia, I thought... But I could not remember the end of the dream.

In the evening my aunt took me with her to visit the house of mourning. It was after sunset; but the window-panes of the houses that looked to the west reflected the tawny gold of a great bank of clouds. Nannie received us in the hall; and, as it would have been unseemly to have shouted at her, my aunt shook hands with her for all. The old woman pointed upwards interrogatively and, on my aunt's nodding, proceeded to toil up the narrow staircase before us, her bowed head being scarcely above the level of the banister-rail. At the first landing she stopped and beckoned us forward encouragingly towards the open door of the dead-room. My aunt went in and the old woman, seeing that I hesitated to enter, began to beckon to me again repeatedly with her hand.

I went in on tiptoe. The room through the lace end of the blind was suffused with dusky golden light amid which the candles looked like pale thin flames. He had been coffined. Nannie gave the lead and we three knelt down at the foot of the bed. I pretended to pray but I could not gather my thoughts because the old woman's mutterings distracted me. I noticed how clumsily her skirt was hooked at the back and how the heels of her cloth boots were trodden down all to one side. The fancy came to me that the old priest was smiling as he lay there in his coffin.

But no. When we rose and went up to the head of the bed I saw that he was not smiling. There he lay, solemn and copious, vested as for the altar, his large hands loosely retaining a chalice. His face was very truculent, grey and massive, with black cavernous nostrils and circled by a scanty white fur. There was a heavy odour in the room—the flowers.

We crossed ourselves and came away. In the little room downstairs we found Eliza seated in his arm-chair in state. I groped my way towards my usual chair in the corner while Nannie went to the sideboard and brought out a decanter of sherry and some wine-glasses. She set these on the table and invited us to take a little glass of wine. Then, at her sister's bidding, she filled out the sherry into the glasses and passed them to us. She pressed me to take some cream crackers also but I declined because I thought I would make too much noise eating them. She seemed to be somewhat disappointed at my refusal and went over quietly to the sofa where she sat down behind her sister. No one spoke: we all gazed at the empty fireplace.

My aunt waited until Eliza sighed and then said:

"Ah, well, he's gone to a better world."

Eliza sighed again and bowed her head in assent. My aunt fingered the stem of her wine-glass before sipping a little.

"Did he… peacefully?" she asked.

"Oh, quite peacefully, ma'am," said Eliza. "You couldn't tell when the breath went out of him. He had a beautiful death, God be praised."

"And everything...?"

"Father O'Rourke was in with him a Tuesday and anointed him and prepared him and all."

"He knew then?"

"He was quite resigned."

"He looks quite resigned," said my aunt.

"That's what the woman we had in to wash him said. She said he just looked as if he was asleep, he looked that peaceful and resigned. No one would think he'd make such a beautiful corpse."

"Yes, indeed," said my aunt.

She sipped a little more from her glass and said:

"Well, Miss Flynn, at any rate it must be a great comfort for you to know that you did all you could for him. You were both very kind to him, I must say."

Eliza smoothed her dress over her knees.

"Ah, poor James!" she said. "God knows we done all we could, as poor as we are—we wouldn't see him want anything while he was in it."

Nannie had leaned her head against the sofa-pillow and seemed about to fall asleep.

"There's poor Nannie," said Eliza, looking at her, "she's wore out. All the work we had, she and me, getting in the woman to wash him and then laying him out and then the coffin and then arranging about the Mass in the chapel. Only for Father O'Rourke I don't know what we'd done at all. It was him brought us all them flowers and them two candlesticks out of the chapel and wrote out the notice for the *Freeman's General*[4] and took charge of all the papers for the cemetery and poor James's insurance."

"Wasn't that good of him?" said my aunt.

Eliza closed her eyes and shook her head slowly.

"Ah, there's no friends like the old friends," she said, "when all is said and done, no friends that a body can trust."

"Indeed, that's true," said my aunt. "And I'm sure now that he's gone to his eternal reward he won't forget you and all your kindness to him."

---

[4] Malapropism. Eliza's mistake is calling *Freeman's Journal* "*Freeman's General.*"

"Ah, poor James!" said Eliza. "He was no great trouble to us. You wouldn't hear him in the house any more than now. Still, I know he's gone and all to that…"

"It's when it's all over that you'll miss him," said my aunt.

"I know that," said Eliza. "I won't be bringing him in his cup of beef-tea any more, nor you, ma'am, sending him his snuff. Ah, poor James!"

She stopped, as if she were communing with the past and then said shrewdly:

"Mind you, I noticed there was something queer coming over him latterly. Whenever I'd bring in his soup to him there I'd find him with his breviary fallen to the floor, lying back in the chair and his mouth open."

She laid a finger against her nose and frowned: then she continued:

"But still and all he kept on saying that before the summer was over he'd go out for a drive one fine day just to see the old house again where we were all born down in Irishtown and take me and Nannie with him. If we could only get one of them new-fangled carriages that makes no noise that Father O'Rourke told him about, them with the rheumatic wheels,[5] for the day cheap—he said, at Johnny Rush's over the way there and drive out the three of us together of a Sunday evening. He had his mind set on that… Poor James!"

"The Lord have mercy on his soul!" said my aunt.

Eliza took out her handkerchief and wiped her eyes with it. Then she put it back again in her pocket and gazed into the empty grate for some time without speaking.

"He was too scrupulous always," she said. "The duties of the priesthood was too much for him. And then his life was, you might say, crossed."

"Yes," said my aunt. "He was a disappointed man. You could see that."

A silence took possession of the little room and, under cover of it, I approached the table and tasted my sherry and then returned quietly to my chair in the corner. Eliza seemed to have fallen into a deep revery. We waited respectfully for her to break the silence: and after a long pause she said slowly:

---

[5] Malapropism. She means pneumatic wheels.

"It was that chalice he broke... That was the beginning of it. Of course, they say it was all right, that it contained nothing, I mean. But still... They say it was the boy's[6] fault. But poor James was so nervous, God be merciful to him!"

"And was that it?" said my aunt. "I heard something..."

Eliza nodded.

"That affected his mind," she said. "After that he began to mope by himself, talking to no one and wandering about by himself. So one night he was wanted for to go on a call and they couldn't find him anywhere. They looked high up and low down; and still they couldn't see a sight of him anywhere. So then the clerk suggested to try the chapel. So then they got the keys and opened the chapel and the clerk and Father O'Rourke and another priest that was there brought in a light for to look for him... And what do you think but there he was, sitting up by himself in the dark in his confession-box, wide-awake and laughing-like softly to himself?"

She stopped suddenly as if to listen. I too listened; but there was no sound in the house: and I knew that the old priest was lying still in his coffin as we had seen him, solemn and truculent in death, an idle chalice on his breast.

Eliza resumed:

"Wide-awake and laughing-like to himself... So then, of course, when they saw that, that made them think that there was something gone wrong with him..."

---

[6] Meaning altar boy.

CRAFT: THE SISTERS

Premise or *Donnée*
With a Note about "Theme"

Every time a student says something like, "Joyce creates a theme of isolation in *Dubliners*," I always ask the same question: "What do you mean?" Some of them can answer it very well. They might tell me about his symbolic use of islands, the rhetorical motif of the word "prisoner," or the fact that many of his characters—from the narrator of "The Sisters" to Gabriel in "The Dead"—spend much of their time separated from those who surround them, reflecting about themselves. Other students, however, glaze over because they're not sure what exactly they mean by the word "theme." They have a sense that Joyce puts some emphasis and meaning on isolation, but they use the word to dodge the details, either because they don't want to do the work or haven't learned how to unpack a narrative and articulate the elements of craft.

While many writers and readers use the word **"theme"** as a blanket term in conversations about fiction, its definition is so vague that, when speaking of the specifics of narrative, more precise terms like "idea," "symbol," "motif," "objective correlative," and "premise" more accurately describe elements of the writer's craft. Some define a theme as a topic for discourse. Others define it as the core subject of a work of art. Others say it is an implicit idea in a piece of fiction. And yet others define it as the moral or message of a story. While those are all fine definitions and ideas, we have far more precise and indicative terms to categorize topic, subject, message, and implicit ideas in fiction that pinpoint and illuminate craft rather than obscure it.

Because we are attempting to refine our understanding and language of craft, I will avoid using the word theme. This serves as an invitation to all readers to leave "theme" behind and replace it with more precise craft vocabulary.

We will start refining our vocabulary with a craft element often confused with theme. Henry James used the word **donnée** (something given) to indicate the central premise of a literary work.[1] The **premise** is the proposition or **"contract"** that each writer establishes in a fictional work. That premise often appears as **exposition** in the beginning or the **setup** of the story. While some use the word to suggest broader categorizations like *coming of age story* or *love story* or *detective's fiction*, a more detailed explanation of a story's premise allows us to question whether or not the writer remains true to it or takes full advantage of it—whether he or she fulfills his or her "contract."

The opening paragraph of "The Sisters" begins to set up the story's **premise**: "There was no hope for him this time ... Every night as I gazed up at the window I said softly to myself the word *paralysis*." That word, he admits, "filled me with fear, and yet I longed to be nearer to it and to look upon its deadly work."

After we learn that Father Flynn has indeed died, we know that the **premise** of "The Sisters" goes something like this: *A boy in a religious Irish family struggles with the emotional paralysis caused by the death of a priest with whom he had a personal relationship.* The narrator's sudden anger at Old Cotter—"Tiresome old red-nosed imbecile!"— the ellipses in narration, and the unresolved ending all indicate emotional turmoil, tension, and paralysis that fulfill the contract Joyce created with his premise.

Some readers may think it absurd that anyone would call the premise of this story a "theme," but imagine someone saying it this way: "The boy's emotional paralysis is a major theme here." To an untrained ear, that sounds pretty good. But what does it mean? By calling it a "major theme" all this person is saying is that the emotional paralysis is somehow important. He's not telling us how or why. He's not telling us how it operates. By calling it the premise, however, we establish that the writer has proposed the subject matter of the

---

[1] Edgar Roberts and Henry Jacobs, *Literature: An Introduction to Reading and Writing*, 2nd ed. (New Jersey: Prentice Hall, 2003), 60.

narrative and can analyze the contract he has made with the reader. Unlike many short narratives, there is no concrete **goal** in this story that forms the premise. This character is not out to win a fight or get a girl or find his long-lost mother. The premise here is far more recondite, and by unpacking it carefully we can easily examine the ways in which Joyce has constructed it.

Whether we are reading a story or writing a story, we can ask ourselves: What story is this writer setting out to tell? It seems like such a simple question, but if the answer is different at the end of the story than it was at the beginning, there's often a problem. A narrative that does not tell the story set up by its premise often leaves readers feeling as though the writer has misled them.

Idea

While a **premise** indicates the central proposition of the narrative, an **idea** deals with the abstract and often implicit concept that inspires it. In "The Sisters" we can differentiate the idea from premise this way:

> The **premise**: A boy in a religious Irish family struggles with the emotional paralysis caused by the death of a priest with whom he had a personal relationship.

> The **idea**: Characters in various states of emotional, vocational, and ideological paralysis.

The paralysis that defines the idea reaches deeply into the lives and actions of all the characters in this story. The paralysis that defines the premise focuses on the narrator's emotional grief, and his inability to accurately express his feelings. The premise of this character's paralysis confines itself, by contract, to *this* story and its **protagonist**. The more abstract idea of paralysis, however, will be an important concept that appears implicitly throughout many, if not all, of the stories in *Dubliners*.

Most readers will, by now, see the trappings of "theme"—which is often used indiscriminately to describe both concrete and abstract ideas in fiction. While the word "idea" may seem like an equally broad term, we often use it to differentiate from premise.

If you've ever read a novel or a short story and are left wondering, "What exactly was that all about?" it usually means the narrative lacks a core idea. It may have been entertaining or even well-written, but when you reach the end you're left feeling as though something was missing. Likewise, if you've ever read a story and felt, "Yes, I get it already!" or "Enough, enough!" it usually means that the idea of the narrative has become more important than the plot or characters. It's easy to imagine ways in which the idea of paralysis could become either lost too deeply in the narrative or forced too hard down the reader's throat. A story about a man injured in a car accident, overcome with indecision about his future, unable to find a job, severely claustrophobic, and jailed for a crime he did not commit may be pushing the idea of paralysis a bit too far. A story about a man injured in a car accident on the other hand could easily fall short on connecting with the idea of paralysis if the writer does not find other ways to indicate or explore that idea.

However, this does not suggest that narrative events are the only way in which writers communicate an idea. Characters, objects, word choice, tone, symbolism can all communicate one or many abstract ideas.

I know that many readers dearly love the novel *Catcher in the Rye*, by J.D. Salinger, and I too find the novel humorous, full of interesting details and observations, and crackling with dynamic dialogue. Many of the novel's moments are wonderful, and Holden Caulfield's character exemplifies teenage angst. But *Catcher in the Rye* lacks an idea. Even its title, though it sounds heady and profound, leads us to a dead end. While the book does have "ideas" (teenage angst, urban anonymity, sexual discovery, class), the novel lacks an abstract and implicit idea that inspires it.

This does not mean that *Catcher in the Rye* is a bad book. Simple evaluations are not part of our conversation here about craft. It means that *Catcher the Rye*, while very entertaining, fails to capture what James Joyce did in *Portrait of the Artist as a Young Man*—a novel with a very similar premise to *Catcher in the Rye*. Stephen Dedalus, like Holden Caulfield, sets out alone in the world to experience adult life. The idea in *Portrait of the Artist as a Young Man* is clear: Curiosity, adventure, discomfort, and nuanced experiences inspire the creativity needed to become an artist. You'd be hard-pressed to come up with a core idea for *Catcher in the Rye*. If you manage to do it, you will have a hard time proving it. That's because with a book that lacks an idea, we often try to invent one for it, especially if we like the book. If you've ever read a critical perspective of a novel that left you rolling your eyes—"This is about the slow radicalization of the youth culture toward nihilism, systemized by a dangerous cocktail of hierarchical education and negligent parenting"—it's often because the critic is inventing an idea for a novel that probably is not there.

In a short story like "The Sisters," the more we think about that idea of the characters' emotional paralysis, the more elements we discover in Joyce's rendering of it. The more I think about *Catcher in the Rye*, the more I'm left wondering, "What is this book all about?"

We can all describe a character or an object or a landscape—some can do it better than others, but we can all do it. But capturing and expressing an abstract idea through fiction is another thing entirely. In "The Sisters," after the narrator and his aunt view the deceased Father Flynn, they accompany Eliza downstairs to a small room, where they all sit. Joyce writes, "No one spoke: we all gazed at the empty fireplace." What better way to communicate that idea of emotional and ideological paralysis than a group of grieving people unable to speak, looking at a fire that's not there?

Point of View

Every story has a **narrator,** or a person who tells the story (in rare cases some authors have used animals or even inanimate objects to tell the story). That narrator tells the story from a certain perspective. Perhaps she's the main character and tells the story about herself. Maybe she's not a character at all and tells it about someone else. Maybe she's even the author and tells it about the characters she has created. We call this function **point of view,** and it refers to who narrates the story and how he or she does it. There are three main categories that cover point of view in fiction: **first person**, **second person**, and **third person**.

> First Person: *I experience emotional paralysis.*
> Second Person: *You experience emotional paralysis.*
> Third Person: *He experiences emotional paralysis.*

In each of these three categories are various subcategories. For example, first person plural uses "we" instead of "I": *We experience emotional paralysis.*

Adam Johnson, the novelist and short story writer[2] once said that point of view is the most important choice an author makes when writing a piece of fiction because it determines and colors all the information the narrator relays to the reader. If a writer chooses the first person, he or she is confined to the voice, ethos, and attitude of one character who can be unreliable. What the author thinks and knows must be filtered through the character of the narrator before it reaches the reader. If the author chooses the second person, it can sound instructional or even presumptuous (*You experience emotional paralysis*), and often reminds the reader that he or she is reading a fictional story. If the author chooses **close third person**, where the writer limits him- or herself to only one character's movements and actions (and often inner thoughts), the author is again restricting him- or herself to one character; whereas if the author uses the third person **omniscient** and has access to all characters' actions and inner thoughts, he or she has far more information to control and must avoid getting carried away with so much narrative freedom.

In "The Sisters" the first person point of view is restricting—it acts to leave much up for interpretation, not just about the narrator, who is frustratingly unable to convey his true feelings in the story, but about Father Flynn, his death, and the past. When the narrator suggests that he "puzzled" his head to "extract meaning from [Old Cotter's] unfinished sentences," it mirrors the relationship we as readers have with this first person narrator, who, in fact, ends the story with an unfinished sentence. James Joyce knows what Old Cotter is trying to

---

[2] *Emporium, Parasites Like Us*

say and what he thinks, but Joyce's narrator does not. That authorial restriction can be both frustrating and wonderfully dramatic.

It's no mystery why Joyce chose this point of view for the story. If you take the **idea** of emotional, vocational and ideological paralysis, what better narrator than a boy unable to understand and articulate his feelings about the death of a priest? Not only is he paralyzed by his own feelings, he is paralyzed by his failure to understand and communicate the nuances and meanings of others' feelings and actions as well.

The **backstory** the reader receives about that narrator's relationship with Father Flynn comes filtered through his grief and nostalgia, leaving the reader to question the reliability of his memory in such a distraught and confused state of mind: "Sometimes he had amused himself by putting difficult questions to me, asking me what one should do in certain circumstances or whether such and such sins were mortal or venial or only imperfections." We are unable to fully comprehend the nuances of Father Flynn's amusement. Is he amused by the narrator's ignorance or do his innocence, curiosity and anxiousness to learn charm him? Does the amusement suggest his condescension or his admiration?

When Old Cotter suggests that the narrator's relationship with the priest was unhealthy, and that he would not like his own children to "'have too much to say to a man like that,'" the reader desires to know more about the nature of the narrator's relationship with "a man like that," knowing that the narrator is incapable of accurately and objectively portraying it. The lack of reliability from this first person point of view adds tension to the relationship between the narrator and the reader, and is a hallmark of first person narrators throughout literature, from Fyodor Dostoevsky's *Notes from the Underground*, to F. Scott Fitzgerald's *The Great Gatsby*, to J.D. Salinger's *Catcher in the Rye*.

Point of view is often categorized under the broader term **narrative mode**, which most writers use interchangeably with point of view. In *Dubliners*, Joyce employs a variety of first person and third person points of view that we will discuss throughout. For an example of the second person point of view, see Lorrie Moore's collection of short stories *Self Help*. For an example of the first person plural, see Jeffrey Eugenides's novel *The Virgin Suicides* or Joshua Ferris's *And Then We Came to the End*.

Symbolism
Pick a Symbol, Any Symbol

The use of symbols in fiction has become one of the most important parts of literary analysis. Many of the countless books and articles written about Joyce's *Dubliners* explore the meanings indicated by his use of symbols. James S. Atherton, in his essay "The Joyce of *Dubliners*," writes that "there is scarcely a factual detail in his stories which some critic has not found symbolic."[3] In fact, an incredible amount of scholarship about literature follows the same pattern. Read a couple books or articles about *The Great Gatsby*, for example, and you'll find yourself tangled in one scholar's interpretation of Fitzgerald's symbolism—the green light, Eckleburg's eyes, how unlighted candles represent Gatsby's impotence... As readers, writers and scholars, we gravitate toward symbols because they're ripe for interpretation, and they can help provide analytic support for arguments about implicit meanings in literary texts. However, all writers, readers and scholars must beware of over-amplified interpretations.

Put simply, a **symbol** is something, like an object, that represents something else, like an idea or an emotion. When the narrator of "The Sisters" looks for "the reflection of candles on the darkened blind," he does so because he knows that two candles placed "at the head of a corpse" symbolize death. This symbol is fairly obvious, particular to the cultural milieu.

However, many symbols in fiction work more covertly. Joyce uses symbols in "The Sisters" to communicate ideas that his narrator is incapable of communicating. This can be an effective technique when paired with the first person point of view because it allows the author to, in a way, bypass the narrator and communicate subtle meanings to the reader. As the narrator, his aunt, and Eliza all stare

---

[3] Thomas F. Staley, ed., *James Joyce Today: Essays on the Major Works* (Bloomington and London: Indiana University Press, 1966), 41.

at the absent fire in the empty fireplace, the absent fire symbolizes the absent Father Flynn, continuing the symbol of the candles at the beginning of the story and creating what I call the **"symbolic architecture"** particular to this narrative—a set or design of symbols, tropes and motifs that represent an idea in the narrative.

The chalice on Father Flynn's chest as he lies in his coffin and the chalice Eliza informs us he broke may symbolize broken faith, corruption, and religious paralysis. Eliza suggests that the broken chalice was the "beginning of it," indicating Father Flynn's mental decline. The "idle chalice on his breast" may indicate that in death all of that mysterious corruption Joyce alludes to will be forgotten and replaced. That narrator remains unaware of the symbolic meaning of the chalice, despite the fact that the reader obtains knowledge about its existence from him.

I will discuss symbols further in response to "Araby" and throughout this text, and will describe more specific types of symbolism, such as **motifs** and **objective correlatives** in following stories.

Synthesis

As I suggested about point of view, writers often use symbolism to further develop and deepen the idea of the narrative. Both the empty fireplace and the broken chalice communicate to us that sense of paralysis. While it's important for us to isolate and analyze various elements of craft, it's also important that we synthesize, and I hope that readers begin to see how Joyce synthesizes his point of view, symbolism, and prose to his idea and premise.

It's easy to imagine a writer with a great idea, premise, point of view, and set of symbols, but a narrative that fails to connect those elements into one story. One of the first and most effective questions we can all ask about a narrative might be: How does the writer synthesize the point of view and symbolic architecture of the narrative with the premise and idea?

Questions

1. After Joyce establishes the **premise** of this narrator's emotional paralysis in the story, how does he follow through on his **contract**? What specific parts of the narrative support his fulfillment of that contract or failure to fulfill it?

2. How does Joyce communicate the abstract **idea** of paralysis in his characters and situations?

3. Where does the **first person narration** expose a lack of reliability, and what is the effect of that unreliability on the reader?

4. What other possible **symbols** does Joyce insert into "The Sisters" and what purpose does their inclusion serve? How do they enrich the reading experience? How do they contribute to the depth of the story's **idea**?

5. While we may argue that "paralysis" becomes both part of this story's **premise** and **idea**, we can also argue that it works as a **symbol**. What might paralysis symbolize here?

An Encounter

It was Joe Dillon who introduced the Wild West to us. He had a little library made up of old numbers of *The Union Jack, Pluck* and *The Halfpenny Marvel*. Every evening after school we met in his back garden and arranged Indian battles. He and his fat young brother Leo, the idler, held the loft of the stable while we tried to carry it by storm; or we fought a pitched battle on the grass. But, however well we fought, we never won siege or battle and all our bouts ended with Joe Dillon's war dance of victory. His parents went to eight-o'clock mass every morning in Gardiner Street and the peaceful odour of Mrs Dillon was prevalent in the hall of the house. But he played too fiercely for us who were younger and more timid. He looked like some kind of an Indian when he capered round the garden, an old tea-cosy[1] on his head, beating a tin with his fist and yelling:

"Ya! yaka, yaka, yaka!"

Everyone was incredulous when it was reported that he had a vocation for the priesthood. Nevertheless it was true.

A spirit of unruliness diffused itself among us and, under its influence, differences of culture and constitution were waived. We banded ourselves together, some boldly, some in jest and some almost in fear: and of the number of these latter, the reluctant Indians who were afraid to seem studious or lacking in robustness, I was one. The adventures related in the literature of the Wild West were remote from my nature but, at least, they opened doors of escape. I liked better some American detective stories which were traversed from time to time by unkempt fierce and beautiful girls. Though there was nothing wrong in these stories and though their intention was sometimes literary they were circulated secretly at school. One day when Father Butler was hearing the four pages of Roman History clumsy Leo Dillon was discovered with a copy of *The Halfpenny Marvel*.

"This page or this page? This page? Now, Dillon, up! 'Hardly had the day'... Go on! What day? 'Hardly had the day dawned'... Have you studied it? What have you there in your pocket?"

---

[1] Piece of cloth meant to insulate a tea pot.

Everyone's heart palpitated as Leo Dillon handed up the paper and everyone assumed an innocent face. Father Butler turned over the pages, frowning.

"What is this rubbish?" he said. "*The Apache Chief!* Is this what you read instead of studying your Roman History? Let me not find any more of this wretched stuff in this college. The man who wrote it, I suppose, was some wretched fellow who writes these things for a drink. I'm surprised at boys like you, educated, reading such stuff. I could understand it if you were... National School boys. Now, Dillon, I advise you strongly, get at your work or..."

This rebuke during the sober hours of school paled much of the glory of the Wild West for me and the confused puffy face of Leo Dillon awakened one of my consciences. But when the restraining influence of the school was at a distance I began to hunger again for wild sensations, for the escape which those chronicles of disorder alone seemed to offer me. The mimic warfare of the evening became at last as wearisome to me as the routine of school in the morning because I wanted real adventures to happen to myself. But real adventures, I reflected, do not happen to people who remain at home: they must be sought abroad.

The summer holidays were near at hand when I made up my mind to break out of the weariness of school life for one day at least. With Leo Dillon and a boy named Mahony I planned a day's miching.[2] Each of us saved up sixpence. We were to meet at ten in the morning on the Canal Bridge. Mahony's big sister was to write an excuse for him and Leo Dillon was to tell his brother to say he was sick. We arranged to go along the Wharf Road until we came to the ships, then to cross in the ferryboat and walk out to see the Pigeon House. Leo Dillon was afraid we might meet Father Butler or someone out of the college; but Mahony asked, very sensibly, what would Father Butler be doing out at the Pigeon House. We were reassured: and I brought the first stage of the plot to an end by collecting sixpence from the other two, at the same time showing them my own sixpence. When we were making the last arrangements on the eve we were all vaguely excited. We shook hands, laughing, and Mahony said:

"Till to-morrow, mates!"

That night I slept badly. In the morning I was first-comer to the bridge as I lived nearest. I hid my books in the long grass near the

---

[2] Skulking. Evading obligations.

ashpit at the end of the garden where nobody ever came and hurried along the canal bank. It was a mild sunny morning in the first week of June. I sat up on the coping of the bridge admiring my frail canvas shoes which I had diligently pipeclayed[3] overnight and watching the docile horses pulling a tramload of business people up the hill. All the branches of the tall trees which lined the mall were gay with little light green leaves and the sunlight slanted through them on to the water. The granite stone of the bridge was beginning to be warm and I began to pat it with my hands in time to an air in my head. I was very happy.

When I had been sitting there for five or ten minutes I saw Mahony's grey suit approaching. He came up the hill, smiling, and clambered up beside me on the bridge. While we were waiting he brought out the catapult which bulged from his inner pocket and explained some improvements which he had made in it. I asked him why he had brought it and he told me he had brought it to have some gas with the birds. Mahony used slang freely, and spoke of Father Butler as Old Bunser. We waited on for a quarter of an hour more but still there was no sign of Leo Dillon. Mahony, at last, jumped down and said:

"Come along. I knew Fatty'd funk it."

"And his sixpence…?" I said.

"That's forfeit," said Mahony. "And so much the better for us—a bob[4] and a tanner[5] instead of a bob."

We walked along the North Strand Road till we came to the Vitriol Works and then turned to the right along the Wharf Road. Mahony began to play the Indian as soon as we were out of public sight. He chased a crowd of ragged girls, brandishing his unloaded catapult and, when two ragged boys began, out of chivalry, to fling stones at us, he proposed that we should charge them. I objected that the boys were too small and so we walked on, the ragged troop screaming after us: "*Swaddlers! Swaddlers!*" thinking that we were Protestants because Mahony, who was dark-complexioned, wore the silver badge of a cricket club in his cap. When we came to the Smoothing Iron we arranged a siege; but it was a failure because you must have at least three. We revenged ourselves on Leo Dillon by

---

[3] Cleaned.
[4] Shilling.
[5] Sixpence.

saying what a funk he was and guessing how many he would get at three o'clock from Mr Ryan.

We came then near the river. We spent a long time walking about the noisy streets flanked by high stone walls, watching the working of cranes and engines and often being shouted at for our immobility by the drivers of groaning carts. It was noon when we reached the quays and as all the labourers seemed to be eating their lunches, we bought two big currant buns and sat down to eat them on some metal piping beside the river. We pleased ourselves with the spectacle of Dublin's commerce—the barges signaled from far away by their curls of woolly smoke, the brown fishing fleet beyond Ringsend, the big white sailing vessel which was being discharged on the opposite quay. Mahony said it would be right skit[6] to run away to sea on one of those big ships and even I, looking at the high masts, saw, or imagined, the geography which had been scantily dosed to me at school gradually taking substance under my eyes. School and home seemed to recede from us and their influences upon us seemed to wane.

We crossed the Liffey in the ferryboat, paying our toll to be transported in the company of two labourers and a little Jew with a bag. We were serious to the point of solemnity, but once during the short voyage our eyes met and we laughed. When we landed we watched the discharging of the graceful three-master[7] which we had observed from the other quay. Some bystander said that she was a Norwegian vessel. I went to the stern and tried to decipher the legend upon it but, failing to do so, I came back and examined the foreign sailors to see had any of them green eyes for I had some confused notion…The sailors' eyes were blue and grey and even black. The only sailor whose eyes could have been called green was a tall man who amused the crowd on the quay by calling out cheerfully every time the planks fell:

"All right! All right!"

When we were tired of this sight we wandered slowly into Ringsend. The day had grown sultry, and in the windows of the grocers' shops musty biscuits lay bleaching. We bought some biscuits and chocolate which we ate sedulously as we wandered through the squalid streets where the families of the fishermen live. We could find no dairy and so we went into a huckster's shop and bought a bottle of

---

[6] Fun.
[7] Ship with three masts.

raspberry lemonade each. Refreshed by this, Mahony chased a cat down a lane, but the cat escaped into a wide field. We both felt rather tired and when we reached the field we made at once for a sloping bank over the ridge of which we could see the Dodder.

It was too late and we were too tired to carry out our project of visiting the Pigeon House. We had to be home before four o'clock lest our adventure should be discovered. Mahony looked regretfully at his catapult and I had to suggest going home by train before he regained any cheerfulness. The sun went in behind some clouds and left us to our jaded thoughts and the crumbs of our provisions.

There was nobody but ourselves in the field. When we had lain on the bank for some time without speaking I saw a man approaching from the far end of the field. I watched him lazily as I chewed one of those green stems on which girls tell fortunes. He came along by the bank slowly. He walked with one hand upon his hip and in the other hand he held a stick with which he tapped the turf lightly. He was shabbily dressed in a suit of greenish-black and wore what we used to call a jerry hat with a high crown. He seemed to be fairly old for his moustache was ashen-grey. When he passed at our feet he glanced up at us quickly and then continued his way. We followed him with our eyes and saw that when he had gone on for perhaps fifty paces he turned about and began to retrace his steps. He walked towards us very slowly, always tapping the ground with his stick, so slowly that I thought he was looking for something in the grass.

He stopped when he came level with us and bade us good-day. We answered him and he sat down beside us on the slope slowly and with great care. He began to talk of the weather, saying that it would be a very hot summer and adding that the seasons had changed greatly since he was a boy—a long time ago. He said that the happiest time of one's life was undoubtedly one's schoolboy days and that he would give anything to be young again. While he expressed these sentiments which bored us a little we kept silent. Then he began to talk of school and of books. He asked us whether we had read the poetry of Thomas Moore or the works of Sir Walter Scott and Lord Lytton. I pretended that I had read every book he mentioned so that in the end he said:

"Ah, I can see you are a bookworm like myself. Now," he added, pointing to Mahony who was regarding us with open eyes, "he is different; he goes in for games."

He said he had all Sir Walter Scott's works and all Lord Lytton's works at home and never tired of reading them. "Of course," he said, "there were some of Lord Lytton's works which boys couldn't read." Mahony asked why couldn't boys read them—a question which agitated and pained me because I was afraid the man would think I was as stupid as Mahony. The man, however, only smiled. I saw that he had great gaps in his mouth between his yellow teeth. Then he asked us which of us had the most sweethearts. Mahony mentioned lightly that he had three totties.[8] The man asked me how many I had. I answered that I had none. He did not believe me and said he was sure I must have one. I was silent.

"Tell us," said Mahony pertly to the man, "how many have you yourself?"

The man smiled as before and said that when he was our age he had lots of sweethearts.

"Every boy," he said, "has a little sweetheart."

His attitude on this point struck me as strangely liberal in a man of his age. In my heart I thought that what he said about boys and sweethearts was reasonable. But I disliked the words in his mouth and I wondered why he shivered once or twice as if he feared something or felt a sudden chill. As he proceeded I noticed that his accent was good. He began to speak to us about girls, saying what nice soft hair they had and how soft their hands were and how all girls were not so good as they seemed to be if one only knew. There was nothing he liked, he said, so much as looking at a nice young girl, at her nice white hands and her beautiful soft hair. He gave me the impression that he was repeating something which he had learned by heart or that, magnetised by some words of his own speech, his mind was slowly circling round and round in the same orbit. At times he spoke as if he were simply alluding to some fact that everybody knew, and at times he lowered his voice and spoke mysteriously as if he were telling us something secret which he did not wish others to overhear. He repeated his phrases over and over again, varying them and surrounding them with his monotonous voice. I continued to gaze towards the foot of the slope, listening to him.

After a long while his monologue paused. He stood up slowly, saying that he had to leave us for a minute or so, a few minutes, and, without changing the direction of my gaze, I saw him walking slowly

---

[8] Girlfriends.

away from us towards the near end of the field. We remained silent when he had gone. After a silence of a few minutes I heard Mahony exclaim:

"I say! Look what he's doing!"

As I neither answered nor raised my eyes Mahony exclaimed again:

"I say... He's a queer old josser!"[9]

"In case he asks us for our names," I said, "let you be Murphy and I'll be Smith."

We said nothing further to each other. I was still considering whether I would go away or not when the man came back and sat down beside us again. Hardly had he sat down when Mahony, catching sight of the cat which had escaped him, sprang up and pursued her across the field. The man and I watched the chase. The cat escaped once more and Mahony began to throw stones at the wall she had escaladed. Desisting from this, he began to wander about the far end of the field, aimlessly.

After an interval the man spoke to me. He said that my friend was a very rough boy and asked did he get whipped often at school. I was going to reply indignantly that we were not National School boys to be whipped, as he called it; but I remained silent. He began to speak on the subject of chastising boys. His mind, as if magnetised again by his speech, seemed to circle slowly round and round its new centre. He said that when boys were that kind they ought to be whipped and well whipped. When a boy was rough and unruly there was nothing would do him any good but a good sound whipping. A slap on the hand or a box on the ear was no good: what he wanted was to get a nice warm whipping. I was surprised at this sentiment and involuntarily glanced up at his face. As I did so I met the gaze of a pair of bottle-green eyes peering at me from under a twitching forehead. I turned my eyes away again.

The man continued his monologue. He seemed to have forgotten his recent liberalism. He said that if ever he found a boy talking to girls or having a girl for a sweetheart he would whip him and whip him; and that would teach him not to be talking to girls. And if a boy had a girl for a sweetheart and told lies about it then he would give him such a whipping as no boy ever got in this world. He said that there was nothing in this world he would like so well as that.

---

[9] Foolish man.

He described to me how he would whip such a boy as if he were unfolding some elaborate mystery. He would love that, he said, better than anything in this world; and his voice, as he led me monotonously through the mystery, grew almost affectionate and seemed to plead with me that I should understand him.

I waited till his monologue paused again. Then I stood up abruptly. Lest I should betray my agitation I delayed a few moments pretending to fix my shoe properly and then, saying that I was obliged to go, I bade him good-day. I went up the slope calmly but my heart was beating quickly with fear that he would seize me by the ankles. When I reached the top of the slope I turned round and, without looking at him, called loudly across the field:

"Murphy!"

My voice had an accent of forced bravery in it and I was ashamed of my paltry stratagem. I had to call the name again before Mahony saw me and hallooed[10] in answer. How my heart beat as he came running across the field to me! He ran as if to bring me aid. And I was penitent; for in my heart I had always despised him a little.

---

[10] Shouted.

CRAFT: AN ENCOUNTER

The Joycean Gnomon

There's no perfect craft word to indicate what writers leave off the page. There are many words that approach the concept—words like inference, indication, understatement, suggestion, subtext, and implicitness—but they fail to precisely describe a writer's conscious choice to leave something unsaid or up to the reader's imagination. However, because numerous critics have written about Joyce's careful and disciplined literary sense when it comes to this very technique, many have come to call Joyce's implicit meanings "gnomons" because of his own inclusion of the word in the first paragraph of "The Sisters."

His narrator refers to gnomon as a word that "sounded strange." Literally, **gnomon** refers to an object that casts a shadow, as the stylus of a sundial casts a shadow that indicates the time of day. In terms of the writer's craft, gnomon refers to something that is implicit rather than explicit in the text. This differs from various kinds of understatement. Something understated is either deemphasized or incompletely expressed—but partially expressed nonetheless. A gnomon, however, is something deliberately left off the page. In "The Sisters," the nature of the narrator's and Father Flynn's relationship is a gnomon—its implicit "styling" casts a dark shadow that the reader struggles to interpret. Similarly, in "An Encounter," when the man who approaches the narrator and Mahony in the field retreats, Joyce leaves his actions up for interpretation. Mahony says, "I say! Look what he's doing!" While the narrator never tells us that he is masturbating, we perhaps infer it. Joyce has "styled" this inference, but chosen to leave it in shadow.

This technique is effective, particularly in "An Encounter," because it expects the reader to make an interpretive choice without sufficient evidence. Like in "The Sisters," this narrator is unreliable. Therefore, we never know for sure when it comes to this man if the narrator exaggerates a sense of danger that isn't there or if he underestimates the danger that would be so obvious if it were you or me in the situation. That danger, that malicious intent that we infer, could also be classified as a Joycean gnomon.

Many readers feel frustrated when put in such a position. They want the narrator to tell us what the stranger is up to when Mahony says, "Look what he's doing!" Other readers may feel Joyce's hand here—may sense that Joyce is playing with us. We all know that Joyce intentionally leaves this event in shadow, forcing us to make an assumption. Because we don't absolutely know what is happening, the tension increases. That unknown gnomon actively involves the reader in the characters' dilemma and conflict. Often, what writers don't tell us has more impact than what they do tell us.

Pun

A **pun** is a play on words, and often plays on different meanings of the same word. Authors may use puns for humorous effect, or as a literary **trope**. If I had just finished chopping wood and said, "I have a *splitting* headache," I'm creating a pun out of the word *splitting* because it can refer to both the splitting of wood and the intensity of my headache. Try this one: "A metaphor is kind of *like* a simile." The word *like* has a "double meaning." It creates a comparison between a metaphor and a simile, but it also forms a simile because a simile is a comparison that uses the word "like."

In "An Encounter" the man says to the narrator and Mahony, "Every boy ... has a little sweetheart." This exemplifies both Joyce's use of a **pun**, a play on words, and **gnomon**. By this point in the story, we are already suspicious of this man. First, he starts talking to the boys using a string of clichés—the weather, his own past, whether or not they have "sweethearts"... We wonder if this stranger has sexual intentions for these two boys. Because we sense that gnomon of sexual danger, we might read the man's statement like this: *Every boy* *has a little sweet heart*. By splitting "sweetheart" into "sweet heart," this play on words suggests that this man might perhaps fancy boys' innocence, naiveté, and lack of development. Because the man's sexual intention is left in shadow, the pun furthers the sense of the gnomon.

Many writers—one might suggest lesser writers—would craft this play on words differently. Consider this example: "'Every boy has a little sweetheart,' the man said, but he said the word 'sweetheart' differently from before, almost like it was two words." This would leave much less up to the reader to infer. While some writers might argue that most readers would miss Joyce's play on words, others would say that even when readers miss it, it still has that mysterious, unconscious effect of creating tension. It gives us a bad feeling. Every individual writer makes a decision about how deeply he or she wants the reader to dig in order to unearth implicit meanings.

Protagonist and Antagonist

A **protagonist** is the main character of the narrative. The narrator of "An Encounter" is the protagonist. An **antagonist** is a character who opposes the main character. Every story has a main character (or sometimes multiple main characters), but not every story has an antagonist. In "The Sisters," the narrator is the main character, but there is no opposing character. The conflict the main character faces has to do with his grief over the death of Father Flynn. However, in "An Encounter," the protagonist's conflict centers around the strange man. While that man doesn't directly or overtly oppose the protagonist—he doesn't threaten or harm him, for example—he certainly *poses* a threat, causes fear, and may have harmful intentions. He acts as the antagonist.

This relationship between protagonist and antagonist has become so fundamental and formulaic in fiction that we often call it simply "good guy/bad guy" or "hero/villain." Writers find this protagonist/antagonist relationship appealing because it is the easiest and often most satisfying way to create conflict. Things start to get sticky and tense when one human being has an unequal advantage over the other, like wealth, strength, age, sex, weapons, secrets, or friends in high places.

In a narrative, the main character often has a goal. What could be easier and more fraught with tension than a person who stands between that main character and his or her goal? In "An Encounter," the boys skip school with the goal of having a fun adventure. The stranger then stands between the main character and his goal. The main character may experience an adventure, but it certainly wasn't any fun: "my heart was beating quickly with fear." I suppose you could argue that the stranger is not an antagonist because he is necessary in creating the protagonist's adventure. In fact, he makes the protagonist's goal possible. And yet, the reader also knows that a boy's perception of adventure—the kind of adventure he reads about it in comics—has a naïve and innocent bent. In fact, what this narrator may learn is that true adventure is not as romantic as he previously believed.

Story versus Plot

In *Aspects of the Novel*, E.M. Forster states that causality defines the core difference between plot and story. A **plot** has causality. A **story** does not. His famous example goes like this: "The king died, and then the queen died." That's a story. "The king died, and then the queen died of grief." That's a plot. Because the second example tells us why the queen died—because it contains causality—it's a plot.

Obviously, we all use "story" as a blanket term that applies to any kind of narrative form. We call television shows, films, novels, and personal anecdotes stories. But put simply, a story is a series of sequential events. Like Forster suggests, a story describes things that happened in the order they happened (like "history"). However, writers do not always tell stories in the order they happened. Some writers start in the middle of the conflict and then backtrack in time. Other writers reveal the end, then return to the beginning. That defines the difference between story and plot. The plot of a story is what appears on the page. It's the part of the story that a writer chooses to present in the order he or she chooses to structure it. Forster provides this example: "The queen died, no one knew why, until it was discovered that it was through grief at the death of the king." The story remains the same ("The king died, and then the queen died"), but he has altered the sequential events in his presentation of it, and provided causality. While in the story the king died first, in this plot the writer begins with the queen's death. This way of plotting the story adds a sense of mystery that compels readers to continue. We want to know why the queen died.[1]

The way a writer plots a story can differ greatly from the way the story actually happened. And unless you're reading Charles Dickens—Chapter One: "I am born"[2]—you're not going to get every part of the story in the plot. The reason this remains confusing stems partly from the continual misuse of the terms. Even James Atherton, whose essay on *Dubliners* I have referenced previously, offers a brief analysis of the structure of "The Boarding House" that demonstrates the problem. He writes that "the plot is simple enough,"[3] and then goes on to describe the story. Later he writes, "It is, indeed, the order of presentation which is surprising."[4] What he means of course is that the *story* is simple enough and that the *plot* is surprising. His mixing up of these two terms is representative of the confusion that still exists around them.

I am not suggesting that we all use the term plot to describe a story on the page (even if it's more accurate). But I am suggesting that we know the difference between story and plot, and that we do not use the term plot to describe the story. Story has become a blanket term, but plot refers to something very specific.

In Joyce's "An Encounter," we can easily say that the story is about a boy who grows up in a Dublin neighborhood. He attends private school and plays Wild West games with friends. Just before summer holiday he and his two friends decide to skip school and go on an adventure.

---

[1] E.M. Forster, *Aspects of the Novel* (Rosetta Books, 2010).
[2] Charles Dickens, *David Copperfield*.
[3] Thomas F. Staley, ed., *James Joyce Today: Essays on the Major Works* (Bloomington and London: Indiana University Press, 1966), 51.
[4] Ibid., 52.

While the plot of "An Encounter" does not deviate from the sequence of the story, like all writers must, Joyce chooses moments to present (or to "plot"). He doesn't begin with the birth of the main character, but he does begin by summarizing the games he played with Joe Dillon. At one moment, Joyce zooms in: "One day when Father Butler was hearing the four pages of Roman history clumsy Leo Dillon was discovered with a copy of *The Halfpenny Marvel*." Then the readers are thrown into a short scene. That scene is part of Joyce's plot. He has handpicked this scene to precede what becomes the central "moment" or **action** of this narrative—this character's encountering of the stranger—in order to suggest the causality between them. When Father Butler chastises Leo Dillon for reading this comic, the narrator admits that the "rebuke during the sober hours of school paled much of the glory of the Wild West for me." He needs a new outlet, which drives this narrator to skip school. Therefore, this plot indicates the motivations, the causes and effects of the moments Joyce chooses to present.

One of the easiest ways to remember the difference goes like this: The story is always bigger than the plot.

Narrative Structure

When a writer "plots" a story, he or she creates a structure that more often than not follows a pattern or formula. While there are many ways to disrupt that formula, most narratives either follow it or only slightly deviate from it. "An Encounter" acts as an ideal story to examine typical narrative structure because it follows this formula. It starts with a **setup**, moves into a **conflict**, and finishes with at least a partial **resolution**.

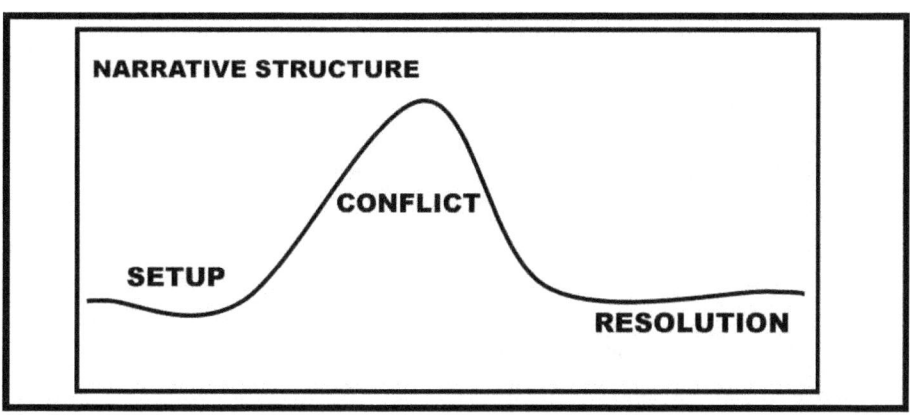

This fundamental narrative structure in fiction is very similar to Gustav Freytag's dramatic structure, which starts with **exposition**, rises to **climax**, and resolves in **dénouement**. In fact, those terms are often used interchangeably with the narrative structure of fiction.

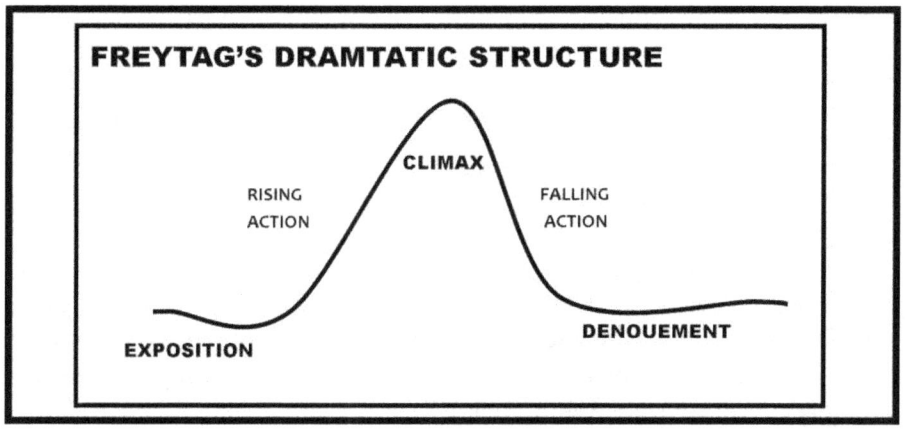

In "An Encounter" the narrative structure might be reflected like this:

Setup:	A schoolboy and his two friends decide to play hooky for the day.
Conflict:	They meet a stranger (**antagonist**) who scares both of them and acts in a very subtle, threatening manner, and the narrator (**protagonist**) is left alone with him in a field.
Resolution:	The narrator escapes the man and is relieved when he is reunited with his friend.

Joyce intensifies this narrative structure by dwelling on the innocence of the narrator in the setup of the story. This narrator likes the Wild West and reads typical boys' magazines. "Every evening after school we met in [Joe Dillon's] back garden and arranged Indian battles." This innocence is then thrown into conflict by the man who approaches the narrator and Mahony in the middle of the story. When this man is talking, the narrator admits, "I disliked the words in his mouth and I wondered why he shivered once or twice as if he feared something or felt a sudden chill." As Joyce ratchets up the **tension**, we feel all the more relieved for this narrator in the brief resolution when he escapes and reunites with Mahony. "How my heart beat as he came running across the field to me!"

In "The Sisters," however, Joyce creates a far subtler structure. Although he begins with a setup and rises to conflict, he does not create an explicit resolution, and shows us one example of how writers often disrupt the typical formula of narrative structure.

Narrative Structure, Sequence, Story, and Plot All Together Now

When I was in a fiction workshop discussion, the instructor brought up **narrative structure** to the writer whose story we were discussing. She didn't understand how the beginning or **setup** of his **story** established the **conflict**. His response was typical of a misunderstanding between story sequence and the structure of **plot**. He threw up his arms and said, "I don't want to start my story at the beginning. That's the whole point!"

We often confuse time with structure because we use the same words to talk about both. We talk about the beginning of a story to suggest the earliest event in time and we talk about the beginning of a plot to talk about the setup, which does not have to be the earliest event in time. This writer was confusing plot or narrative structure with story. Just because you have a setup, conflict, and **resolution** does not mean that those elements have to follow sequentially in time.

Let's take a look at this writer's story:

Story: In the year 2000 the sister of the mayor died of leukemia. Five years later, in 2005, the mayor himself was diagnosed with pancreatic cancer. He spent five years fighting it, but died of cancer in 2010.

Now, when this writer was turning this story into a plot, he had to face how to structure these elements sequentially, whether or not he wanted to include all those elements in the plot, and how to show the causal relationship between the events. For example, the writer might choose to begin the plot with the mayor's diagnosis (2005) and end with his death (2010). The earlier death of the sister (2000) may be told through dialogue between characters or through **exposition** and **backstory** at some point, but may never be plotted in scene.

However, that's not how this writer attempted to structure the plot. He wanted to structure it nonsequentially in reverse order, starting with the mayor's death (2010), then the mayor's diagnosis (2005), and finally the death of the mayor's sister (2000). What got him into trouble was not this reverse structure; it was the fact that he never properly established that the mayor actually died in the setup of his plot. If you arrange your setup to establish the premise of the story, and the premise of the story is the death of the mayor, then you have to follow through, be brave, and plot his death in the setup. This writer wanted it both ways. He wanted the mystery of not knowing if the mayor dies or not, and the premise of the mayor's death. He needed to choose.

Let's take a look at how he ended up revising the plot. Here's how this writer turned that sequential story into a nonsequential plot, following the formula of narrative structure:

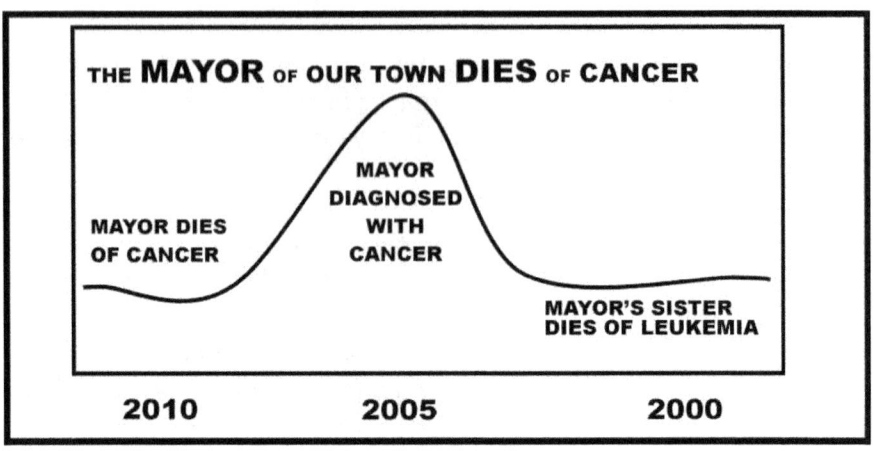

He has kept his reverse order, and as long as he can create a causal relationship between these elements, narrative structure remains intact. For example, even though the reader would know from the setup that the mayor dies, the writer creates conflict after his diagnosis with an **antagonistic** political foe, the complications of his mayoral duties, his feelings of failure as a politician, and his declining relationship with his wife. Then, as a resolution, the mayor's sister's death ten years earlier suggests that he learned how to cope with pain, suffering, and death through empathy in his past. The resolution establishes that even though he died young, the things he learned when he experienced his sister's death allowed him to die gracefully. When this writer was finished, he had turned his story into an elegant plot.

Foreshadowing

Because readers are familiar with how narratives work, foreshadowing often relies on readers' assumptions. **Foreshadowing** is a subtle and implicit indication of things to come. An instance of foreshadowing does not state "this character is going to die at the end of this story" but instead implies it: "It was as though the cold ground was calling his name, inviting him into it." Because readers often suspect (but aren't sure) about foreshadowing in a story, it often creates tension and a sense of mystery.

If you had never read a story before, it would be difficult to interpret an instance of foreshadowing in the setup. That kind of foreshadowing automatically assumes a certain amount of knowledge from the reader. In "An Encounter," early in the story, Joyce foreshadows the coming conflict when his narrator says, "I wanted real adventures to happen to myself." A savvy reader knows immediately that the narrator's desire for adventure is going to be thrown into conflict, and it works as an effective device to increase tension—the reader wondering if this hunger for adventure will get him into terrible trouble or lead to some magical discovery.

Later in the story, just as the man approaches the narrator and Mahony in the field, the narrator says, "I watched him lazily as I chewed one of those green stems on which girls tell fortunes." Here, Joyce does two things. First, the reader is already starting to feel apprehensive about this approaching stranger. We may feel that way because we know stories need conflict. But the narrator doesn't know that. He is relaxed. He watches the man "lazily." Therefore, this moment exemplifies a case of both foreshadowing and **dramatic irony** in the fiction because we know more than the character does: We know that danger is ahead for him. This dramatic irony only increases as the narrator enters conversation with the man, because we know that he is making a mistake, and that he should escape as soon as possible.

Secondly, Joyce sneaks in a reference to the romantic fortunes young people tell with flowers.   Unlike the earlier instance of foreshadowing, even a savvy reader would miss the significance and subtlety of the foreshadowing here. Those innocent fortunes about young love are about to be thrown into conflict with the suggestions of pedophilia and the threat of sexual molestation that follow. Yet, even though readers would miss the reference on a first reading, it works on the surface level too—one minute the narrator is lazily and innocently chewing on flowers, the next he feels threatened and afraid and invents false names for himself and Mahony to mislead this suspicious man.

Questions

1. What is your interpretation of the man who approaches the narrator and Mahony? What elements in the story cause you to question his intentions for these two boys? Why does Joyce decide to leave the danger implicit?

2. Notice how Joyce's language in "An Encounter" differs from the language in "The Sisters." This narrator has more control of language. Some might even argue that Joyce invades the narrator's voice. Consider this sentence: "But when the restraining influence of the school was at a distance I began to hunger again for the wild sensations, for the escape which those chronicles of disorder alone seemed to offer me." Not only is this a complex subordinate clause, it's a beautiful sentence with a wonderful sound that begins with a lulling "began to hunger again" and moves into the disruptive "chronicles of disorder…" As a sentence, it's a great one to read and read again, to appreciate for its meaning and lyrical beauty. But does it sound like the narrator of this story? The same narrator who fails to describe exactly what the strange man is doing in the field? Or does it sound like James Joyce? When comparing the **first person narrator** of "The Sisters" and the first person narrator of "An Encounter," how do they differ in terms of reliability, **tone**, and the **idea** of the narratives?

3. We know that the narrator is relieved to be reunited with Mahony, but we have no idea how these two boys will react to the event. Why does Joyce choose to end the **plot** before the **conflict** has been fully **resolved**? In "The Sisters" Joyce does not even begin to resolve the narrative, and ends in the middle of the conflict, in the middle of the narrator's emotional paralysis. Why?

Araby

North Richmond Street, being blind,[1] was a quiet street except at the hour when the Christian Brothers' School set the boys free. An uninhabited house of two storeys stood at the blind end, detached from its neighbours in a square ground. The other houses of the street, conscious of decent lives within them, gazed at one another with brown imperturbable faces.

The former tenant of our house, a priest, had died in the back drawing-room. Air, musty from having been long enclosed, hung in all the rooms, and the waste room behind the kitchen was littered with old useless papers. Among these I found a few paper-covered books, the pages of which were curled and damp: *The Abbot*, by Walter Scott, *The Devout Communnicant* and *The Memoirs of Vidocq*. I liked the last best because its leaves were yellow. The wild garden behind the house contained a central apple-tree and a few straggling bushes under one of which I found the late tenant's rusty bicycle-pump. He had been a very charitable priest; in his will he had left all his money to institutions and the furniture of his house to his sister.

When the short days of winter came dusk fell before we had well eaten our dinners. When we met in the street the houses had grown sombre. The space of sky above us was the colour of ever-changing violet and towards it the lamps of the street lifted their feeble lanterns. The cold air stung us and we played till our bodies glowed. Our shouts echoed in the silent street. The career of our play brought us through the dark muddy lanes behind the houses where we ran the gantlet[2] of the rough tribes from the cottages, to the back doors of the dark dripping gardens where odours arose from the ashpits, to the dark odorous stables where a coachman smoothed and combed the horse or shook music from the buckled harness. When we returned to the street, light from the kitchen windows had filled the areas. If my uncle was seen turning the corner we hid in the shadow until we had seen him safely housed. Or if Mangan's sister came out on the doorstep to call her brother in to his tea we watched her from our shadow peer up and down the street. We waited to see

---

[1] Cul-de-sac or dead end.
[2] Archaic form of "gauntlet."

whether she would remain or go in and, if she remained, we left our shadow and walked up to Mangan's steps resignedly. She was waiting for us, her figure defined by the light from the half-opened door. Her brother always teased her before he obeyed and I stood by the railings looking at her. Her dress swung as she moved her body and the soft rope of her hair tossed from side to side.

Every morning I lay on the floor in the front parlour watching her door. The blind was pulled down to within an inch of the sash so that I could not be seen. When she came out on the doorstep my heart leaped. I ran to the hall, seized my books and followed her. I kept her brown figure always in my eye and, when we came near the point at which our ways diverged, I quickened my pace and passed her. This happened morning after morning. I had never spoken to her, except for a few casual words, and yet her name was like a summons to all my foolish blood.

Her image accompanied me even in places the most hostile to romance. On Saturday evenings when my aunt went marketing I had to go to carry some of the parcels. We walked through the flaring streets, jostled by drunken men and bargaining women, amid the curses of labourers, the shrill litanies of shop-boys who stood on guard by the barrels of pigs' cheeks, the nasal chanting of street-singers, who sang a *come-all-you* about O'Donovan Rossa, or a ballad about the troubles in our native land. These noises converged in a single sensation of life for me: I imagined that I bore my chalice safely through a throng of foes. Her name sprang to my lips at moments in strange prayers and praises which I myself did not understand. My eyes were often full of tears (I could not tell why) and at times a flood from my heart seemed to pour itself out into my bosom. I thought little of the future. I did not know whether I would ever speak to her or not or, if I spoke to her, how I could tell her of my confused adoration. But my body was like a harp and her words and gestures were like fingers running upon the wires.

One evening I went into the back drawing-room in which the priest had died. It was a dark rainy evening and there was no sound in the house. Through one of the broken panes I heard the rain impinge upon the earth, the fine incessant needles of water playing in the sodden beds. Some distant lamp or lighted window gleamed below me. I was thankful that I could see so little. All my senses seemed to desire to veil themselves and, feeling that I was about to slip from them, I pressed the palms of my hands together until they trembled, murmuring: *"O love! O love!"* many times.

At last she spoke to me. When she addressed the first words to me I was so confused that I did not know what to answer. She asked me was I going to *Araby*. I forgot whether I answered yes or no. It would be a splendid bazaar, she said she would love to go.

"And why can't you?" I asked.

While she spoke she turned a silver bracelet round and round her wrist. She could not go, she said, because there would be a retreat that week in her convent. Her brother and two other boys were fighting for their caps and I was alone at the railings. She held one of the spikes, bowing her head towards me. The light from the lamp opposite our door caught the white curve of her neck, lit up her hair that rested there and, falling, lit up the hand upon the railing. It fell over one side of her dress and caught the white border of a petticoat, just visible as she stood at ease.

"It's well for you," she said.

"If I go," I said, "I will bring you something."

What innumerable follies laid waste my waking and sleeping thoughts after that evening! I wished to annihilate the tedious intervening days. I chafed against the work of school. At night in my bedroom and by day in the classroom her image came between me and the page I strove to read. The syllables of the word *Araby* were called to me through the silence in which my soul luxuriated and cast an Eastern enchantment over me. I asked for leave to go to the bazaar on Saturday night. My aunt was surprised and hoped it was not some Freemason affair. I answered few questions in class. I watched my master's face pass from amiability to sternness; he hoped I was not beginning to idle. I could not call my wandering thoughts together. I had hardly any patience with the serious work of life which, now that it stood between me and my desire, seemed to me child's play, ugly monotonous child's play.

On Saturday morning I reminded my uncle that I wished to go to the bazaar in the evening. He was fussing at the hallstand, looking for the hat-brush, and answered me curtly:

"Yes, boy, I know."

As he was in the hall I could not go into the front parlour and lie at the window. I left the house in bad humour and walked slowly towards the school. The air was pitilessly raw and already my heart misgave me.

When I came home to dinner my uncle had not yet been home. Still it was early. I sat staring at the clock for some time and, when its ticking began to irritate me, I left the room. I mounted the staircase and gained the upper part of the house. The high, cold, empty, gloomy rooms liberated me and I went from room to room singing. From the front window I saw my companions playing below in the street. Their cries reached me weakened and indistinct and, leaning my forehead against the cool glass, I looked over at the dark house where she lived. I may have stood there for an hour, seeing nothing but the brown-clad figure cast by my imagination, touched discreetly by the lamplight at the curved neck, at the hand upon the railings and at the border below the dress.

When I came downstairs again I found Mrs Mercer sitting at the fire. She was an old garrulous woman, a pawnbroker's widow, who collected used stamps for some pious purpose. I had to endure the gossip of the tea-table. The meal was prolonged beyond an hour and still my uncle did not come. Mrs Mercer stood up to go: she was sorry she couldn't wait any longer, but it was after eight o'clock and she did not like to be out late as the night air was bad for her. When she had gone I began to walk up and down the room, clenching my fists. My aunt said:

"I'm afraid you may put off your bazaar for this night of Our Lord."

At nine o'clock I heard my uncle's latchkey in the hall door. I heard him talking to himself and heard the hallstand rocking when it had received the weight of his overcoat. I could interpret these signs. When he was midway through his dinner I asked him to give me the money to go to the bazaar. He had forgotten.

"The people are in bed and after their first sleep now," he said.

I did not smile. My aunt said to him energetically:

"Can't you give him the money and let him go? You've kept him late enough as it is."

My uncle said he was very sorry he had forgotten. He said he believed in the old saying: "All work and no play makes Jack a dull boy." He asked me where I was going and, when I had told him a second time he asked me did I know *The Arab's Farewell to his Steed*. When I left the kitchen he was about to recite the opening lines of the piece to my aunt.

I held a florin[3] tightly in my hand as I strode down Buckingham Street towards the station. The sight of the streets thronged with buyers and glaring with gas recalled to me the purpose of my journey. I took my seat in a third-class carriage of a deserted train. After an intolerable delay the train moved out of the station slowly. It crept onward among ruinous houses and over the twinkling river. At Westland Row Station a crowd of people pressed to the carriage doors; but the porters moved them back, saying that it was a special train for the bazaar. I remained alone in the bare carriage. In a few minutes the train drew up beside an improvised wooden platform. I passed out on to the road and saw by the lighted dial of a clock that it was ten minutes to ten. In front of me was a large building which displayed the magical name.

I could not find any sixpenny entrance and, fearing that the bazaar would be closed, I passed in quickly through a turnstile, handing a shilling to a weary-looking man. I found myself in a big hall girdled at half its height by a gallery. Nearly all the stalls were closed and the greater part of the hall was in darkness. I recognised a silence like that which pervades a church after a service. I walked into the centre of the bazaar timidly. A few people were gathered about the stalls which were still open. Before a curtain, over which the words *Café Chantant* were written in coloured lamps, two men were counting money on a salver.[4] I listened to the fall of the coins.

Remembering with difficulty why I had come I went over to one of the stalls and examined porcelain vases and flowered tea-sets. At the door of the stall a young lady was talking and laughing with two young gentlemen. I remarked their English accents and listened vaguely to their conversation.

"O, I never said such a thing!"
"O, but you did!"
"O, but I didn't!"
"Didn't she say that?"
"Yes. I heard her."
"O, there's a... fib!"

Observing me the young lady came over and asked me did I wish to buy anything. The tone of her voice was not encouraging; she seemed to have spoken to me out of a sense of duty. I looked humbly

---

[3] Coin worth two shillings.
[4] Tray.

at the great jars that stood like eastern guards at either side of the dark entrance to the stall and murmured:

"No, thank you."

The young lady changed the position of one of the vases and went back to the two young men. They began to talk of the same subject. Once or twice the young lady glanced at me over her shoulder.

I lingered before her stall, though I knew my stay was useless, to make my interest in her wares seem the more real. Then I turned away slowly and walked down the middle of the bazaar. I allowed the two pennies to fall against the sixpence in my pocket. I heard a voice call from one end of the gallery that the light was out. The upper part of the hall was now completely dark.

Gazing up into the darkness I saw myself as a creature driven and derided by vanity; and my eyes burned with anguish and anger.

CRAFT: ARABY

Image and Imagery

The word "Araby" is an archaic form of "Arabian Peninsula," and its usage here as both the title of the story and the name of the bazaar **symbolizes** the narrator's intrigue with the exotic and things that juxtapose with his own life. Here, the narrator's intrigue with the exotic applies to both the bazaar and to Mangan's sister.

Joyce crafts this symbol by beginning the story with an "uninhabited house of two storeys" that "stood at the blind end, detached from its neighbours." This image remains with us throughout the story, primarily because we are continually reminded of the narrator's neighborhood. By the end, Joyce reveals the deeper meaning of this symbolic house. The narrator arrived too late at the bazaar, failed in his attempt to buy a gift for Mangan's sister, and is left empty and alone in the dark. His spirit is, in effect, "uninhabited" and he is detached from his neighbors.

But the symbolism of that house works in a much bigger way in "Araby," as many symbols often do in fiction. We imagine this uninhabited house as dead and dark, and Joyce continues this **imagery** throughout "Araby" in the "dark muddy lanes behind the houses," and the "dark dripping gardens," and the "dark odorous stables." When the narrator finally arrives at the bazaar, "the hall was in darkness" and the "upper part of the hall was now completely dark." This imagery deepens that original symbol of the uninhabited house, creating for the reader a sense of gloom, secrecy, and loneliness.

The **image** that Joyce creates of Mangan's sister focuses primarily on her dress, the "soft rope of her hair," and her "brown figure." "Her image accompanied me even in places the most hostile to romance."

What differentiates an image from imagery in fiction relies solely on frequency. An **image** is something that appears once (and by appear I mean that the writer creates the image, usually with descriptive language), and **imagery** appears more than once throughout a fictional work. While the image of Mangan's sister accompanies the narrator everywhere, he provides the reader with that brief image only once. However, the imagery of darkness and shadow appear throughout the story.

Personification

After the narrator mentions the uninhabited house at the "blind end," he **personifies**—or represents inanimate objects with human qualities—the other houses in the neighborhood, which he imagines are "conscious of the decent lives within them" and that "gazed at one another with brown imperturbable faces." This does a couple important things. First, it juxtaposes the narrator's description of the dead, blind, uninhabited house with the others that are alive and able to gaze.

Second, it adds weight and depth to the symbolic function of the uninhabited house, and comments on the narrator's emotional conflict. His fantasies, in the end, fail to find any of the life he sees in those houses, and instead find only darkness and loneliness. His own gaze, which is focused on Mangan's sister's door, finds only disappointment. This character feels more dead than alive. Instead of finding life at the bazaar, instead of capturing the image of Mangan's sister he has longed for, he remains "blind" in the dark.

Sentence Length

Often, the simplest observations about writing have an incredible effect on reading. As we dig deep into the meanings of the symbolism and imagery, as we analyze the effects of the point of view and choices the author makes in plotting the narrative, we often overlook some of the stylistic techniques that enrich our reading experience. As you review the following example of prose from "Araby," notice the length of the sentences:

> Her image accompanied me even in places the most hostile to romance. On Saturday evenings when my aunt went marketing I had to go to carry some of the parcels. *We walked through the flaring streets, jostled by drunken men and bargaining women, amid the curses of labourers, the shrill litanies of shop-boys who stood on guard by the barrels of pigs' cheeks, the nasal chanting of street-singers, who sang a come-all-you about O'Donovan Rossa, or a ballad about the troubles in our native land.* [Italics mine]

When we reach the italicized sentence, we have no idea when it might end. It seems to careen on and on, wanders just like the narrator and his aunt as they festoon through the market. The sentence, in effect, reflects the action.

Many writers talk a lot about the importance of varying sentence length, and I don't disagree that varying sentence length can easily bring **dynamism** and energy to **static** and monotonous prose. However, varying sentence length can often be inappropriate if the **action** in the story requires a different semantic effect or meaning. When a writer crafts a story, he or she attempts to align the style of the prose with the action or meaning in the narrative. And in the previous example from "Araby" we can see how Joyce not only aligns the style with the action, but heightens the meaning and experience with the length of his sentence.

Below, Joyce accomplishes a different effect when he describes the narrator's uncle finally returning home:

> At nine o'clock I heard my uncle's latchkey in the halldoor. I heard him talking to himself and heard the hallstand rocking when it had received the weight of his overcoat. *I could interpret these signs.* When he was midway through his dinner I asked him to give me the money to go to the bazaar. *He had forgotten.* [Italics mine]

Just before, the narrator had been pacing "up and down the room, clenching [his] fists." The simple, declarative sentences in italics match perfectly the frank, testy, and anxious mood of the narrator.

The narrator doesn't tell us how he knows his uncle had forgotten; he just declares it. The staccato sentence length and structure amplifies his impatience and fury.

Questions

1. "Araby" overflows with **symbolism, images,** and **imagery.** Isolate examples of each. Are all the images and imagery that Joyce creates symbolic? How would you describe the **"symbolic architecture"** of this story, or the story's symbolic design?

2. Where else does Joyce pair the sentence length and structure to events that occur in the story? Can you articulate why and how those sentences affect your experience of the events?

Eveline

She sat at the window watching the evening invade the avenue. Her head was leaned against the window curtains and in her nostrils was the odour of dusty cretonne.[1] She was tired.

Few people passed. The man out of the last house passed on his way home; she heard his footsteps clacking along the concrete pavement and afterwards crunching on the cinder path before the new red houses. One time there used to be a field there in which they used to play every evening with other people's children. Then a man from Belfast bought the field and built houses in it—not like their little brown houses but bright brick houses with shining roofs. The children of the avenue used to play together in that field—the Devines, the Waters, the Dunns, little Keogh the cripple, she and her brothers and sisters. Ernest, however, never played: he was too grown up. Her father used often to hunt them in out of the field with his blackthorn stick; but usually little Keogh used to keep nix[2] and call out when he saw her father coming. Still they seemed to have been rather happy then. Her father was not so bad then; and besides, her mother was alive. That was a long time ago; she and her brothers and sisters were all grown up; her mother was dead. Tizzie Dunn was dead, too, and the Waters had gone back to England. Everything changes. Now she was going to go away like the others, to leave her home.

Home! She looked round the room, reviewing all its familiar objects which she had dusted once a week for so many years, wondering where on earth all the dust came from. Perhaps she would never see again those familiar objects from which she had never dreamed of being divided. And yet during all those years she had never found out the name of the priest whose yellowing photograph hung on the wall above the broken harmonium beside the coloured print of the promises made to Blessed Margaret Mary Alacoque. He had been a school friend of her father. Whenever he showed the photograph to a visitor her father used to pass it with a casual word:

"He is in Melbourne now."

---

[1] A type of heavy fabric.
[2] Lookout.

She had consented to go away, to leave her home. Was that wise? She tried to weigh each side of the question. In her home anyway she had shelter and food; she had those whom she had known all her life about her. Of course she had to work hard, both in the house and at business. What would they say of her in the Stores when they found out that she had run away with a fellow? Say she was a fool, perhaps; and her place would be filled up by advertisement. Miss Gavan would be glad. She had always had an edge on her, especially whenever there were people listening.

"Miss Hill, don't you see these ladies are waiting?"

"Look lively, Miss Hill, please."

She would not cry many tears at leaving the Stores.

But in her new home, in a distant unknown country, it would not be like that. Then she would be married—she, Eveline. People would treat her with respect then. She would not be treated as her mother had been. Even now, though she was over nineteen, she sometimes felt herself in danger of her father's violence. She knew it was that that had given her the palpitations. When they were growing up he had never gone for her like he used to go for Harry and Ernest, because she was a girl, but latterly he had begun to threaten her and say what he would do to her only for her dead mother's sake. And now she had nobody to protect her. Ernest was dead and Harry, who was in the church decorating business, was nearly always down somewhere in the country. Besides, the invariable squabble for money on Saturday nights had begun to weary her unspeakably. She always gave her entire wages—seven shillings—and Harry always sent up what he could but the trouble was to get any money from her father. He said she used to squander the money, that she had no head, that he wasn't going to give her his hard-earned money to throw about the streets, and much more, for he was usually fairly bad on Saturday night. In the end he would give her the money and ask her had she any intention of buying Sunday's dinner. Then she had to rush out as quickly as she could and do her marketing, holding her black leather purse tightly in her hand as she elbowed her way through the crowds and returning home late under her load of provisions. She had hard work to keep the house together and to see that the two young children who had been left to her charge went to school regularly and got their meals regularly. It was hard work—a hard life—but now that she was about to leave it she did not find it a wholly undesirable life.

She was about to explore another life with Frank. Frank was very kind, manly, open-hearted. She was to go away with him by the night-boat to be his wife and to live with him in Buenos Ayres where he had a home waiting for her. How well she remembered the first time she had seen him; he was lodging in a house on the main road where she used to visit. It seemed a few weeks ago. He was standing at the gate, his peaked cap pushed back on his head and his hair tumbled forward over a face of bronze. Then they had come to know each other. He used to meet her outside the Stores every evening and see her home. He took her to see *The Bohemian Girl* and she felt elated as she sat in an unaccustomed part of the theatre with him. He was awfully fond of music and sang a little. People knew that they were courting and, when he sang about the lass that loves a sailor, she always felt pleasantly confused. He used to call her Poppens out of fun. First of all it had been an excitement for her to have a fellow and then she had begun to like him. He had tales of distant countries. He had started as a deck boy at a pound a month on a ship of the Allan Line going out to Canada. He told her the names of the ships he had been on and the names of the different services. He had sailed through the Straits of Magellan and he told her stories of the terrible Patagonians. He had fallen on his feet in Buenos Ayres, he said, and had come over to the old country just for a holiday. Of course, her father had found out the affair and had forbidden her to have anything to say to him.

"I know these sailor chaps," he said.

One day he had quarrelled with Frank and after that she had to meet her lover secretly.

The evening deepened in the avenue. The white of two letters in her lap grew indistinct. One was to Harry; the other was to her father. Ernest had been her favourite but she liked Harry too. Her father was becoming old lately, she noticed; he would miss her. Sometimes he could be very nice. Not long before, when she had been laid up for a day, he had read her out a ghost story and made toast for her at the fire. Another day, when their mother was alive, they had all gone for a picnic to the Hill of Howth. She remembered her father putting on her mother's bonnet to make the children laugh.

Her time was running out but she continued to sit by the window, leaning her head against the window curtain, inhaling the odour of dusty cretonne. Down far in the avenue she could hear a street organ playing. She knew the air.[3] Strange that it should come that very night to remind her of the promise to her mother, her promise to keep the home together as long as she could. She remembered the last night of her mother's illness; she was again in the close dark room at the other side of the hall and outside she heard a melancholy air of Italy. The organ-player had been ordered to go away and given sixpence. She remembered her father strutting back into the sickroom saying:

"Damned Italians! coming over here!"

As she mused the pitiful vision of her mother's life laid its spell on the very quick of her being—that life of commonplace sacrifices closing in final craziness. She trembled as she heard again her mother's voice saying constantly with foolish insistence:

"Derevaun Seraun! Derevaun Seraun!"[4]

She stood up in a sudden impulse of terror. Escape! She must escape! Frank would save her. He would give her life, perhaps love, too. But she wanted to live. Why should she be unhappy? She had a right to happiness. Frank would take her in his arms, fold her in his arms. He would save her.

She stood among the swaying crowd in the station at the North Wall. He held her hand and she knew that he was speaking to her, saying something about the passage over and over again. The station was full of soldiers with brown baggages. Through the wide doors of the sheds she caught a glimpse of the black mass of the boat, lying in beside the quay wall, with illumined portholes. She answered nothing. She felt her cheek pale and cold and, out of a maze of distress, she prayed to God to direct her, to show her what was her duty. The boat blew a long mournful whistle into the mist. If she went, to-morrow she would be on the sea with Frank, steaming towards Buenos Ayres. Their passage had been booked. Could she still draw back after all he had done for her? Her distress awoke a nausea in her body and she kept moving her lips in silent fervent prayer.

A bell clanged upon her heart. She felt him seize her hand:

"Come!"

All the seas of the world tumbled about her heart. He was drawing her into them: he would drown her. She gripped with both hands at the iron railing.

---

[3] Song.
[4] Gibberish.

"Come!"

No! No! No! It was impossible. Her hands clutched the iron in frenzy. Amid the seas she sent a cry of anguish.

"Eveline! Evvy!"

He rushed beyond the barrier and called to her to follow. He was shouted at to go on but he still called to her. She set her white face to him, passive, like a helpless animal. Her eyes gave him no sign of love or farewell or recognition.

CRAFT: EVELINE

Verbal Irony: Character Names

Epifanio San Juan, Jr. in his analysis of *Dubliners*, suggests that what makes Eveline's "panicked recoil in the end lose its quality of abject and repulsive cowardice" stems from "the consistency of her portrayal as a woman whose response to life takes place on a basic, elemental plane."[1] He argues that she is open-minded and impressionable and therefore vulnerable. Many critics have claimed that Eveline's choice to stay behind points to her failure, fear, and lack of a sense of adventure.

However, while her doubts in the first half of the story about leaving her familiar household objects and her aging father seem timid, her doubts about Frank in the second half of the story seem more justified. Just as the reader begins to believe that Eveline is overanxious, Joyce provides us with this sentence: "She was about to explore another life with Frank."

The sentence is short, suggests a shift in tone, and the name acts as a **pun**. Frank means honest and straightforward, and the sentence itself is bold and straightforward. However, we begin to learn that there's nothing straightforward about Frank. He has traveled widely. He lives in Buenos Aires. He has "sailed through the Straits of Magellan." Their relationship has been fraught with trouble. Eveline's father disapproves of Frank and she has to "meet her lover secretly." There's nothing immediately suspicious about Frank—except for his quarreling with Eveline's father—but the reader wonders why Eveline has chosen a man so different from her.

---

[1] Epifanio San Juan, Jr., *James Joyce and the Craft of Fiction* (New Jersey: Associated University Presses, Inc., 1972), 72.

Joyce has chosen Frank's name carefully. The **pun** is **ironic**. It's a form of **verbal irony** in which the word expresses an idea different from its meaning. Similarly, Joyce's ironic choice of the name "Eveline," which contains that loaded name "Eve," might indicate that instead of biting into the forbidden fruit, this Eve has walked away from the temptation and stayed in the garden.

Joyce deprives us of Frank's voice until the end. "She felt him seize her hand: 'Come!'" While it might be "frank" to scream such a command at your lover, it is far from reassuring.

We as readers are left to consider what we know as the **idea** of this short story collection (paralysis) with practicality. On the one hand, Eveline shirks adventure and change, and seems to willingly choose incarceration in a life that does not fulfill her. On the other hand, Frank may not be the savior who will escort her out of that prison into fulfillment. Joyce's development of the idea of paralysis creates tension and a real dilemma for both the characters and the readers, who may themselves be left paralyzed, trying to decide if Eveline made the right or wrong choice.

Close Third Person & Point of View Inflection

Before "Eveline," all three stories—"The Sisters," "An Encounter," and "Araby"—are told from the first person point of view of nameless male characters. In "Eveline" we have our first instance of the **third person point of view,** and because Joyce tells the story through Eveline's experiences, we call this the **close third person.** It is also often called the **limited third person point of view**. The close third indicates a difference from the **omniscient third person point of view,** in which the narrator has access to multiple characters' actions and thoughts.

While we're at it, let's define the difference between **subjective third person** and **objective third person.** In "Eveline" we have an example of subjective third person because the narrator has access to the character's inner thoughts. An objective close third person narrator would follow one character through the narrative, but would not have access to her inner thoughts. That narrator, though remaining "close," would remain unbiased.

In "Eveline" Joyce isolates us in Eveline's experiences and thoughts, her point of view. We do not have access to Frank's or Eveline's father's thoughts, for example. While the narrator remains anonymous, as is typical of many third person narrators, the narrator does not hold Eveline at a distance or describe her objectively. In fact, much of the story revolves around her inner thoughts.

To complicate things even further, Joyce employs a very subtle technique called **point of view inflection**, which should not be confused with subjectivity. Point of view inflection describes an instance in which the character's voice actually invades the narrator's voice. "Then she would be married—she, Eveline." In this example, because we are now familiar with Joyce's writing, we know that he as the author would never add a dash and follow it with "she, Eveline." That's not the author's voice, nor is it the narrator's. That is Eveline's voice creeping into the third person point of view. The narrator's voice here is inflecting to further reflect Eveline's inner thoughts. While point of view inflection often occurs with subjective third person narrators, a subjective third person narrator does not require point of view inflection.

Sounds confusing, doesn't it? Think of this way: When it comes to the close third person point of view, a writer must decide on his or her scope, or how close he or she will get to the character. The widest scope is an objective close third person narrator who does not have access to the character's inner thoughts. A narrower scope is a subjective narrator who does have access to the character's inner thoughts. And an even narrower scope is a subjective narrator who employs point of view inflection.

Let's examine a few sentences of "Eveline" to illustrate Joyce's use of subjectivity, objectivity and point of view inflection.

Subjective Narration: **Bold**
Objective Narration: *Italics*
Point of View Inflection: Underline

> <u>Home!</u> *She looked round the room, reviewing all its familiar objects which she had dusted once a week for so many years,* **wondering where on earth all the dust came from. Perhaps she would never see again those familiar objects from which she had never dreamed of being divided.**

It probably seems like a lot of terminology, so let's sum up. "Eveline" is an example of the **close third person point of view**, because we follow one character throughout the narrative. This close third person narrator is **subjective**, because he has access to Eveline's inner thoughts. Because those inner thoughts are so important to this story, the narrator uses **point of view inflection,** allowing Eveline's voice to invade the narration in order to further embed us in Eveline's perspective.

I'm going to go out on a limb here and suggest that when Joyce set out to write Eveline he did not say to himself, "I'm going to include significant point of view inflection in this story." Most likely it just happened. I mention this to suggest to both readers and writers that many of the ways in which we analyze narratives do not necessarily come from the author's conscious intention. Whether Joyce intended to use point of view inflection or not doesn't really matter. What matters is that it's there and it has an effect. If you're a writer, you probably aren't going to make conscious decisions about point of view inflection before you write a story or even while you write a story. It's after you write it that you detect it and ask yourself if your own use of point of view inflection creates the desired effect.

Here's a secret for you readers out there: Even writers don't always know what their intentions are until they read their own work.

Choice and Discourse

The **premise** of this story involves Eveline's choice to follow Frank to Buenos Aires. **Choice** is an important idea in fiction, and it often either creates or strengthens a character's goal. Here, at the beginning of the story, Eveline has already decided to go with Frank to Buenos Aires. Therefore, the tension comes from the suggestion that she might change her mind—a tension that first surfaces with the sentences: "She had consented to go away, to leave her home. Was that wise?"

We all know what a choice is. **Discourse**, however, is a more complex idea. Simply put, it's written or spoken communication, expression, and reasoning. "Eveline" exemplifies the relationship between choice and discourse very well. The narrator reveals that Eveline may not have actually *chosen* to accompany Frank to Buenos Aires, but "consented." After the reader understands Eveline's consent, a long discourse follows that deals with both sides of that choice. On the one hand, Eveline admits that she has shelter, food, and friends at home. On the other hand, she's had to work very hard, and she will be respected as a married woman if she goes with Frank. Her father is there at home in Ireland, but he's old and she has grown afraid of his threats and violence. Her life will be easier with Frank, who has money. Then again she admits that while she has had to work hard "she did not find it a wholly undesirable life." There is the mystery and adventure of traveling with Frank to Buenos Aires, but there is the fear that things will not turn out as well as Eveline might hope.

As I pointed out earlier, the reader, like Eveline, engages in this discourse, and must participate in the choice. The reader goes back and forth, wondering, like Eveline does, if this choice is wise. Joyce includes Eveline's reasoning to create tension surrounding the choice—a choice that becomes far less straightforward as the story progresses to the end and into the height of **conflict** or **crisis**. After Frank yells "Come!" to Eveline twice, he then calls, "Eveline! Evvy!" It's a softer tone, more tender, and it suggests to the reader that perhaps Frank might not be so bad, so aggressive and cold. Too late. We are now isolated in Eveline's choice.

Questions

1. Where else does Joyce use **point of view inflection** in "Eveline"? Do you find that such instances allow you to more intimately connect with Eveline's voice and character, or do you find the inflection jarring, distracting, and/or ineffective?

2. When it comes to Eveline's **choice** to go to Buenos Aires with Frank, what side are you on at the beginning, middle, and end of the story? What elements of Joyce's **discourse** persuade you one way or the other? If the narrator managed to change your mind, how did he do it?

3. How "close" is this **close third person narrator**? How close do you feel to Eveline? Do you feel like someone viewing this story from a distance? From above? From later in time? Or do you feel right next to Eveline? Do you feel as though the narrator has a character or personality or is more like Eveline herself? Find several examples that support your opinion about the closeness of the narrator. How does the narrator's distance affect the way you understand Eveline?

After the Race

The cars came scudding in towards Dublin, running evenly like pellets in the groove of the Naas Road. At the crest of the hill at Inchicore sightseers had gathered in clumps to watch the cars careering homeward and through this channel of poverty and inaction the Continent sped its wealth and industry. Now and again the clumps of people raised the cheer of the gratefully oppressed. Their sympathy, however, was for the blue cars—the cars of their friends, the French.

The French, moreover, were virtual victors. Their team had finished solidly; they had been placed second and third and the driver of the winning German car was reported a Belgian. Each blue car, therefore, received a double measure of welcome as it topped the crest of the hill and each cheer of welcome was acknowledged with smiles and nods by those in the car. In one of these trimly built cars was a party of four young men whose spirits seemed to be at present well above the level of successful Gallicism: in fact, these four young men were almost hilarious. They were Charles Ségouin, the owner of the car; André Rivière, a young electrician of Canadian birth; a huge Hungarian named Villona and a neatly groomed young man named Doyle. Ségouin was in good humour because he had unexpectedly received some orders in advance (he was about to start a motor establishment in Paris) and Rivière was in good humour because he was to be appointed manager of the establishment; these two young men (who were cousins) were also in good humour because of the success of the French cars. Villona was in good humour because he had had a very satisfactory luncheon; and besides he was an optimist by nature. The fourth member of the party, however, was too excited to be genuinely happy.

He was about twenty-six years of age, with a soft, light brown moustache and rather innocent-looking grey eyes. His father, who had begun life as an advanced Nationalist, had modified his views early. He had made his money as a butcher in Kingstown and by opening shops in Dublin and in the suburbs he had made his money many times over. He had also been fortunate enough to secure some of the police contracts and in the end he had become rich enough to be alluded to in the Dublin newspapers as a merchant prince. He had sent his son to England to be educated in a big Catholic college and had afterwards sent him to Dublin University to study law. Jimmy did not study very earnestly and took to bad courses for a while. He had money and he was popular; and he divided his time curiously between musical and motoring circles. Then he had been sent for a term to Cambridge to see a little life. His father, remonstrative, but covertly proud of the excess, had paid his bills and brought him home. It was at Cambridge that he had met Ségouin. They were not much more than acquaintances as yet but Jimmy found great pleasure in the society of one who had seen so much of the world and was reputed to own some of the biggest hotels in France. Such a person (as his father agreed) was well worth knowing, even if he had not been the charming companion he was. Villona was entertaining also—a brilliant pianist—but, unfortunately, very poor.

The car ran on merrily with its cargo of hilarious youth. The two cousins sat on the front seat; Jimmy and his Hungarian friend sat behind. Decidedly Villona was in excellent spirits; he kept up a deep bass hum of melody for miles of the road. The Frenchmen flung their laughter and light words over their shoulders and often Jimmy had to strain forward to catch the quick phrase. This was not altogether pleasant for him, as he had nearly always to make a deft guess at the meaning and shout back a suitable answer in the face of a high wind. Besides Villona's humming would confuse anybody; the noise of the car, too.

Rapid motion through space elates one; so does notoriety; so does the possession of money. These were three good reasons for Jimmy's excitement. He had been seen by many of his friends that day in the company of these Continentals. At the control Ségouin had presented him to one of the French competitors and, in answer to his confused murmur of compliment, the swarthy face of the driver had disclosed a line of shining white teeth. It was pleasant after that honour to return to the profane world of spectators amid nudges and significant looks. Then as to money—he really had a great sum under his control. Ségouin, perhaps, would not think it a great sum but Jimmy who, in spite of temporary errors, was at heart the inheritor of solid instincts knew well with what difficulty it had been got together. This knowledge had previously kept his bills within the limits of reasonable recklessness, and if he had been so conscious of the labour latent in money when there had been question merely of some freak of the higher intelligence, how much more so now when he was about to stake the greater part of his substance! It was a serious thing for him.

Of course, the investment was a good one and Ségouin had managed to give the impression that it was by a favour of friendship the mite of Irish money was to be included in the capital of the concern. Jimmy had a respect for his father's shrewdness in business matters and in this case it had been his father who had first suggested the investment; money to be made in the motor business, pots of money. Moreover Ségouin had the unmistakable air of wealth. Jimmy set out to translate into days' work that lordly car in which he sat. How smoothly it ran. In what style they had come careering along the country roads! The journey laid a magical finger on the genuine pulse of life and gallantly the machinery of human nerves strove to answer the bounding courses of the swift blue animal.

They drove down Dame Street. The street was busy with unusual traffic, loud with the horns of motorists and the gongs of impatient tram-drivers. Near the bank Ségouin drew up and Jimmy and his friend alighted. A little knot of people collected on the footpath to pay homage to the snorting motor. The party was to dine together that evening in Ségouin's hotel and, meanwhile, Jimmy and his friend, who was staying with him, were to go home to dress. The car steered out slowly for Grafton Street while the two young men pushed their way through the knot of gazers. They walked northward with a curious feeling of disappointment in the exercise, while the city hung its pale globes of light above them in a haze of summer evening.

In Jimmy's house this dinner had been pronounced an occasion. A certain pride mingled with his parents' trepidation, a certain eagerness, also, to play fast and loose for the names of great foreign cities have at least this virtue. Jimmy, too, looked very well when he was dressed and, as he stood in the hall giving a last equation to the bows of his dress tie, his father may have felt even commercially satisfied at having secured for his son qualities often unpurchaseable. His father, therefore, was unusually friendly with Villona and his manner expressed a real respect for foreign accomplishments; but this subtlety of his host was probably lost upon the Hungarian, who was beginning to have a sharp desire for his dinner.

The dinner was excellent, exquisite. Ségouin, Jimmy decided, had a very refined taste. The party was increased by a young

Englishman named Routh whom Jimmy had seen with Ségouin at Cambridge. The young men supped¹ in a snug room lit by electric candle lamps. They talked volubly and with little reserve. Jimmy, whose imagination was kindling, conceived the lively youth of the Frenchmen twined elegantly upon the firm framework of the Englishman's manner. A graceful image of his, he thought, and a just one. He admired the dexterity with which their host directed the conversation. The five young men had various tastes and their tongues had been loosened. Villona, with immense respect, began to discover to the mildly surprised Englishman the beauties of the English madrigal,² deploring the loss of old instruments. Rivière, not wholly ingenuously, undertook to explain to Jimmy the triumph of the French mechanicians. The resonant voice of the Hungarian was about to prevail in ridicule of the spurious lutes of the romantic painters when Ségouin shepherded his party into politics. Here was congenial ground for all. Jimmy, under generous influences, felt the buried zeal of his father wake to life within him: he aroused the torpid Routh at last. The room grew doubly hot and Ségouin's task grew harder each moment: there was even danger of personal spite. The alert host at an opportunity lifted his glass to Humanity and, when the toast had been drunk, he threw open a window significantly.

That night the city wore the mask of a capital. The five young men strolled along Stephen's Green in a faint cloud of aromatic smoke. They talked loudly and gaily and their cloaks dangled from their shoulders. The people made way for them. At the corner of Grafton Street a short fat man was putting two handsome ladies on a car in charge of another fat man. The car drove off and the short fat man caught sight of the party.

"André."

"It's Farley!"

A torrent of talk followed. Farley was an American. No one knew very well what the talk was about. Villona and Rivière were the noisiest, but all the men were excited. They got up on a car, squeezing themselves together amid much laughter. They drove by the crowd, blended now into soft colours, to a music of merry bells. They took the train at Westland Row and in a few seconds, as it seemed to Jimmy, they were walking out of Kingstown Station. The ticket-collector saluted Jimmy; he was an old man:

---

¹ Ate supper.
² A type of song for two or more singers.

"Fine night, sir!"

It was a serene summer night; the harbour lay like a darkened mirror at their feet. They proceeded towards it with linked arms, singing *Cadet Roussel* in chorus, stamping their feet at every:

"Ho! Ho! Hohé, vraiment!"

They got into a rowboat at the slip and made out for the American's yacht. There was to be supper, music, cards. Villona said with conviction:

"It is delightful!"

There was a yacht piano in the cabin. Villona played a waltz for Farley and Rivière, Farley acting as cavalier and Rivière as lady. Then an impromptu square dance, the men devising original figures. What merriment! Jimmy took his part with a will; this was seeing life, at least. Then Farley got out of breath and cried, "*Stop!*" A man brought in a light supper, and the young men sat down to it for form's sake. They drank, however: it was Bohemian. They drank[3] Ireland, England, France, Hungary, the United States of America. Jimmy made a speech, a long speech, Villona saying: "*Hear! hear!*" whenever there was a pause. There was a great clapping of hands when he sat down. It must have been a good speech. Farley clapped him on the back and laughed loudly. What jovial fellows! What good company they were!

Cards! cards! The table was cleared. Villona returned quietly to his piano and played voluntaries[4] for them. The other men played game after game, flinging themselves boldly into the adventure. They drank the health of the Queen of Hearts and of the Queen of Diamonds. Jimmy felt obscurely the lack of an audience: the wit was flashing. Play ran very high and paper began to pass. Jimmy did not know exactly who was winning but he knew that he was losing. But it was his own fault for he frequently mistook his cards and the other men had to calculate his I.O.U.'s for him. They were devils of fellows but he wished they would stop: it was getting late. Someone gave the toast of the yacht *The Belle of Newport* and then someone proposed one great game for a finish.

The piano had stopped; Villona must have gone up on deck. It was a terrible game. They stopped just before the end of it to drink for luck. Jimmy understood that the game lay between Routh and Ségouin. What excitement! Jimmy was excited too; he would lose, of

---

[3] As in "drank to."
[4] Improvised songs.

course. How much had he written away? The men rose to their feet to play the last tricks, talking and gesticulating. Routh won. The cabin shook with the young men's cheering and the cards were bundled together. They began then to gather in what they had won. Farley and Jimmy were the heaviest losers.

He knew that he would regret in the morning but at present he was glad of the rest, glad of the dark stupor that would cover up his folly. He leaned his elbows on the table and rested his head between his hands, counting the beats of his temples. The cabin door opened and he saw the Hungarian standing in a shaft of grey light:

"Daybreak, gentlemen!"

CRAFT: After the Race

CRAFT: AFTER THE RACE

Trope: Metaphor and Simile

Literary **tropes** are figurative words or expressions used in a symbolic or nonliteral way. The most common tropes are **metaphors** and **similes**, and the strongest writing in "After the Race" employs tropes and **images**. In fact, Joyce begins the story with an image and a simile: "The cars came scudding in towards Dublin, running evenly like pellets in the groove of the Naas Road." Later in the story, Joyce writes, "It was a serene summer night; the harbor lay like a darkened mirror at their feet." These similes allow the reader to see the images—the cars as they come "scudding" or moving swiftly toward the city, and the water of the harbor.

The use of "like" or "as" differentiate a simile from a metaphor. For example, Joyce's simile about the harbor—"the harbor lay *like* a darkened mirror"—could be changed into a metaphor by removing the word "like": *The harbor was a darkened mirror*. While this may seem elementary, writers do agonize over whether they should create a simile or a metaphor. By using the words like or as, a simile declares itself a comparison, but a metaphor boldly creates a comparison without instructing the reader—a reader is expected to understand the comparison implicitly. Metaphors have the added bonus of not requiring like or as, which many writers consider clunky, but similes have the added bonus of safety. Readers are far more likely to doubt the effectiveness of the metaphor "the harbor was a darkened mirror" than the simile "the harbor was like a darkened mirror."

One of Joyce's simple metaphors in "After the Race" offers a good example of how a writer provides an image for a reader: "The car steered out slowly for Grafton Street while the two young men pushed their way through the knot of gazers." The "knot" metaphor indicates that the crowd is full and tight, and suggests not only that there are numerous people, but that they are enthusiastic. While we don't actually imagine the crowd as a "knot," we do visualize the image of a crowd as "knot-like."

But leave it to James Joyce, however, to pack numerous metaphors into one sentence—so many that it is often difficult to keep track of not only the images and symbolism, but the sentence structure and meaning too. "The journey laid a magical finger on the genuine pulse of life and gallantly the machinery of human nerves strove to answer the bounding courses of the swift blue animal."

The "swift blue animal" metaphor provides an effective image for the reader. Joyce's metaphor for the "machinery of human nerves" earlier in the sentence makes it that much more powerful. This forms a **chiasmus** of images in the sentence, as Joyce reverses metaphors—the human is a machine and the machine is an animal (for a detailed analysis of chiasmus see "Grace"). However, the first set of metaphors—"The journey laid a magical finger on the genuine pulse of life..."—seems less precise and effective. The journey's act of laying a finger on something is a bit of a stretch, but to lay a finger on the "pulse of life" seems almost ridiculous. In effect, it lessens the strength of the stronger metaphors that follow in the sentence.

Writers adore tropes. They painstakingly invent and construct them. They use them like badges of honor. They admire the tropes of other writers and think, "How did she come up with that? Brilliant!" But a lot of writers—Joyce included—sometimes overuse tropes and especially metaphors. Many books I read have poor description and too many tropes that try to take the place of description and detail. If you're trying to describe someone's eyes, you could say, "His eyes were two ponds reflecting the moon at midnight" or you could say, "His eyes were dark blue, and they reflected the light of the candle beside him in small triangles of white beside his black pupils."

There are times, I suppose, when the writer wants the reader to think about two ponds at midnight. But tropes can be like close-ups in a film. If you overuse them, the whole narrative seems overwrought and claustrophobic. If you use them precisely and sparingly, they can do wonders. The "swift blue animal" is an effective metaphor. So is the "knot of gazers." But the journey laying a "magical finger" falls flat.

Show versus Tell

Writers often use the terms **"show"** and **"tell"** to indicate how the writer presents a narrative event. **Tell** refers to an event that the writer summarizes using **exposition**. In "After the Race" the narrator says, "Jimmy made a speech, a long speech." The narrator is **telling** us that Jimmy spoke, but not **showing** us the scene. If I were to tell you that a character had an argument with his mother, it would have a different effect than if I actually included the argument in the story, or "showed" it.

While Warren Beck in his book on Joyce's *Dubliners* argues that "After the Race" suffers from a lack of pathos and Joyce's lack of knowledge about the context and characters, his error in craft comes down to his failure to show much of anything in the story.[1] When the men play cards, Joyce writes:

> What excitement! Jimmy was excited too; he would lose, of course. How much had he written away? The men rose to their feet to play the last tricks, talking and gesticulating. Routh won. The cabin shook with the young men's cheering and the cards were bundled together.

While Joyce tells us that there's excitement in this scene, we certainly don't see it or feel it. He doesn't provide us with the necessary details that will allow us to "enter" the scene. Earlier in the story, Joyce writes that the car "ran on merrily with its cargo of hilarious youth," but never shows us any of the hilarity.

Beck may be right that Joyce's lack of familiarity with the subject matter led to the awkwardness and distance of the narration, which may remind writers of a marginally helpful cliché that circles like a

---

[1] Warren Beck, *Joyce's Dubliners: Substance, Vision and Art* (Durham N.C.: Duke University Press, 1969), 123-124.

vulture over the imaginative heads of beginning writers, warning that if you don't "write what you know" you may perish. However, the more helpful mantra might be, "When in murky and unknown waters, show instead of tell."

Questions

1. How does Joyce use literary **tropes** in "After the Race"? When closely analyzing the meanings of several similes or metaphors, do you find them effective? How do they affect the way you experience the story?

2. Choose a moment in "After the Race" you think is or should be a moment of high tension and narrative importance. First, how does Joyce construct the moment? Does he **"show"** or does he **"tell"**? Does the moment include concrete, specific, and detailed information and/or description? How effectively does his construction of the moment communicate the tension and/or narrative change?

3. Returning to **narrative structure**, can you summarize the **setup**, **conflict**, and **resolution** in "After the Race"? In your attempt to summarize, how might we assess the narrative structure and **plot**?

4. Earlier, I suggested that some stories suffer from over-amplifying the **idea**. In "After the Race," I find that Joyce's idea of international class structures and political power—as exemplified by the characters—overpowers the importance of **narrative structure**, character, and **plot**. Can you find examples of Joyce's idea in this story? What particularly do you find successful or lacking in those examples? How might Joyce have more effectively created characters and a dramatic plot?

Two Gallants

The grey warm evening of August had descended upon the city and a mild warm air, a memory of summer, circulated in the streets. The streets, shuttered for the repose of Sunday, swarmed with a gaily coloured crowd. Like illumined pearls the lamps shone from the summits of their tall poles upon the living texture below which, changing shape and hue unceasingly, sent up into the warm grey evening air an unchanging unceasing murmur.

Two young men came down the hill of Rutland Square. One of them was just bringing a long monologue to a close. The other, who walked on the verge of the path and was at times obliged to step on to the road, owing to his companion's rudeness, wore an amused listening face. He was squat and ruddy. A yachting cap was shoved far back from his forehead and the narrative to which he listened made constant waves of expression break forth over his face from the corners of his nose and eyes and mouth. Little jets of wheezing laughter followed one another out of his convulsed body. His eyes, twinkling with cunning enjoyment, glanced at every moment towards his companion's face. Once or twice he rearranged the light waterproof[1] which he had slung over one shoulder in toreador[2] fashion. His breeches, his white rubber shoes and his jauntily slung waterproof expressed youth. But his figure fell into rotundity at the waist, his hair was scant and grey and his face, when the waves of expression had passed over it, had a ravaged look.

When he was quite sure that the narrative had ended he laughed noiselessly for fully half a minute. Then he said:

"Well!... That takes the biscuit!"

His voice seemed winnowed of vigour; and to enforce his words he added with humour:

"That takes the solitary, unique, and, if I may so call it, recherché[3] biscuit!"

He became serious and silent when he had said this. His tongue was tired for he had been talking all the afternoon in a public-

---

[1] Raincoat.
[2] Bullfighter.
[3] Exquisite, rare.

house[4] in Dorset Street. Most people considered Lenehan a leech but, in spite of this reputation, his adroitness and eloquence had always prevented his friends from forming any general policy against him. He had a brave manner of coming up to a party of them in a bar and of holding himself nimbly at the borders of the company until he was included in a round. He was a sporting vagrant armed with a vast stock of stories, limericks and riddles. He was insensitive to all kinds of discourtesy. No one knew how he achieved the stern task of living, but his name was vaguely associated with racing tissues.[5]

"And where did you pick her up, Corley?" he asked.

Corley ran his tongue swiftly along his upper lip.

"One night, man," he said, "I was going along Dame Street and I spotted a fine tart under Waterhouse's clock and said goodnight, you know. So we went for a walk round by the canal and she told me she was a slavey[6] in a house in Baggot Street. I put my arm round her and squeezed her a bit that night. Then next Sunday, man, I met her by appointment. We went out to Donnybrook and I brought her into a field there. She told me she used to go with a dairyman... It was fine, man. Cigarettes every night she'd bring me and paying the tram out and back. And one night she brought me two bloody fine cigars—O, the real cheese, you know, that the old fellow used to smoke... I was afraid, man, she'd get in the family way. But she's up to the dodge."

"Maybe she thinks you'll marry her," said Lenehan.

"I told her I was out of a job," said Corley. "I told her I was in Pim's. She doesn't know my name. I was too hairy[7] to tell her that. But she thinks I'm a bit of class, you know."

Lenehan laughed again, noiselessly.

"Of all the good ones ever I heard," he said, "that emphatically takes the biscuit."

Corley's stride acknowledged the compliment. The swing of his burly body made his friend execute a few light skips from the path to the roadway and back again. Corley was the son of an inspector of police and he had inherited his father's frame and gut. He walked with his hands by his sides, holding himself erect and swaying his head from side to side. His head was large, globular and oily; it

---

[4] Pub.
[5] Pamphlets about horse racing.
[6] Servant or maid.
[7] Smart.

sweated in all weathers; and his large round hat, set upon it sideways, looked like a bulb which had grown out of another. He always stared straight before him as if he were on parade and, when he wished to gaze after someone in the street, it was necessary for him to move his body from the hips. At present he was about town.[8] Whenever any job was vacant a friend was always ready to give him the hard word. He was often to be seen walking with policemen in plain clothes, talking earnestly. He knew the inner side of all affairs and was fond of delivering final judgments. He spoke without listening to the speech of his companions. His conversation was mainly about himself—what he had said to such a person and what such a person had said to him and what he had said to settle the matter. When he reported these dialogues he aspirated the first letter of his name after the manner of Florentines.[9]

Lenehan offered his friend a cigarette. As the two young men walked on through the crowd Corley occasionally turned to smile at some of the passing girls but Lenehan's gaze was fixed on the large faint moon circled with a double halo. He watched earnestly the passing of the grey web of twilight across its face. At length he said:

"Well... tell me, Corley, I suppose you'll be able to pull it off all right, eh?"

Corley closed one eye expressively as an answer.

"Is she game for that?" asked Lenehan dubiously. "You can never know women."

"She's all right," said Corley. "I know the way to get around her, man. She's a bit gone on me."

"You're what I call a gay Lothario," said Lenehan. "And the proper kind of a Lothario, too!"

A shade of mockery relieved the servility of his manner. To save himself he had the habit of leaving his flattery open to the interpretation of raillery.[10] But Corley had not a subtle mind.

"There's nothing to touch a good slavey," he affirmed. "Take my tip for it."

"By one who has tried them all," said Lenehan.

"First I used to go with girls, you know," said Corley, unbosoming; "Girls off the South Circular. I used to take them out, man, on the tram somewhere and pay the tram or take them to a

---

[8] Unemployed.
[9] As in "Horley."
[10] Ridicule, teasing.

band or a play at the theatre or buy them chocolate and sweets or something that way. I used to spend money on them right enough," he added, in a convincing tone, as if he was conscious of being disbelieved.

But Lenehan could well believe it; he nodded gravely.

"I know that game," he said, "and it's a mug's[11] game."

"And damn the thing I ever got out of it," said Corley.

"Ditto here," said Lenehan.

"Only off of one of them," said Corley.

He moistened his upper lip by running his tongue along it. The recollection brightened his eyes. He too gazed at the pale disc of the moon, now nearly veiled, and seemed to meditate.

She was... a bit of all right," he said regretfully.

He was silent again. Then he added:

"She's on the turf[12] now. I saw her driving down Earl Street one night with two fellows with her in a car."

"I suppose that's your doing," said Lenehan.

"There was others at her before me," said Corley philosophically.

This time Lenehan was inclined to disbelieve. He shook his head to and fro and smiled.

"You know you can't kid me, Corley," he said.

"Honest to God!" said Corley. "Didn't she tell me herself?"

Lenehan made a tragic gesture.

"Base betrayer!" he said.

As they passed along the railings of Trinity College, Lenehan skipped out into the road and peered up at the clock.

"Twenty after," he said.

"Time enough," said Corley. "She'll be there all right. I always let her wait a bit."

Lenehan laughed quietly.

"Ecod![13] Corley, you know how to take them," he said.

"I'm up to all their little tricks," Corley confessed.

"But tell me," said Lenehan again, "are you sure you can bring it off all right? You know it's a ticklish job. They're damn close on that point. Eh?... What?"

---

[11] Fool's.
[12] A prostitute.
[13] Variant of "Egad!" or "Oh God!"

His bright, small eyes searched his companion's face for reassurance. Corley swung his head to and fro as if to toss aside an insistent insect, and his brows gathered.

"I'll pull it off," he said. "Leave it to me, can't you?"

Lenehan said no more. He did not wish to ruffle his friend's temper, to be sent to the devil and told that his advice was not wanted. A little tact was necessary. But Corley's brow was soon smooth again. His thoughts were running another way.

"She's a fine decent tart," he said, with appreciation; "that's what she is."

They walked along Nassau Street and then turned into Kildare Street. Not far from the porch of the club a harpist stood in the roadway, playing to a little ring of listeners. He plucked at the wires heedlessly, glancing quickly from time to time at the face of each new-comer and from time to time, wearily also, at the sky. His harp, too, heedless that her coverings had fallen about her knees, seemed weary alike of the eyes of strangers and of her master's hands. One hand played in the bass the melody of *Silent, O Moyle*, while the other hand careered in the treble after each group of notes. The notes of the air sounded deep and full.

The two young men walked up the street without speaking, the mournful music following them. When they reached Stephen's Green they crossed the road. Here the noise of trams, the lights and the crowd released them from their silence.

"There she is!" said Corley.

At the corner of Hume Street a young woman was standing. She wore a blue dress and a white sailor hat. She stood on the curbstone, swinging a sunshade in one hand. Lenehan grew lively.

"Let's have a look at her, Corley," he said.

Corley glanced sideways at his friend and an unpleasant grin appeared on his face.

"Are you trying to get inside[14] me?" he asked.

"Damn it!" said Lenehan boldly. "I don't want an introduction. All I want is to have a look at her. I'm not going to eat her."

"O... A look at her?" said Corley, more amiably. "Well... I'll tell you what. I'll go over and talk to her and you can pass by."

"Right!" said Lenehan.

---

[14] As in "get the inside track" in horse racing.

Corley had already thrown one leg over the chains when Lenehan called out:

"And after? Where will we meet?"

"Half ten,"[15] answered Corley, bringing over his other leg.

"Where?"

"Corner of Merrion Street. We'll be coming back."

"Work it all right now," said Lenehan in farewell.

Corley did not answer. He sauntered across the road swaying his head from side to side. His bulk, his easy pace, and the solid sound of his boots had something of the conqueror in them. He approached the young woman and, without saluting, began at once to converse with her. She swung her umbrella more quickly and executed half turns on her heels. Once or twice when he spoke to her at close quarters she laughed and bent her head.

Lenehan observed them for a few minutes. Then he walked rapidly along beside the chains at some distance and crossed the road obliquely. As he approached Hume Street corner he found the air heavily scented and his eyes made a swift anxious scrutiny of the young woman's appearance. She had her Sunday finery on. Her blue serge skirt was held at the waist by a belt of black leather. The great silver buckle of her belt seemed to depress the centre of her body, catching the light stuff of her white blouse like a clip. She wore a short black jacket with mother-of-pearl buttons and a ragged black boa. The ends of her tulle collarette[16] had been carefully disordered and a big bunch of red flowers was pinned in her bosom stems upwards. Lenehan's eyes noted approvingly her stout short muscular body. Frank rude health glowed in her face, on her fat red cheeks and in her unabashed blue eyes. Her features were blunt. She had broad nostrils, a straggling mouth which lay open in a contented leer, and two projecting front teeth. As he passed Lenehan took off his cap and, after about ten seconds, Corley returned a salute to the air. This he did by raising his hand vaguely and pensively changing the angle of position of his hat.

Lenehan walked as far as the Shelbourne Hotel where he halted and waited. After waiting for a little time he saw them coming towards him and, when they turned to the right, he followed them, stepping lightly in his white shoes, down one side of Merrion Square. As he walked on slowly, timing his pace to theirs, he watched Corley's

---

[15] 10:30
[16] Collar

head which turned at every moment towards the young woman's face like a big ball revolving on a pivot. He kept the pair in view until he had seen them climbing the stairs of the Donnybrook tram; then he turned about and went back the way he had come.

Now that he was alone his face looked older. His gaiety seemed to forsake him and, as he came by the railings of the Duke's Lawn, he allowed his hand to run along them. The air which the harpist had played began to control his movements. His softly padded feet played the melody while his fingers swept a scale of variations idly along the railings after each group of notes.

He walked listlessly round Stephen's Green and then down Grafton Street. Though his eyes took note of many elements of the crowd through which he passed they did so morosely. He found trivial all that was meant to charm him and did not answer the glances which invited him to be bold. He knew that he would have to speak a great deal, to invent and to amuse and his brain and throat were too dry for such a task. The problem of how he could pass the hours till he met Corley again troubled him a little. He could think of no way of passing them but to keep on walking. He turned to the left when he came to the corner of Rutland Square and felt more at ease in the dark quiet street, the sombre look of which suited his mood. He paused at last before the window of a poor-looking shop over which the words *Refreshment Bar* were printed in white letters. On the glass of the window were two flying inscriptions: *Ginger Beer* and *Ginger Ale*. A cut ham was exposed on a great blue dish while near it on a plate lay a segment of very light plum-pudding. He eyed this food earnestly for some time and then, after glancing warily up and down the street, went into the shop quickly.

He was hungry for, except some biscuits which he had asked two grudging curates[17] to bring him, he had eaten nothing since breakfast-time. He sat down at an uncovered wooden table opposite two work-girls and a mechanic. A slatternly girl waited on him.

"How much is a plate of peas?" he asked.

"Three halfpence, sir," said the girl.

"Bring me a plate of peas," he said, "and a bottle of ginger beer."

He spoke roughly in order to belie his air of gentility for his entry had been followed by a pause of talk. His face was heated. To

---

[17] Waiter or bartender.

appear natural he pushed his cap back on his head and planted his elbows on the table. The mechanic and the two work-girls examined him point by point before resuming their conversation in a subdued voice. The girl brought him a plate of grocer's hot peas, seasoned with pepper and vinegar, a fork and his ginger beer. He ate his food greedily and found it so good that he made a note of the shop mentally. When he had eaten all the peas he sipped his ginger beer and sat for some time thinking of Corley's adventure. In his imagination he beheld the pair of lovers walking along some dark road; he heard Corley's voice in deep energetic gallantries and saw again the leer of the young woman's mouth. This vision made him feel keenly his own poverty of purse and spirit. He was tired of knocking about, of pulling the devil by the tail,[18] of shifts and intrigues. He would be thirty-one in November. Would he never get a good job? Would he never have a home of his own? He thought how pleasant it would be to have a warm fire to sit by and a good dinner to sit down to. He had walked the streets long enough with friends and with girls. He knew what those friends were worth: he knew the girls too. Experience had embittered his heart against the world. But all hope had not left him. He felt better after having eaten than he had felt before, less weary of his life, less vanquished in spirit. He might yet be able to settle down in some snug corner and live happily if he could only come across some good simple-minded girl with a little of the ready.[19]

    He paid twopence halfpenny to the slatternly girl and went out of the shop to begin his wandering again. He went into Capel Street and walked along towards the City Hall. Then he turned into Dame Street. At the corner of George's Street he met two friends of his and stopped to converse with them. He was glad that he could rest from all his walking. His friends asked him had he seen Corley and what was the latest. He replied that he had spent the day with Corley. His friends talked very little. They looked vacantly after some figures in the crowd and sometimes made a critical remark. One said that he had seen Mac an hour before in Westmoreland Street. At this Lenehan said that he had been with Mac the night before in Egan's. The young man who had seen Mac in Westmoreland Street asked was

---

[18] Being poor.
[19] Money.

it true that Mac had won a bit over a billiard match. Lenehan did not know: he said that Holohan had stood[20] them drinks in Egan's.

He left his friends at a quarter to ten and went up George's Street. He turned to the left at the City Markets and walked on into Grafton Street. The crowd of girls and young men had thinned and on his way up the street he heard many groups and couples bidding one another good-night. He went as far as the clock of the College of Surgeons: it was on the stroke of ten. He set off briskly along the northern side of the Green hurrying for fear Corley should return too soon. When he reached the corner of Merrion Street he took his stand in the shadow of a lamp and brought out one of the cigarettes which he had reserved and lit it. He leaned against the lamp-post and kept his gaze fixed on the part from which he expected to see Corley and the young woman return.

His mind became active again. He wondered had Corley managed it successfully. He wondered if he had asked her yet or if he would leave it to the last. He suffered all the pangs and thrills of his friend's situation as well as those of his own. But the memory of Corley's slowly revolving head calmed him somewhat: he was sure Corley would pull it off all right. All at once the idea struck him that perhaps Corley had seen her home by another way and given him the slip. His eyes searched the street: there was no sign of them. Yet it was surely half-an-hour since he had seen the clock of the College of Surgeons. Would Corley do a thing like that? He lit his last cigarette and began to smoke it nervously. He strained his eyes as each tram stopped at the far corner of the square. They must have gone home by another way. The paper of his cigarette broke and he flung it into the road with a curse.

Suddenly he saw them coming towards him. He started with delight and keeping close to his lamp-post tried to read the result in their walk. They were walking quickly, the young woman taking quick short steps, while Corley kept beside her with his long stride. They did not seem to be speaking. An intimation of the result pricked him like the point of a sharp instrument. He knew Corley would fail; he knew it was no go.

They turned down Baggot Street and he followed them at once, taking the other footpath. When they stopped he stopped too. They talked for a few moments and then the young woman went

---

[20] Bought.

down the steps into the area of a house. Corley remained standing at the edge of the path, a little distance from the front steps. Some minutes passed. Then the hall-door was opened slowly and cautiously. A woman came running down the front steps and coughed. Corley turned and went towards her. His broad figure hid hers from view for a few seconds and then she reappeared running up the steps. The door closed on her and Corley began to walk swiftly towards Stephen's Green.

Lenehan hurried on in the same direction. Some drops of light rain fell. He took them as a warning and, glancing back towards the house which the young woman had entered to see that he was not observed, he ran eagerly across the road. Anxiety and his swift run made him pant. He called out:

"Hallo, Corley!"

Corley turned his head to see who had called him, and then continued walking as before. Lenehan ran after him, settling the waterproof on his shoulders with one hand.

"Hallo, Corley!" he cried again.

He came level with his friend and looked keenly in his face. He could see nothing there.

"Well?" he said. "Did it come off?"

They had reached the corner of Ely Place. Still without answering, Corley swerved to the left and went up the side street. His features were composed in stern calm. Lenehan kept up with his friend, breathing uneasily. He was baffled and a note of menace pierced through his voice.

"Can't you tell us?" he said. "Did you try her?"

Corley halted at the first lamp and stared grimly before him. Then with a grave gesture he extended a hand towards the light and, smiling, opened it slowly to the gaze of his disciple. A small gold coin shone in the palm.

CRAFT: TWO GALLANTS

Foil and Epiphany

If an **antagonist** is one who opposes the **protagonist**, it wouldn't be absurd to call Corley in "Two Gallants" Lenehan's antagonist. While Corley does not directly challenge Lenehan—they are not entangled in some conflict or competition that pits one against the other—Corley does stand in opposition to Lenehan. While they are friends, they are different and have drastically divided attitudes and outlooks. But because the reader comes to understand Lenehan better through the comparison or reflection we see to Corley, we can categorize Corley as a **foil** character rather than an antagonist. A foil is a minor character meant to highlight or reflect the traits of a major character.

Even before the two characters have been named, the narrator suggests the differences between the two:

> Two young men came down the hill of Rutland Square. One of them was just bringing a long monologue to a close. The other, who walked on the verge of the path and was at times obliged to step on the road, owing to his companion's rudeness, wore an amused listening face.

Already the reader sees a dynamic developing between these two nameless characters. As we get to know Corley and Lenehan, it becomes obvious that Corley is the rude character—Lenehan's foil. Later in the story, the narrator reveals that Lenehan is "insensitive to all discourtesy," suggesting that he is merely tolerating Corley's rudeness for some greater purpose.

When Lenehan and Corley separate, Lenehan grows morose. "He found trivial all that was meant to charm him" and becomes troubled about "how he could pass the hours till he met Corley." When he stops in a refreshment bar he thinks wistfully of "Corley's adventure" with the girl, and imagines "Corley's voice in deep energetic gallantries."

> This vision made [Lenehan] feel keenly his own poverty of purse and spirit. He was tired of knocking about, of pulling the devil by the tail, of shifts and intrigues. He would be thirty-one in November. Would he never get a good job? Would he never have a home of his own?

Joyce motivates this introspection through Lenehan's own comparison to Corley, and the reader understands Lenehan's conflicts, doubts, and dreams when reflected by Corley's enthusiastic spirit.

Joyce uses Corley as a **foil** to transport his protagonist to an **epiphany**. "But all hope had not left him," Joyce writes. Lenehan feels better and optimistic that he will "live happily" and find a "good simple-minded girl with a little of the ready." Corley causes Lenehan to both doubt himself and strive for a better life.

The most common type of foil character in all of fiction is the seemingly perfect man or woman who makes a major character feel jealous about any number of things, from beauty to wealth to career to confidence (Jay Gatsby reflecting Nick Carraway). The other most common type of foil is the "dynamic duo" (Robin reflecting Batman, Sancho Panza reflecting Don Quixote, Doctor Watson reflecting Sherlock Holmes). Many confuse a foil character with a greatly misunderstood term known as the **doppelganger**. But the difference is simple. While a foil reflects something in a major character, a doppelganger is a double—a paranormal copy. If Corley looked like Lenehan, talked like him, walked like him, and *was* him, he'd be a doppelganger. What causes the confusion between the two terms is simple. A doppelganger can be a foil, but a foil is not a doppelganger. Corley is in no way Lenehan's double, but one can imagine how a double could reflect Lenehan's traits and lead him to some kind of realization.

For a great example of a complex doppelganger, see the novel *Atmospheric Disturbances*, by Rivka Galchen. Other doppelgangers appear in Fydor Dostoyevsky's story, "The Double: The Petersburg Poem," Edgar Allan Poe's "William Wilson," and Phillip Roth's novel, *Operation Shylock*.

Idiom

An **idiom** is a phrase that has a vernacular meaning that isn't always obvious to those who have not heard it. The idioms "hang out" or "chill out," though very familiar to us, would mystify someone not acquainted with contemporary American vernacular.

Joyce uses idioms heavily in "Two Gallants," primarily in order to characterize Corley. Lenehan has remarkably few idioms in his speech, and this has the effect of further distinguishing the two characters. Nevertheless, when Lenehan responds to Corley's monologue in the beginning of the story, he *does* use a common idiom: "Well!... That takes the biscuit!" However, he follows that up with this reinvention of the idiom: "That takes the solitary unique, and, if I may so call it, *recherché* biscuit!" This immediately communicates to the reader that Lenehan is sophisticated and articulate. One of Corley's early pieces of dialogue follows: "One night, man, I was going along Dame Street and I spotted a fine tart under Waterhouse's clock and said goodnight, you know." In comparison to Corley, Lenehan's dialogue is refined and aloof. Even his idioms are ironically transformed. But Corley follows with a long list of street-wise, idiomatic vernacular: "the real cheese," "get in the family way," "up to the dodge," "too hairy," "I'm a bit of class," and "on the turf." In a way, these, along with Joyce's humorous descriptions of Corley's "large, globular" head that "sweated in all weathers," function to turn Corley into a comic character. In comparison to Lenehan, Corley is simple and straightforward—a man who seems to have no doubts and will not change.

Questions

1. Where else in *Dubliners* has Joyce used a **foil** character? How does that character help to sharpen our knowledge of the **protagonist**?

2. In opposition to the comic **idioms** in "Two Gallants" how does Joyce use idioms elsewhere in *Dubliners* to create believable or **round** characters, or connect those characters with their settings?

3. How does Joyce communicate the implicit and core **idea** of this story? First, what is your interpretation of the **idea**? Second, how does that idea operate to inform the characters and events?

The Boarding House

Mrs Mooney was a butcher's daughter. She was a woman who was quite able to keep things to herself: a determined woman. She had married her father's foreman and opened a butcher's shop near Spring Gardens. But as soon as his father-in-law was dead Mr Mooney began to go to the devil. He drank, plundered the till, ran headlong into debt. It was no use making him take the pledge:[1] he was sure to break out again a few days after. By fighting his wife in the presence of customers and by buying bad meat he ruined his business. One night he went for his wife with the cleaver and she had to sleep at a neighbour's house.

After that they lived apart. She went to the priest and got a separation from him with care of the children. She would give him neither money nor food nor house-room; and so he was obliged to enlist himself as a sheriff's man. He was a shabby stooped little drunkard with a white face and a white moustache and white eyebrows, pencilled above his little eyes, which were veined and raw; and all day long he sat in the bailiff's room, waiting to be put on a job. Mrs Mooney, who had taken what remained of her money out of the butcher business and set up a boarding house in Hardwicke Street, was a big imposing woman. Her house had a floating population made up of tourists from Liverpool and the Isle of Man and, occasionally, *artistes* from the music halls. Its resident population was made up of clerks from the city. She governed the house cunningly and firmly, knew when to give credit, when to be stern and when to let things pass. All the resident young men spoke of her as *The Madam*.

Mrs Mooney's young men paid fifteen shillings a week for board and lodgings (beer or stout at dinner excluded). They shared in common tastes and occupations and for this reason they were very chummy with one another. They discussed with one another the chances of favourites and outsiders. Jack Mooney, the Madam's son, who was clerk to a commission agent in Fleet Street, had the reputation of being a hard case. He was fond of using soldiers' obscenities: usually he came home in the small hours. When he met

---

[1] To quit drinking.

his friends he had always a good one to tell them and he was always sure to be on to a good thing—that is to say, a likely horse or a likely *artiste*. He was also handy with the mits[2] and sang comic songs. On Sunday nights there would often be a reunion in Mrs Mooney's front drawing-room. The music-hall *artistes* would oblige; and Sheridan played waltzes and polkas and vamped accompaniments. Polly Mooney, the Madam's daughter, would also sing. She sang:

> I'm a... naughty girl.
> You needn't sham:
> You know I am.

Polly was a slim girl of nineteen; she had light soft hair and a small full mouth. Her eyes, which were grey with a shade of green through them, had a habit of glancing upwards when she spoke with anyone, which made her look like a little perverse madonna. Mrs Mooney had first sent her daughter to be a typist in a corn-factor's[3] office but, as a disreputable sheriff's man used to come every other day to the office, asking to be allowed to say a word to his daughter, she had taken her daughter home again and set her to do housework. As Polly was very lively the intention was to give her the run of the young men. Besides young men like to feel that there is a young woman not very far away. Polly, of course, flirted with the young men but Mrs Mooney, who was a shrewd judge, knew that the young men were only passing the time away: none of them meant business. Things went on so for a long time and Mrs Mooney began to think of sending Polly back to typewriting when she noticed that something was going on between Polly and one of the young men. She watched the pair and kept her own counsel.

Polly knew that she was being watched, but still her mother's persistent silence could not be misunderstood. There had been no open complicity between mother and daughter, no open understanding but, though people in the house began to talk of the affair, still Mrs Mooney did not intervene. Polly began to grow a little strange in her manner and the young man was evidently perturbed. At last, when she judged it to be the right moment, Mrs Mooney intervened. She dealt with moral problems as a cleaver deals with meat: and in this case she had made up her mind.

---

[2] Boxing gloves.
[3] Grain dealer.

It was a bright Sunday morning of early summer, promising heat, but with a fresh breeze blowing. All the windows of the boarding house were open and the lace curtains ballooned gently towards the street beneath the raised sashes. The belfry of George's Church sent out constant peals and worshippers, singly or in groups, traversed the little circus before the church, revealing their purpose by their self-contained demeanour no less than by the little volumes in their gloved hands. Breakfast was over in the boarding house and the table of the breakfast-room was covered with plates on which lay yellow streaks of eggs with morsels of bacon-fat and bacon-rind. Mrs Mooney sat in the straw arm-chair and watched the servant Mary remove the breakfast things. She made Mary collect the crusts and pieces of broken bread to help to make Tuesday's bread-pudding. When the table was cleared, the broken bread collected, the sugar and butter safe under lock and key, she began to reconstruct the interview which she had had the night before with Polly. Things were as she had suspected: she had been frank in her questions and Polly had been frank in her answers. Both had been somewhat awkward, of course. She had been made awkward by her not wishing to receive the news in too cavalier a fashion or to seem to have connived and Polly had been made awkward not merely because allusions of that kind always made her awkward but also because she did not wish it to be thought that in her wise innocence she had divined the intention behind her mother's tolerance.

Mrs Mooney glanced instinctively at the little gilt clock on the mantelpiece as soon as she had become aware through her revery that the bells of George's Church had stopped ringing. It was seventeen minutes past eleven: she would have lots of time to have the matter out with Mr Doran and then catch short twelve at Marlborough Street. She was sure she would win. To begin with she had all the weight of social opinion on her side: she was an outraged mother. She had allowed him to live beneath her roof, assuming that he was a man of honour and he had simply abused her hospitality. He was thirty-four or thirty-five years of age, so that youth could not be pleaded as his excuse; nor could ignorance be his excuse since he was a man who had seen something of the world. He had simply taken advantage of Polly's youth and inexperience: that was evident. The question was: What reparation would he make?

There must be reparation made in such cases. It is all very well for the man: he can go his ways as if nothing had happened, having had his moment of pleasure, but the girl has to bear the brunt. Some mothers would be content to patch up such an affair for a sum of money; she had known cases of it. But she would not do so. For her only one reparation could make up for the loss of her daughter's honour: marriage.

    She counted all her cards again before sending Mary up to Doran's room to say that she wished to speak with him. She felt sure she would win. He was a serious young man, not rakish[4] or loud-voiced like the others. If it had been Mr Sheridan or Mr Meade or Bantam Lyons her task would have been much harder. She did not think he would face publicity. All the lodgers in the house knew something of the affair; details had been invented by some. Besides, he had been employed for thirteen years in a great Catholic winemerchant's office and publicity would mean for him, perhaps, the loss of his sit.[5] Whereas if he agreed all might be well. She knew he had a good screw[6] for one thing and she suspected he had a bit of stuff put by.[7]

    Nearly the half-hour! She stood up and surveyed herself in the pier-glass.[8] The decisive expression of her great florid face satisfied her and she thought of some mothers she knew who could not get their daughters off their hands.

    Mr Doran was very anxious indeed this Sunday morning. He had made two attempts to shave but his hand had been so unsteady that he had been obliged to desist. Three days' reddish beard fringed his jaws and every two or three minutes a mist gathered on his glasses so that he had to take them off and polish them with his pocket-handkerchief. The recollection of his confession of the night before was a cause of acute pain to him; the priest had drawn out every ridiculous detail of the affair and in the end had so magnified his sin that he was almost thankful at being afforded a loophole of reparation. The harm was done. What could he do now but marry her or run away? He could not brazen it out. The affair would be sure to be talked of and his employer would be certain to hear of it. Dublin is such a small city: everyone knows everyone else's business. He felt his heart leap warmly in his throat as he heard in his excited imagination

---

[4] Immoral.
[5] Job.
[6] Salary.
[7] Money put away.
[8] Mirror.

old Mr Leonard calling out in his rasping voice: *Send Mr Doran here, please.*

All his long years of service gone for nothing! All his industry and diligence thrown away! As a young man he had sown his wild oats, of course; he had boasted of his free-thinking and denied the existence of God to his companions in public-houses. But that was all passed and done with... nearly. He still bought a copy of *Reynolds's Newspaper* every week but he attended to his religious duties and for nine-tenths of the year lived a regular life. He had money enough to settle down on; it was not that. But the family would look down on her. First of all there was her disreputable father and then her mother's boarding house was beginning to get a certain fame. He had a notion that he was being had. He could imagine his friends talking of the affair and laughing. She *was* a little vulgar; sometimes she said *I seen* and *If I had've known*. But what would grammar matter if he really loved her? He could not make up his mind whether to like her or despise her for what she had done. Of course he had done it too. His instinct urged him to remain free, not to marry. Once you are married you are done for, it said.

While he was sitting helplessly on the side of the bed in shirt and trousers she tapped lightly at his door and entered. She told him all, that she had made a clean breast of it to her mother and that her mother would speak with him that morning. She cried and threw her arms round his neck, saying:

"O Bob! Bob! What am I to do? What am I to do at all?"

She would put an end to herself, she said.

He comforted her feebly, telling her not to cry, that it would be all right, never fear. He felt against his shirt the agitation of her bosom.

It was not altogether his fault that it had happened. He remembered well, with the curious patient memory of the celibate, the first casual caresses her dress, her breath, her fingers had given him. Then late one night as he was undressing for bed she had tapped at his door, timidly. She wanted to relight her candle at his for hers had been blown out by a gust. It was her bath night. She wore a loose open combing-jacket[9] of printed flannel. Her white instep shone in the opening of her furry slippers and the blood glowed warmly

---

[9] Robe.

behind her perfumed skin. From her hands and wrists too as she lit and steadied her candle a faint perfume arose.

On nights when he came in very late it was she who warmed up his dinner. He scarcely knew what he was eating feeling her beside him alone, at night, in the sleeping house. And her thoughtfulness! If the night was anyway cold or wet or windy there was sure to be a little tumbler of punch ready for him. Perhaps they could be happy together...

They used to go upstairs together on tiptoe, each with a candle, and on the third landing exchange reluctant good-nights. They used to kiss. He remembered well her eyes, the touch of her hand and his delirium...

But delirium passes. He echoed her phrase, applying it to himself: *What am I to do?* The instinct of the celibate warned him to hold back. But the sin was there; even his sense of honour told him that reparation must be made for such a sin.

While he was sitting with her on the side of the bed Mary came to the door and said that the missus wanted to see him in the parlour. He stood up to put on his coat and waistcoat, more helpless than ever. When he was dressed he went over to her to comfort her. It would be all right, never fear. He left her crying on the bed and moaning softly: *O my God!*

Going down the stairs his glasses became so dimmed with moisture that he had to take them off and polish them. He longed to ascend through the roof and fly away to another country where he would never hear again of his trouble, and yet a force pushed him downstairs step by step. The implacable faces of his employer and of the Madam stared upon his discomfiture. On the last flight of stairs he passed Jack Mooney who was coming up from the pantry nursing two bottles of *Bass*. They saluted coldly; and the lover's eyes rested for a second or two on a thick bulldog face and a pair of thick short arms. When he reached the foot of the staircase he glanced up and saw Jack regarding him from the door of the return-room.[10]

Suddenly he remembered the night when one of the music-hall *artistes*, a little blond Londoner, had made a rather free allusion to Polly. The reunion had been almost broken up on account of Jack's violence. Everyone tried to quiet him. The music-hall *artiste*, a little paler than usual, kept smiling and saying that there was no harm

---

[10] Where one returns bottles to the seller.

meant: but Jack kept shouting at him that if any fellow tried that sort of a game on with his sister he'd bloody well put his teeth down his throat, so he would.

*****

Polly sat for a little time on the side of the bed, crying. Then she dried her eyes and went over to the looking-glass. She dipped the end of the towel in the water-jug and refreshed her eyes with the cool water. She looked at herself in profile and readjusted a hairpin above her ear. Then she went back to the bed again and sat at the foot. She regarded the pillows for a long time and the sight of them awakened in her mind secret, amiable memories. She rested the nape of her neck against the cool iron bed-rail and fell into a reverie. There was no longer any perturbation visible on her face.

She waited on patiently, almost cheerfully, without alarm. Her memories gradually giving place to hopes and visions of the future. Her hopes and visions were so intricate that she no longer saw the white pillows on which her gaze was fixed or remembered that she was waiting for anything.

At last she heard her mother calling. She started to her feet and ran to the banisters.

"Polly! Polly!"

"Yes, mamma?"

"Come down, dear. Mr Doran wants to speak to you."

Then she remembered what she had been waiting for.

CRAFT: THE BOARDING HOUSE

Narrative Mode: Omniscience

"The Boarding House" comes at a perfect time for us to expand on previous discussions of **point of view** under a broad term called **narrative mode**. Writers use narrative modes to indicate the set of craft methods employed as a means to communicate plot to a reader. Most often, writers use the term narrative mode to refer to the point of view, but it also includes the narrative tense (past, present, or future) and the narrative voice or form, which describes how the writer constructs the plot (dialogue versus exposition, epistolary, stream of consciousness...).

While "The Boarding House" doesn't provide a straightforward **omniscient** narrator as does an Austen or Dickens novel, we can nevertheless categorize this story as omniscient, meaning that the narrator has access to all the characters' points of view and can navigate freely through space and time (many writers think of the omniscient narrator as God—all knowing and all powerful). At the beginning of the story, the narrator broadly and objectively provides the reader with background. In terms of the **narrative structure**, this forms a classic **setup** with **objective** omniscient **exposition**:

> Mrs Mooney was a butcher's daughter. She was a woman who was quite able to keep things to herself: a determined woman. She had married her father's foreman and opened a butcher's shop near Spring Gardens. But as soon as his father-in-law was dead Mr Mooney began to go to the devil. He drank, plundered the till, ran headlong into debt.

In this example, we can detect the narrator's omniscient shift from Mrs. Mooney to Mr. Mooney.

Gradually the narrative zooms in closer and closer to Mrs. Mooney's point of view and becomes **limited** and **subjective** as the narrator plunges us into the story's **premise**—Mrs. Mooney's goal of convincing Mr. Doran to marry her daughter, Polly. "She was sure she would win." However, just as the reader is getting settled in what seems to have gradually narrowed from omniscient to **close third person**, Joyce abruptly shifts point of view: "Mr Doran was very anxious indeed this Sunday morning."

We remain in Mr. Doran's point of view as he mulls over the **choice** he knows he has to make, which invites the reader into the **discourse**. Then, yet again, just before Mr. Doran faces Mrs. Mooney, Joyce shifts the narrative focus to Polly.

These omniscient narrative shifts illuminate Mrs. Mooney's **conflict**, goal, and **challenge** to convince Mr. Doran to marry her daughter. By understanding Mrs. Mooney's determination, Mr. Doran's indecision, and Polly's affected desperation, we understand the subtle way that mother and daughter have connived to persuade Mr. Doran to marry.

This omniscient narrator effectively carries out the premise of this story. The main challenge a writer faces when employing the omniscient narrator is getting carried away with the freedom of being able to enter the mind of any character and leap around through space and time. In "The Boarding House," we can see Joyce's careful control of that omniscience—his deliberate shifts and the deepening of the premise through those shifts. It's easy to imagine how Joyce might get sidetracked by Mr. Doran, for example—how he might start to tell Mr. Doran's **backstory**, his coming to the boarding house, his previous relationships, the details of his relationship with Polly... Because he shifts from Mrs. Mooney to Mr. Doran, it would be tempting to write more about Mr. Doran's and Polly's relationship. But Joyce exhibits perfect control over this impulse, always keeping in mind the contract he made with his premise.

Rhetorical Motif

Unlike the symbol of the chalice in "The Sisters," Joyce effectively uses the word "reparation" symbolically in "The Boarding House" as a **rhetorical motif** (motifs are symbols that reoccur. For more about motifs see the following story, "A Little Cloud"). Most importantly, this rhetorical motif indicates and complicates the shifts in narrative focus. "Reparations" means one thing to Mrs. Mooney, another thing to Mr. Doran, and yet another thing to Polly.

As Mrs. Mooney plans her strategy, she wonders: "What reparation would [Mr. Doran] make?" This reparation refers to Mr. Doran's and Polly's affair in the boarding house. Mrs. Mooney knows that other mothers in similar situations have accepted money as reparation, but her definition of the term in this matter is set. "For her only one reparation could make up for the loss of her daughter's honour: marriage."

As Mr. Doran tries to shave, he is unable to concentrate because of his shame about the affair.

The recollection of his confession of the night before was a cause of acute pain to him; the priest had drawn out every ridiculous detail of the affair and in the end had so magnified his sin that he was almost thankful at being afforded a loophole of reparation.

This interesting repetition shows that Mrs. Mooney's definition of the term differs from Mr. Doran's, who obviously feels as though his sin can perhaps be forgiven or at least overlooked through religious penance. This is further confirmed later when he admits to himself that "reparation must be made for such a sin." While Mrs. Mooney's motive clearly is to marry off her daughter—we learn of her interest in doing so early in the story as Mrs. Mooney considers sending Polly back to her job as a typist because the men in the boarding house only flirted and "none of them meant business"—Mr. Doran's motive is to repair his religious sin.

Joyce does not use the motif of reparation when he switches to Polly's point of view, and this is perhaps the most interesting shade of the rhetorical motif—its absence. It seems the entire concept of reparations does not interest Polly, who clearly operates on a far more detached level. Her tears and appeals to Mr. Doran appear somewhat disingenuous. When he leaves the room, she simply dries her eyes and waits patiently. She is a detached actor in the drama—perhaps a victim, perhaps a seductress and operator, probably a bit of both. The idea of reparation does not apply to her character.

Details

It may seem to many readers and writers that the rhetorical motif of reparations in "The Boarding House" exists only as a trivial detail, or that its subtlety is such that it barely warrants inclusion in this text. But what many readers never understand, even though they may have read thousands of books, is that most of the craft elements that move us, that engage us, that keep us turning those pages, are invisible. They are the smallest details.

Often what differentiates a beginning writer from a practiced writer are generalizations. Beginning writers often haven't learned how to use subtle details to create big explosions. Just that one word, reparations, works in so many different ways. First, it differentiates the characters. Second, it informs the **idea** of the story—the paralysis that each character faces because of the affair. Third, the repetition creates continuity—though we may not consciously recognize the repetition, our minds still recognize the word as being part of the "world" of this story. Fourth, it acts to fulfill the **contract** set up by the **premise**: Without Mr. Doran's guilt and his need to repair his sin, Mrs. Mooney might fail in trapping him into her own repair, which is Mr. Doran's marriage to Polly.

That one detail, though so seemingly insignificant on the surface, has an important and multifaceted function in the narrative. We often tend to think of details as small, material items that a writer describes—a piece of fingernail on the floor, the broken lead in a pencil—but details can range from words to ideas to tropes to stylistic choices. While you can always tell a writer to include more details, it's difficult to articulate how a writer can use them. Details are particular. **Narrative structure**, for example, is not a detail and not particular. It is universal. While you need narrative structure to create a **plot**, it doesn't provide you with details. However, while **symbolism** is universal, the symbols you create don't have to be. When we speak of craft, what we often mean by details are the small particulars that make the writing unique.

In "The Boarding House" Joyce uses descriptive details to invite us into the setting: "Breakfast was over in the boarding house and the table of the breakfast-room was covered with plates on which lay yellow streaks of eggs with morsels of bacon-fat and bacon-rind." These details stimulate our senses and help us visualize the space. But let's look at another, subtler kind of detail. As Mr. Doran walks down the stairs to face Mrs. Mooney, he passes Polly's brother Jack:

> Suddenly he remembered the night when one of the music-hall *artistes*, a little blond Londoner, had made a rather free allusion to Polly. The reunion had been almost broken up on account of Jack's violence. Everyone tried to quiet him. The music-hall *artiste*, a little paler than usual, kept smiling and saying that there was no harm meant: but Jack kept shouting at him that if any fellow tried that sort of a game on with his sister he'd bloody well put his teeth down his throat, so he would.

A lesser writer might simply write, "Mr. Doran was scared of what Jack might do to him if he didn't do the right thing." Or even worse: "Mr. Doran feared the consequences of his not marrying Polly." Instead, Joyce chooses to insert a detail—a particular event—in order to communicate his fear of Jack's violence if he does the wrong thing. Joyce doesn't need to say it because the detail communicates it. Furthermore, though Joyce never writes that Mr. Doran agrees to marry Polly—another example of a Joycean **gnomon**—this detail, by exposing his paralyzing fear, both indicates and **foreshadows** Mrs. Mooney's bullying him into marriage.

Questions

1. If we consider *Dubliners* as a whole, how do these shifting techniques in **narrative mode** affect the reading experience? Why would Joyce begin with nameless **first person narrators** in "The Sisters," "An Encounter," and "Araby" and then shift to **third person narrators** in later stories?

2. How does Joyce use the **rhetorical motif** of "reparations" as a way to comment on a larger **idea** in this story? More specifically, what might this motif say about Polly?

3. Try to pick out some **details** in "The Boarding House" that are not described objects. Look for particulars that are concrete and specific, rather than abstract or general. How does Joyce use those details to communicate something bigger?

A Little Cloud

Eight years before he had seen his friend off at the North Wall and wished him godspeed. Gallaher had got on. You could tell that at once by his travelled air, his well-cut tweed suit, and fearless accent. Few fellows had talents like his and fewer still could remain unspoiled by such success. Gallaher's heart was in the right place and he had deserved to win. It was something to have a friend like that.

Little Chandler's thoughts ever since lunch-time had been of his meeting with Gallaher, of Gallaher's invitation and of the great city London where Gallaher lived. He was called Little Chandler because, though he was but slightly under the average stature, he gave one the idea of being a little man. His hands were white and small, his frame was fragile, his voice was quiet and his manners were refined. He took the greatest care of his fair silken hair and moustache and used perfume discreetly on his handkerchief. The half-moons of his nails were perfect and when he smiled you caught a glimpse of a row of childish white teeth.

As he sat at his desk in the King's Inns he thought what changes those eight years had brought. The friend whom he had known under a shabby and necessitous guise had become a brilliant figure on the *London Press*. He turned often from his tiresome writing to gaze out of the office window. The glow of a late autumn sunset covered the grass plots and walks. It cast a shower of kindly golden dust on the untidy nurses and decrepit old men who drowsed on the benches; it flickered upon all the moving figures—on the children who ran screaming along the gravel paths and on everyone who passed through the gardens. He watched the scene and thought of life; and (as always happened when he thought of life) he became sad. A gentle melancholy took possession of him. He felt how useless it was to struggle against fortune, this being the burden of wisdom which the ages had bequeathed to him.

He remembered the books of poetry upon his shelves at home. He had bought them in his bachelor days and many an evening, as he sat in the little room off the hall, he had been tempted to take one down from the bookshelf and read out something to his wife. But shyness had always held him back; and so the books had remained on their shelves. At times he repeated lines to himself and this consoled him.

When his hour had struck he stood up and took leave of his desk and of his fellow-clerks punctiliously. He emerged from under the feudal arch of the King's Inns, a neat modest figure, and walked swiftly down Henrietta Street. The golden sunset was waning and the air had grown sharp. A horde of grimy children populated the street. They stood or ran in the roadway or crawled up the steps before the gaping doors or squatted like mice upon the thresholds. Little Chandler gave them no thought. He picked his way deftly through all that minute vermin-like life and under the shadow of the gaunt spectral mansions in which the old nobility of Dublin had roystered. No memory of the past touched him, for his mind was full of a present joy.

He had never been in Corless's but he knew the value of the name. He knew that people went there after the theatre to eat oysters and drink liqueurs; and he had heard that the waiters there spoke French and German. Walking swiftly by at night he had seen cabs drawn up before the door and richly dressed ladies, escorted by cavaliers,[1] alight and enter quickly. They wore noisy dresses and many wraps. Their faces were powdered and they caught up their dresses, when they touched earth, like alarmed Atalantas.[2] He had always passed without turning his head to look. It was his habit to walk swiftly in the street even by day and whenever he found himself in the city late at night he hurried on his way apprehensively and excitedly. Sometimes, however, he courted the causes of his fear. He chose the darkest and narrowest streets and, as he walked boldly forward, the silence that was spread about his footsteps troubled him, the wandering, silent figures troubled him; and at times a sound of low fugitive laughter made him tremble like a leaf.

He turned to the right towards Capel Street. Ignatius Gallaher on the *London Press*! Who would have thought it possible eight years before? Still, now that he reviewed the past, Little Chandler could remember many signs of future greatness in his friend. People used to say that Ignatius Gallaher was wild. Of course, he did mix with a rakish set of fellows at that time, drank freely and borrowed money on all sides. In the end he had got mixed up in some shady affair, some money transaction: at least, that was one version of his flight.

---

[1] Gentlemen.
[2] Fierce huntress from Greek mythology.

But nobody denied him talent. There was always a certain... something in Ignatius Gallaher that impressed you in spite of yourself. Even when he was out at elbows[3] and at his wits' end for money he kept up a bold face. Little Chandler remembered (and the remembrance brought a slight flush of pride to his cheek) one of Ignatius Gallaher's sayings when he was in a tight corner:

"Half time now, boys," he used to say light-heartedly. "Where's my considering cap?"

That was Ignatius Gallaher all out; and, damn it, you couldn't but admire him for it.

Little Chandler quickened his pace. For the first time in his life he felt himself superior to the people he passed. For the first time his soul revolted against the dull inelegance of Capel Street. There was no doubt about it: if you wanted to succeed you had to go away. You could do nothing in Dublin. As he crossed Grattan Bridge he looked down the river towards the lower quays and pitied the poor stunted houses. They seemed to him a band of tramps, huddled together along the riverbanks, their old coats covered with dust and soot, stupefied by the panorama of sunset and waiting for the first chill of night bid them arise, shake themselves and begone. He wondered whether he could write a poem to express his idea. Perhaps Gallaher might be able to get it into some London paper for him. Could he write something original? He was not sure what idea he wished to express but the thought that a poetic moment had touched him took life within him like an infant hope. He stepped onward bravely.

Every step brought him nearer to London, farther from his own sober inartistic life. A light began to tremble on the horizon of his mind. He was not so old—thirty-two. His temperament might be said to be just at the point of maturity. There were so many different moods and impressions that he wished to express in verse. He felt them within him. He tried to weigh his soul to see if it was a poet's soul. Melancholy was the dominant note of his temperament, he thought, but it was a melancholy tempered by recurrences of faith and resignation and simple joy. If he could give expression to it in a book of poems perhaps men would listen. He would never be popular: he saw that. He could not sway the crowd but he might appeal to a little circle of kindred minds. The English critics, perhaps, would recognise him as one of the Celtic school by reason of the

---

[3] Out of money.

melancholy tone of his poems; besides that, he would put in allusions. He began to invent sentences and phrases from the notice which his book would get. *"Mr Chandler has the gift of easy and graceful verse."*... *"wistful sadness pervades these poems."*...*"The Celtic note."* It was a pity his name was not more Irish-looking. Perhaps it would be better to insert his mother's name before the surname: Thomas Malone Chandler, or better still: T. Malone Chandler. He would speak to Gallaher about it.

    He pursued his revery so ardently that he passed his street and had to turn back. As he came near Corless's his former agitation began to overmaster him and he halted before the door in indecision. Finally he opened the door and entered.

    The light and noise of the bar held him at the doorways for a few moments. He looked about him, but his sight was confused by the shining of many red and green wine-glasses. The bar seemed to him to be full of people and he felt that the people were observing him curiously. He glanced quickly to right and left (frowning slightly to make his errand appear serious), but when his sight cleared a little he saw that nobody had turned to look at him: and there, sure enough, was Ignatius Gallaher leaning with his back against the counter and his feet planted far apart.

    "Hallo, Tommy, old hero, here you are! What is it to be? What will you have? I'm taking whisky: better stuff than we get across the water. Soda? Lithia?[4] No mineral? I'm the same. Spoils the flavour... Here, *garçon*, bring us two halves of malt whisky, like a good fellow... Well, and how have you been pulling along since I saw you last? Dear God, how old we're getting! Do you see any signs of aging in me—eh, what? A little grey and thin on the top—what?"

    Ignatius Gallaher took off his hat and displayed a large closely cropped head. His face was heavy, pale and clean-shaven. His eyes, which were of bluish slate-colour, relieved his unhealthy pallor and shone out plainly above the vivid orange tie he wore. Between these rival features the lips appeared very long and shapeless and colourless. He bent his head and felt with two sympathetic fingers the thin hair at the crown. Little Chandler shook his head as a denial. Ignatius Gallaher put on his hat again.

    "It pulls you down," he said. "Press life. Always hurry and scurry, looking for copy and sometimes not finding it: and then,

---

[4] Mineral water.

always to have something new in your stuff. Damn proofs and printers, I say, for a few days. I'm deuced[5] glad, I can tell you, to get back to the old country. Does a fellow good, a bit of a holiday. I feel a ton better since I landed again in dear dirty Dublin... Here you are, Tommy. Water? Say when."

Little Chandler allowed his whisky to be very much diluted.

"You don't know what's good for you, my boy," said Ignatius Gallaher. "I drink mine neat."

"I drink very little as a rule," said Little Chandler modestly. "An odd half-one or so when I meet any of the old crowd: that's all."

"Ah well," said Ignatius Gallaher, cheerfully, "here's to us and to old times and old acquaintances."

They clinked glasses and drank the toast.

"I met some of the old gang to-day," said Ignatius Gallaher. "O'Hara seems to be in a bad way. What's he doing?"

"Nothing," said Little Chandler. "He's gone to the dogs."

"But Hogan has a good sit, hasn't he?"

"Yes; he's in the Land Commission."

"I met him one night in London and he seemed to be very flush... Poor O'Hara! Boose, I suppose?"

"Other things, too," said Little Chandler shortly.

Ignatius Gallaher laughed.

"Tommy," he said, "I see you haven't changed an atom. You're the very same serious person that used to lecture me on Sunday mornings when I had a sore head and a fur on my tongue. You'd want to knock about a bit in the world. Have you never been anywhere even for a trip?"

"I've been to the Isle of Man," said Little Chandler.

Ignatius Gallaher laughed.

"The Isle of Man!" he said. "Go to London or Paris: Paris, for choice. That'd do you good."

"Have you seen Paris?"

"I should think I have! I've knocked about there a little."

"And is it really so beautiful as they say?" asked Little Chandler.

He sipped a little of his drink while Ignatius Gallaher finished his boldly.

---

[5] As in "darned."

"Beautiful?" said Ignatius Gallaher, pausing on the word and on the flavour of his drink. "It's not so beautiful, you know. Of course, it is beautiful... But it's the life of Paris; that's the thing. Ah, there's no city like Paris for gaiety, movement, excitement..."

Little Chandler finished his whisky and, after some trouble, succeeded in catching the barman's eye. He ordered the same again.

"I've been to the Moulin Rouge," Ignatius Gallaher continued when the barman had removed their glasses, "and I've been to all the Bohemian cafés. Hot stuff! Not for a pious chap like you, Tommy."

Little Chandler said nothing until the barman returned with two glasses: then he touched his friend's glass lightly and reciprocated the former toast. He was beginning to feel somewhat disillusioned. Gallaher's accent and way of expressing himself did not please him. There was something vulgar in his friend which he had not observed before. But perhaps it was only the result of living in London amid the bustle and competition of the Press. The old personal charm was still there under this new gaudy manner. And, after all, Gallaher had lived; he had seen the world. Little Chandler looked at his friend enviously.

"Everything in Paris is gay," said Ignatius Gallaher. "They believe in enjoying life—and don't you think they're right? If you want to enjoy yourself properly you must go to Paris. And, mind you, they've a great feeling for the Irish there. When they heard I was from Ireland they were ready to eat me, man."

Little Chandler took four or five sips from his glass.

"Tell me," he said, "is it true that Paris is so... immoral as they say?"

Ignatius Gallaher made a catholic gesture with his right arm.

"Every place is immoral," he said. "Of course you do find spicy bits in Paris. Go to one of the students' balls, for instance. That's lively, if you like, when the *cocottes*[6] begin to let themselves loose. You know what they are, I suppose?"

"I've heard of them," said Little Chandler.

Ignatius Gallaher drank off his whisky and shook his hand.

"Ah," he said, "you may say what you like. There's no woman like the Parisienne—for style, for go."

"Then it is an immoral city," said Little Chandler, with timid insistence—"I mean, compared with London or Dublin?"

---

[6] Prostitutes.

"London!" said Ignatius Gallaher. "It's six of one and half-a-dozen of the other. You ask Hogan, my boy. I showed him a bit about London when he was over there. He'd open your eye... I say, Tommy, don't make punch of that whisky: liquor up."

"No, really..."

"O, come on, another one won't do you any harm. What is it? The same again, I suppose?"

"Well... all right."

"François, the same again... Will you smoke, Tommy?"

Ignatius Gallaher produced his cigar-case. The two friends lit their cigars and puffed at them in silence until their drinks were served.

"I'll tell you my opinion," said Ignatius Gallaher, emerging after some time from the clouds of smoke in which he had taken refuge, "it's a rum[7] world. Talk of immorality! I've heard of cases—what am I saying?—I've known them: cases of... immorality..."

Ignatius Gallaher puffed thoughtfully at his cigar and then, in a calm historian's tone, he proceeded to sketch for his friend some pictures of the corruption which was rife abroad. He summarized the vices of many capitals and seemed inclined to award the palm to Berlin. Some things he could not vouch for (his friends had told him), but of others he had had personal experience. He spared neither rank nor caste. He revealed many of the secrets of religious houses on the Continent and described some of the practices which were fashionable in high society and ended by telling, with details, a story about an English duchess—a story which he knew to be true. Little Chandler was astonished.

"Ah, well," said Ignatius Gallaher, "here we are in old jog-along Dublin where nothing is known of such things."

"How dull you must find it," said Little Chandler, "after all the other places you've seen!"

"Well," said Ignatius Gallaher, "it's a relaxation to come over here, you know. And, after all, it's the old country, as they say, isn't it? You can't help having a certain feeling for it. That's human nature... But tell me something about yourself. Hogan told me you had... tasted the joys of connubial bliss. Two years ago, wasn't it?"

Little Chandler blushed and smiled.

"Yes," he said. "I was married last May twelve months."

---

[7] Strange.

"I hope it's not too late in the day to offer my best wishes," said Ignatius Gallaher. "I didn't know your address or I'd have done so at the time."

He extended his hand, which Little Chandler took.

"Well, Tommy," he said, "I wish you and yours every joy in life, old chap, and tons of money, and may you never die till I shoot you. And that's the wish of a sincere friend, an old friend. You know that?"

"I know that," said Little Chandler.

"Any youngsters?" said Ignatius Gallaher.

Little Chandler blushed again.

"We have one child," he said.

"Son or daughter?"

"A little boy."

Ignatius Gallaher slapped his friend sonorously on the back.

"Bravo," he said, "I wouldn't doubt you, Tommy."

Little Chandler smiled, looked confusedly at his glass and bit his lower lip with three childishly white front teeth.

"I hope you'll spend an evening with us," he said, "before you go back. My wife will be delighted to meet you. We can have a little music and——"

"Thanks awfully, old chap," said Ignatius Gallaher, "I'm sorry we didn't meet earlier. But I must leave to-morrow night."

"To-night, perhaps...?"

"I'm awfully sorry, old man. You see I'm over here with another fellow, clever young chap he is too, and we arranged to go to a little card-party. Only for that..."

"O, in that case..."

"But who knows?" said Ignatius Gallaher considerately. "Next year I may take a little skip over here now that I've broken the ice. It's only a pleasure deferred."

"Very well," said Little Chandler, "the next time you come we must have an evening together. That's agreed now, isn't it?"

"Yes, that's agreed," said Ignatius Gallaher. "Next year if I come, *parole d'honneur*."[8]

"And to clinch the bargain," said Little Chandler, "we'll just have one more now."

Ignatius Gallaher took out a large gold watch and looked at it.

---

[8] Word of honor.

"Is it to be the last?" he said. "Because you know, I have an a.p."⁹

"O, yes, positively," said Little Chandler.

"Very well, then," said Ignatius Gallaher, "let us have another one as a *deoc an doruis*¹⁰—that's good vernacular for a small whisky, I believe."

Little Chandler ordered the drinks. The blush which had risen to his face a few moments before was establishing itself. A trifle made him blush at any time: and now he felt warm and excited. Three small whiskies had gone to his head and Gallaher's strong cigar had confused his mind, for he was a delicate and abstinent person. The adventure of meeting Gallaher after eight years, of finding himself with Gallaher in Corless's surrounded by lights and noise, of listening to Gallaher's stories and of sharing for a brief space Gallaher's vagrant and triumphant life, upset the equipoise of his sensitive nature. He felt acutely the contrast between his own life and his friend's and it seemed to him unjust. Gallaher was his inferior in birth and education. He was sure that he could do something better than his friend had ever done, or could ever do, something higher than mere tawdry journalism if he only got the chance. What was it that stood in his way? His unfortunate timidity! He wished to vindicate himself in some way, to assert his manhood. He saw behind Gallaher's refusal of his invitation. Gallaher was only patronising him by his friendliness just as he was patronising Ireland by his visit.

The barman brought their drinks. Little Chandler pushed one glass towards his friend and took up the other boldly.

"Who knows?" he said, as they lifted their glasses. "When you come next year I may have the pleasure of wishing long life and happiness to Mr and Mrs Ignatius Gallaher."

Ignatius Gallaher in the act of drinking closed one eye expressively over the rim of his glass. When he had drunk he smacked his lips decisively, set down his glass and said:

"No blooming fear of that, my boy. I'm going to have my fling first and see a bit of life and the world before I put my head in the sack¹¹—if I ever do."

"Some day you will," said Little Chandler calmly.

---

⁹ Appointment.
¹⁰ Drink at door.
¹¹ The hood placed over a person's head before they are hanged.

Ignatius Gallaher turned his orange tie and slate-blue eyes full upon his friend.

"You think so?" he said.

"You'll put your head in the sack," repeated Little Chandler stoutly, "like everyone else if you can find the girl."

He had slightly emphasised his tone and he was aware that he had betrayed himself; but, though the colour had heightened in his cheek, he did not flinch from his friend's gaze. Ignatius Gallaher watched him for a few moments and then said:

"If ever it occurs, you may bet your bottom dollar there'll be no mooning and spooning about it. I mean to marry money. She'll have a good fat account at the bank or she won't do for me."

Little Chandler shook his head.

"Why, man alive," said Ignatius Gallaher, vehemently, "do you know what it is? I've only to say the word and to-morrow I can have the woman and the cash. You don't believe it? Well, I know it. There are hundreds— what am I saying?—thousands of rich Germans and Jews, rotten with money, that'd only be too glad... You wait a while my boy. See if I don't play my cards properly. When I go about a thing I mean business, I tell you. You just wait."

He tossed his glass to his mouth, finished his drink and laughed loudly. Then he looked thoughtfully before him and said in a calmer tone:

"But I'm in no hurry. They can wait. I don't fancy tying myself up to one woman, you know."

He imitated with his mouth the act of tasting and made a wry face.

"Must get a bit stale, I should think," he said.

*****

Little Chandler sat in the room off the hall, holding a child in his arms. To save money they kept no servant but Annie's young sister Monica came for an hour or so in the morning and an hour or so in the evening to help. But Monica had gone home long ago. It was a quarter to nine. Little Chandler had come home late for tea and, moreover, he had forgotten to bring Annie home the parcel of coffee from Bewley's. Of course she was in a bad humour and gave him short answers. She said she would do without any tea but when it came near the time at which the shop at the corner closed she decided to go out herself for a quarter of a pound of tea and two pounds of sugar. She put the sleeping child deftly in his arms and said:

"Here. Don't waken him."

A little lamp with a white china shade stood upon the table and its light fell over a photograph which was enclosed in a frame of crumpled horn. It was Annie's photograph. Little Chandler looked at it, pausing at the thin tight lips. She wore the pale blue summer blouse which he had brought her home as a present one Saturday. It had cost him ten and elevenpence; but what an agony of nervousness it had cost him! How he had suffered that day, waiting at the shop door until the shop was empty, standing at the counter and trying to appear at his ease while the girl piled ladies' blouses before him, paying at the desk and forgetting to take up the odd penny of his change, being called back by the cashier, and finally, striving to hide his blushes as he left the shop by examining the parcel to see if it was securely tied. When he brought the blouse home Annie kissed him and said it was very pretty and stylish; but when she heard the price she threw the blouse on the table and said it was a regular swindle to charge ten and elevenpence for it. At first she wanted to take it back but when she tried it on she was delighted with it, especially with the make of the sleeves, and kissed him and said he was very good to think of her.

Hm!...

He looked coldly into the eyes of the photograph and they answered coldly. Certainly they were pretty and the face itself was pretty. But he found something mean in it. Why was it so unconscious and ladylike? The composure of the eyes irritated him. They repelled him and defied him: there was no passion in them, no rapture. He thought of what Gallaher had said about rich Jewesses. Those dark Oriental eyes, he thought, how full they are of passion, of voluptuous longing!... Why had he married the eyes in the photograph?

He caught himself up at the question and glanced nervously round the room. He found something mean in the pretty furniture which he had bought for his house on the hire[12] system. Annie had chosen it herself and it reminded him of her. It too was prim and pretty. A dull resentment against his life awoke within him. Could he not escape from his little house? Was it too late for him to try to live bravely like Gallaher? Could he go to London? There was the furniture

---

[12] Credit.

still to be paid for. If he could only write a book and get it published, that might open the way for him.

A volume of Byron's poems lay before him on the table. He opened it cautiously with his left hand lest he should waken the child and began to read the first poem in the book:

> Hushed are the winds and still the evening gloom,
>   Not e'en a Zephyr wanders through the grove,
> Whilst I return to view my Margaret's tomb
>   And scatter flowers on the dust I love.

He paused. He felt the rhythm of the verse about him in the room. How melancholy it was! Could he, too, write like that, express the melancholy of his soul in verse? There were so many things he wanted to describe: his sensation of a few hours before on Grattan Bridge, for example. If he could get back again into that mood...

The child awoke and began to cry. He turned from the page and tried to hush it: but it would not be hushed. He began to rock it to and fro in his arms but its wailing cry grew keener. He rocked it faster while his eyes began to read the second stanza:

> Within this narrow cell reclines her clay,
>   That clay where once...

It was useless. He couldn't read. He couldn't do anything. The wailing of the child pierced the drum of his ear. It was useless, useless! He was a prisoner for life. His arms trembled with anger and suddenly bending to the child's face he shouted:

"Stop!"

The child stopped for an instant, had a spasm of fright and began to scream. He jumped up from his chair and walked hastily up and down the room with the child in his arms. It began to sob piteously, losing its breath for four or five seconds, and then bursting out anew. The thin walls of the room echoed the sound. He tried to soothe it but it sobbed more convulsively. He looked at the contracted and quivering face of the child and began to be alarmed. He counted seven sobs without a break between them and caught the child to his breast in fright. If it died!...

The door was burst open and a young woman ran in, panting.

"What is it? What is it?" she cried.

The child, hearing its mother's voice, broke out into a paroxysm of sobbing.

"It's nothing, Annie... it's nothing... He began to cry..."

She flung her parcels on the floor and snatched the child from him.

"What have you done to him?" she cried, glaring into his face.

Little Chandler sustained for one moment the gaze of her eyes and his heart closed together as he met the hatred in them. He began to stammer:

"It's nothing... He... he began to cry... I couldn't... I didn't do anything... What?"

Giving no heed to him she began to walk up and down the room, clasping the child tightly in her arms and murmuring:

"My little man! My little mannie! Was 'ou frightened, love?... There now, love! There now!... Lambabaun![13] Mamma's little lamb of the world!... There now!"

Little Chandler felt his cheeks suffused with shame and he stood back out of the lamplight. He listened while the paroxysm of the child's sobbing grew less and less; and tears of remorse started to his eyes.

---

[13] As in "baby lamb."

CRAFT: A LITTLE CLOUD

Setting

Remember the **idea** of paralysis that Joyce employed in the first paragraph of "The Sisters"? As readers are now aware, Joyce connects that sense of paralysis with place, with Dublin. In "A Little Cloud," Joyce's insertion of actual places and names create a sense of Chandler's paralyzing feeling of isolation.

Joyce makes Chandler's inability to escape Dublin that much more palpable by his detailed descriptions of **setting** and his use of existing place names. We can almost follow Chandler "down Henrietta Street," across the "Grattan Bridge," and into "Corless's" to meet Gallaher. Proper names create his prison—a prison that he himself acknowledges. He wonders if he could "escape from his little house" and acknowledges that he is a "prisoner for life." Chandler's Dublin has become part of his provincial paralysis and ennui.

Like so many elements of craft, the choices an author makes when it comes to setting, language, character, **symbolism**, and **structure** all connect to the **idea** and **premise** of the narrative. Every reader and writer can start by analyzing a narrative for its premise and idea and then synthesize other craft elements with that knowledge. One of the most straightforward ways to evaluate a narrative is to ask: Do the craft elements here align, inform, and connect with the premise and idea?

This conversation about setting will continue after the following story "Counterparts."

Dialogue: Do and Undo

Joyce builds up Chandler's assumptions and expectations about Gallaher, who Chandler hasn't seen in eight years, to such a degree that we, the readers, are not only anxious for Chandler to meet him, but we feel we know him and hope that he might help Chandler overcome some of his personal doubts. Chandler even wonders if Gallaher might advise him on his choice of names as a poet. However, it's through dialogue that Joyce chooses to expose the "real" Gallaher and indicate how he differs from the idealized Gallaher Chandler has created in his mind, based on his memories. In the span of a couple pages, we understand Gallaher's aloofness and arrogance. He calls the bartender "*garçon*," a condescending attempt at sophistication (it means "boy" in French), and he speaks a mile a minute, apparently more interested in exerting his superiority over his old friend than wondering how he has been.

But most pointedly, Joyce creates a drama in the dialogue between these characters that starts with Gallaher's subtle and thinly-veiled insults. After speaking of adventure and high society, he says, "…here we are in old jog-along Dublin where nothing is known of such things." Knowing that Chandler feels trapped in Dublin and has higher hopes for himself, the reader here hopes he will rise to the occasion. Instead, Chandler says, "How dull you must find it … after all the other places you've seen!" Not only does Chandler accept his old friend's patronizing remarks, he legitimizes them. While Gallaher subtly insults Chandler, Chandler exalts Gallaher.

A writer's first impulse when writing dialogue often involves creating conversation that accurately reflects the characters' thoughts and voices and creates **verisimilitude** (or believability). While this is an important aspect of creating believable dialogue, it does not necessarily create dramatic dialogue. Effective writers ask themselves this question: What does this dialogue "do" to the other character(s) and/or how does it "undo" the other character(s)? The best stage and screen actors are actually not actors, but "reactors." Effective and dramatic acting involves the nuances of reacting to another character who is attempting to do or undo something. In fiction, effective dialogue works similarly. Not only does it reflect the voice of the speaker, it "does something" or "undoes something" in the character(s) who must react to it. It might even undo the speaker.

If we return to our previous example from "A Little Cloud," the reader knows that Gallaher "undoes" Chandler by his suggestion that Dublin is unsophisticated. Chandler, as a Dubliner, is therefore unsophisticated too. I call it "undo" because Gallaher's insult is indirect, and it leaves Chandler in a position that does necessarily require a direct reaction. If Gallaher had said, "You know nothing of such things, Chandler," that would be an example of him doing something that would require a similarly direct reaction. But here Chandler's weak and indirect reaction becomes a perfect illustration of Gallaher's point. Chandler, in effect, participates in Gallaher's undoing of him.

Because Joyce uses Gallaher to reflect Chandler's character, Gallaher becomes a **foil**. Like many foil characters, this leads the protagonist to an epiphany. Later in the conversation Chandler realizes that "Gallaher was only patronizing him by his friendliness just as he was patronizing Ireland by his visit." Joyce now brings both character and setting together, linking Chandler to that paralysis, the prison that is Dublin.

This **epiphany**—that Gallaher is patronizing him—leads Chandler to his one moment of revenge, where with one short sentence he attempts to undo Gallaher's arrogance. After Chandler tells Gallaher about his marriage and the birth of his son, Gallaher admits that he's not interested in marriage, not interested in putting his "head in a sack." This attempt to further demean Chandler pushes Chandler's buttons, and he responds, "You'll put your head in the sack ... like everyone else if you can find the girl." Chandler indicates that Gallaher's failure to marry points to his failure in discovering the right person. He is criticizing Gallaher's social skills. And, in fact, this piece of dialogue does work to finally undo that idealized character of Gallaher that Chandler creates earlier in the narrative. Gallaher reacts by becoming overly-confident, insisting that he will marry a rich woman and that he only has to "say the word" and tomorrow he could have it all. By the end of Chandler's and Gallaher's exchange, we understand each of the characters strengths and vulnerabilities very well—not because Joyce **told** us what they were, but because he **showed** us in scene through dramatic dialogue.

Both readers and writers can benefit from asking what certain parts of dialogue are doing to the characters in the narrative. At the end of the story, after Chandler yells at his son and causes him to cry, his wife asks him what he has done to the boy. Chandler responds to his wife, "'It's nothing… He… he began to cry… I couldn't… I didn't do anything… What?'" What Chandler says (that he didn't do anything) is far less important than what he does (attempts to conceal his guilt and shame).

Motif

Joyce often uses **motifs** or **symbols** to start and end stories in *Dubliners*. The "uninhabited house" at the beginning of "Araby" then becomes the narrator's empty spirit by the end of the story, filled only with "anguish and anger." Because that uninhabited house appears only once, we call it a **symbol**. If Joyce had returned to that house again and again, we could call it a **motif**. The chalice in "The Sisters," because it appears twice in the story, may be called a motif. **Motifs** are symbols that reoccur. In "A Little Cloud," the Isle of Man works as a symbol that represents Chandler's feeling of isolation and paralysis, but because islands do not reappear, we cannot call islands a motif (though we could call islands a motif in *Dubliners* as a whole).

Chandler's "Little" suggests his almost doll-like appearance. Joyce describes him as only "slightly under the average stature," but having hands that are "white and small," a "fragile" frame, refined manners, "fair silken hair," perfect "half-moon" nails, and "a row of childish white teeth." It's this last descriptor that holds the most impact. His childishness suggests Chandler's naiveté, provincialism, and self-doubt.

Throughout the story, we come to know Chandler as a little man—one who has cliché dreams to become a poet, one who looks up to his old friend Gallaher as cosmopolitan, and one who has little control of his impulses. When he arrives at the bar, he tells Gallaher that he drinks "very little as a rule," but goes on to have multiple drinks and even suggests a last. However, it's not until the end of the story that we understand Chandler's "littleness." When Annie comes home to find their son crying in his arms after he yelled at the child, she takes the boy from Chandler and begins a series of calming sentences. "My little man! My little mannie! ... Momma's little lamb of the world!"

The motif of "littleness" indicates Chandler's childishness, shame, self-doubt, remorse, and failure as a poet, husband, and father. It goes beyond being just a **rhetorical motif** because Joyce inserts the idea of littleness into various parts of the story in a myriad of different ways. It's the protagonist's name (Little Chandler,) it appears in the title ("A Little Cloud"), Chandler's wife uses it ("little man") and it appears in the descriptions of Chandler's physical characteristics. Joyce is careful to always return to that motif, to imbue every part of the story and Chandler's character with littleness. Even his inner turmoil results from his feelings of "littleness," reflected in both his physical features and his lack of world experience. Joyce, with the relentless intensity and frequency of this motif, traps Chandler in his prison.

Questions

1. Because Joyce implies the importance of **setting** in the title of this collection, how does setting inform the meaning and create **conflict** in "A Little Cloud"? Can you isolate instances in other stories where characters are in conflict with their settings?

2. Choose a dialogue exchange in this story, and analyze it in terms of what each character is **doing** or **undoing**. Are they directly doing something to each other, or is there an indirect undoing? How does the drama in the dialogue affect your understanding of the characters?

3. Critics have pondered over the title "A Little Cloud" ever since it was first published. As a **reference** or **allusion**, what might it refer to? As an **image**, how does it affect the way we visualize events or characters in the story? As a **motif**, how does the idea of littleness affect how we might interpret the title? After investigating all these different angles, what's your interpretation of the title? What makes it an effective or ineffective story title?

Counterparts

The bell rang furiously and, when Miss Parker went to the tube,[1] a furious voice called out in a piercing North of Ireland accent:

"Send Farrington here!"

Miss Parker returned to her machine,[2] saying to a man who was writing at a desk:

"Mr Alleyne wants you upstairs."

The man muttered "*Blast* him!" under his breath and pushed back his chair to stand up. When he stood up he was tall and of great bulk. He had a hanging face, dark wine-coloured, with fair eyebrows and moustache: his eyes bulged forward slightly and the whites of them were dirty. He lifted up the counter and, passing by the clients, went out of the office with a heavy step.

He went heavily upstairs until he came to the second landing, where a door bore a brass plate with the inscription *Mr Alleyne*. Here he halted, puffing with labour and vexation, and knocked. The shrill voice cried:

"Come in!"

The man entered Mr Alleyne's room. Simultaneously, Mr Alleyne, a little man wearing gold-rimmed glasses on a clean-shaven face, shot his head up over a pile of documents. The head itself was so pink and hairless it seemed like a large egg reposing on the papers. Mr Alleyne did not lose a moment:

"Farrington? What is the meaning of this? Why have I always to complain of you? May I ask you why you haven't made a copy of that contract between Bodley and Kirwan? I told you it must be ready by four o'clock."

"But Mr Shelley said, sir——"

"*Mr Shelley said, sir...* Kindly attend to what I say and not to what *Mr Shelley says*, sir. You have always some excuse or another for shirking work. Let me tell you that if the contract is not copied before this evening I'll lay the matter before Mr Crosbie... Do you hear me now?"

"Yes, sir."

---

[1] Intercom.
[2] Typewriter.

"Do you hear me now?... Ay and another little matter! I might as well be talking to the wall as talking to you. Understand once and for all that you get a half an hour for your lunch and not an hour and a half. How many courses do you want, I'd like to know... Do you mind me now?"

"Yes, sir."

Mr Alleyne bent his head again upon his pile of papers. The man stared fixedly at the polished skull which directed the affairs of Crosbie & Alleyne, gauging its fragility. A spasm of rage gripped his throat for a few moments and then passed, leaving after it a sharp sensation of thirst. The man recognised the sensation and felt that he must have a good night's drinking. The middle of the month was passed and, if he could get the copy done in time, Mr Alleyne might give him an order on the cashier.[3] He stood still, gazing fixedly at the head upon the pile of papers. Suddenly Mr Alleyne began to upset all the papers, searching for something. Then, as if he had been unaware of the man's presence till that moment, he shot up his head again, saying:

"Eh? Are you going to stand there all day? Upon my word, Farrington, you take things easy!"

"I was waiting to see..."

"Very good, you needn't wait to see. Go downstairs and do your work."

The man walked heavily towards the door and, as he went out of the room, he heard Mr Alleyne cry after him that if the contract was not copied by evening Mr Crosbie would hear of the matter.

He returned to his desk in the lower office and counted the sheets which remained to be copied. He took up his pen and dipped it in the ink but he continued to stare stupidly at the last words he had written: *In no case shall the said Bernard Bodley be...* The evening was falling and in a few minutes they would be lighting the gas: then he could write. He felt that he must slake[4] the thirst in his throat. He stood up from his desk and, lifting the counter as before, passed out of the office. As he was passing out the chief clerk looked at him inquiringly.

"It's all right, Mr Shelley," said the man, pointing with his finger to indicate the objective of his journey.

---

[3] Advance.
[4] Quench.

The chief clerk glanced at the hat-rack, but, seeing the row complete, offered no remark. As soon as he was on the landing the man pulled a shepherd's plaid cap out of his pocket, put it on his head and ran quickly down the rickety stairs. From the street door he walked on furtively on the inner side of the path towards the corner and all at once dived into a doorway. He was now safe in the dark snug of O'Neill's shop, and filling up the little window that looked into the bar with his inflamed face, the colour of dark wine or dark meat, he called out:

"Here, Pat, give us a g.p.,[5] like a good fellow."

The curate brought him a glass of plain porter. The man drank it at a gulp and asked for a caraway seed. He put his penny on the counter and, leaving the curate to grope for it in the gloom, retreated out of the snug as furtively as he had entered it.

Darkness, accompanied by a thick fog, was gaining upon the dusk of February and the lamps in Eustace Street had been lit. The man went up by the houses until he reached the door of the office, wondering whether he could finish his copy in time. On the stairs a moist pungent odour of perfumes saluted his nose: evidently Miss Delacour had come while he was out in O'Neill's. He crammed his cap back again into his pocket and re-entered the office, assuming an air of absentmindedness.

"Mr Alleyne has been calling for you," said the chief clerk severely. "Where were you?"

The man glanced at the two clients who were standing at the counter as if to intimate that their presence prevented him from answering. As the clients were both male the chief clerk allowed himself a laugh.

"I know that game," he said. "Five times in one day is a little bit... Well, you better look sharp and get a copy of our correspondence in the Delacour case for Mr Alleyne."

This address in the presence of the public, his run upstairs and the porter he had gulped down so hastily confused the man and, as he sat down at his desk to get what was required, he realised how hopeless was the task of finishing his copy of the contract before half past five. The dark damp night was coming and he longed to spend it in the bars, drinking with his friends amid the glare of gas and the clatter of glasses. He got out the Delacour correspondence and

---

[5] Glass of porter.

passed out of the office. He hoped Mr Alleyne would not discover that the last two letters were missing.

The moist pungent perfume lay all the way up to Mr Alleyne's room. Miss Delacour was a middle-aged woman of Jewish appearance. Mr Alleyne was said to be sweet on her or on her money. She came to the office often and stayed a long time when she came. She was sitting beside his desk now in an aroma of perfumes, smoothing the handle of her umbrella and nodding the great black feather in her hat. Mr Alleyne had swivelled his chair round to face her and thrown his right foot jauntily upon his left knee. The man put the correspondence on the desk and bowed respectfully but neither Mr Alleyne nor Miss Delacour took any notice of his bow. Mr Alleyne tapped a finger on the correspondence and then flicked it towards him as if to say: "*That's all right: you can go.*"

The man returned to the lower office and sat down again at his desk. He stared intently at the incomplete phrase: *In no case shall the said Bernard Bodley be...* and thought how strange it was that the last three words began with the same letter. The chief clerk began to hurry Miss Parker, saying she would never have the letters typed in time for post. The man listened to the clicking of the machine for a few minutes and then set to work to finish his copy. But his head was not clear and his mind wandered away to the glare and rattle of the public-house. It was a night for hot punches. He struggled on with his copy, but when the clock struck five he had still fourteen pages to write. Blast it! He couldn't finish it in time. He longed to execrate aloud, to bring his fist down on something violently. He was so enraged that he wrote *Bernard Bernard* instead of *Bernard Bodley* and had to begin again on a clean sheet.

He felt strong enough to clear out the whole office singlehanded. His body ached to do something, to rush out and revel in violence. All the indignities of his life enraged him... Could he ask the cashier privately for an advance? No, the cashier was no good, no damn good: he wouldn't give an advance... He knew where he would meet the boys: Leonard and O'Halloran and Nosey Flynn. The barometer of his emotional nature was set for a spell of riot.

His imagination had so abstracted him that his name was called twice before he answered. Mr Alleyne and Miss Delacour were standing outside the counter and all the clerks had turned round in anticipation of something. The man got up from his desk. Mr Alleyne began a tirade of abuse, saying that two letters were missing. The man answered that he knew nothing about them, that he had made a faithful copy. The tirade continued: it was so bitter and violent that the man could hardly restrain his fist from descending upon the head of the manikin[6] before him:

"I know nothing about any other two letters," he said stupidly.

"*You—know—nothing.* Of course you know nothing," said Mr Alleyne. "Tell me," he added, glancing first for approval to the lady beside him, "do you take me for a fool? Do you think me an utter fool?"

The man glanced from the lady's face to the little egg-shaped head and back again; and, almost before he was aware of it, his tongue had found a felicitous moment:

"I don't think, sir," he said, "that that's a fair question to put to me."

There was a pause in the very breathing of the clerks. Everyone was astounded (the author of the witticism no less than his neighbours) and Miss Delacour, who was a stout amiable person, began to smile broadly. Mr Alleyne flushed to the hue of a wild rose and his mouth twitched with a dwarf's passion. He shook his fist in the man's face till it seemed to vibrate like the knob of some electric machine:

"You impertinent ruffian! You impertinent ruffian! I'll make short work of you! Wait till you see! You'll apologise to me for your impertinence or you'll quit the office instanter![7] You'll quit this, I'm telling you, or you'll apologise to me!"

*****

He stood in a doorway opposite the office watching to see if the cashier would come out alone. All the clerks passed out and finally the cashier came out with the chief clerk. It was no use trying to say a word to him when he was with the chief clerk. The man felt that his position was bad enough. He had been obliged to offer an abject apology to Mr Alleyne for his impertinence but he knew what a hornet's nest the office would be for him. He could remember the way in which Mr Alleyne had hounded little Peake out of the office in order to make room for his own nephew. He felt savage and thirsty

---

[6] A short man.
[7] Instantly or now.

and revengeful, annoyed with himself and with everyone else. Mr Alleyne would never give him an hour's rest; his life would be a hell to him. He had made a proper fool of himself this time. Could he not keep his tongue in his cheek? But they had never pulled together from the first, he and Mr Alleyne, ever since the day Mr Alleyne had overheard him mimicking his North of Ireland accent to amuse Higgins and Miss Parker: that had been the beginning of it. He might have tried Higgins for the money, but sure Higgins never had anything for himself. A man with two establishments to keep up, of course he couldn't...

He felt his great body again aching for the comfort of the public-house. The fog had begun to chill him and he wondered could he touch Pat in O'Neill's. He could not touch him[8] for more than a bob—and a bob was no use. Yet he must get money somewhere or other: he had spent his last penny for the g.p. and soon it would be too late for getting money anywhere. Suddenly, as he was fingering his watch-chain, he thought of Terry Kelly's pawn-office in Fleet Street. That was the dart![9] Why didn't he think of it sooner?

He went through the narrow alley of Temple Bar quickly, muttering to himself that they could all go to hell because he was going to have a good night of it. The clerk in Terry Kelly's said *A crown!*[10] but the consignor held out for six shillings; and in the end the six shillings was allowed him literally. He came out of the pawn-office joyfully, making a little cylinder of the coins between his thumb and fingers. In Westmoreland Street the footpaths were crowded with young men and women returning from business and ragged urchins ran here and there yelling out the names of the evening editions. The man passed through the crowd, looking on the spectacle generally with proud satisfaction and staring masterfully at the office-girls. His head was full of the noises of tram-gongs and swishing trolleys and his nose already sniffed the curling fumes punch. As he walked on he preconsidered the terms in which he would narrate the incident to the boys:

"So, I just looked at him—coolly, you know, and looked at her. Then I looked back at him again—taking my time, you know. 'I don't think that's a fair question to put to me,' says I."

---

[8] Rely on him for a loan.
[9] Idea.
[10] Five shillings.

Nosey Flynn was sitting up in his usual corner of Davy Byrne's and, when he heard the story, he stood[11] Farrington a half-one, saying it was as smart a thing as ever he heard. Farrington stood a drink in his turn. After a while O'Halloran and Paddy Leonard came in and the story was repeated to them. O'Halloran stood tailors[12] of malt, hot, all round and told the story of the retort he had made to the chief clerk when he was in Callan's of Fownes's Street; but, as the retort was after the manner of the liberal shepherds in the eclogues, he had to admit that it was not as clever as Farrington's retort. At this, Farrington told the boys to polish off that and have another.

Just as they were naming their poisons who should come in but Higgins! Of course he had to join in with the others. The men asked him to give his version of it, and he did so with great vivacity for the sight of five small hot whiskies was very exhilarating. Everyone roared laughing when he showed the way in which Mr Alleyne shook his fist in Farrington's face. Then he imitated Farrington, saying, *"And here was my nabs,[13] as cool as you please,"* while Farrington looked at the company out of his heavy dirty eyes, smiling and at times drawing forth stray drops of liquor from his moustache with the aid of his lower lip.

When that round was over there was a pause. O'Halloran had money but neither of the other two seemed to have any; so the whole party left the shop somewhat regretfully. At the corner of Duke Street, Higgins and Nosey Flynn bevelled off to the left while the other three turned back towards the city. Rain was drizzling down on the cold streets and, when they reached the Ballast Office, Farrington suggested the Scotch House. The bar was full of men and loud with the noise of tongues and glasses. The three men pushed past the whining matchsellers at the door and formed a little party at the corner of the counter. They began to exchange stories. Leonard introduced them to a young fellow named Weathers who was performing at the Tivoli as an acrobat and knockabout *artiste*. Farrington stood a drink all round. Weathers said he would take a small Irish and Apollinaris. Farrington, who had definite notions of what was what, asked the boys would they have an Apollinaris too; but the boys told Tim to make theirs hot. The talk became theatrical. O'Halloran stood a round and then Farrington stood another round,

---

[11] Bought.
[12] Three-ounces.
[13] Boss.

Weathers protesting that the hospitality was too Irish. He promised to get them in behind the scenes and introduce them to some nice girls. O'Halloran said that he and Leonard would go, but that Farrington wouldn't go because he was a married man; and Farrington's heavy dirty eyes leered at the company in token that he understood he was being chaffed. Weathers made them all have just one little tincture at his expense and promised to meet them later on at Mulligan's in Poolbeg Street.

When the Scotch House closed they went round to Mulligan's. They went into the parlour at the back and O'Halloran ordered small hot specials all round. They were all beginning to feel mellow. Farrington was just standing another round when Weathers came back. Much to Farrington's relief he drank a glass of bitter this time. Funds were getting low but they had enough to keep them going. Presently two young women with big hats and a young man in a check suit came in and sat at a table close by. Weathers saluted them and told the company that they were out of the Tivoli. Farrington's eyes wandered at every moment in the direction of one of the young women. There was something striking in her appearance. An immense scarf of peacock-blue muslin was wound round her hat and knotted in a great bow under her chin; and she wore bright yellow gloves, reaching to the elbow. Farrington gazed admiringly at the plump arm which she moved very often and with much grace; and when, after a little time, she answered his gaze he admired still more her large dark brown eyes. The oblique staring expression in them fascinated him. She glanced at him once or twice and, when the party was leaving the room, she brushed against his chair and said *"O, pardon!"* in a London accent. He watched her leave the room in the hope that she would look back at him, but he was disappointed. He cursed his want of money and cursed all the rounds he had stood, particularly all the whiskies and Apolinaris which he had stood to Weathers. If there was one thing that he hated it was a sponge. He was so angry that he lost count of the conversation of his friends.

When Paddy Leonard called him he found that they were talking about feats of strength. Weathers was showing his biceps muscle to the company and boasting so much that the other two had called on Farrington to uphold the national honour. Farrington pulled up his sleeve accordingly and showed his biceps muscle to the company. The two arms were examined and compared and finally it was agreed to have a trial of strength. The table was cleared and the two men rested their elbows on it, clasping hands. When Paddy Leonard said "*Go!*" each was to try to bring down the other's hand on to the table. Farrington looked very serious and determined.

The trial began. After about thirty seconds Weathers brought his opponent's hand slowly down on to the table. Farrington's dark wine-coloured face flushed darker still with anger and humiliation at having been defeated by such a stripling.[14]

"You're not to put the weight of your body behind it. Play fair," he said.

"Who's not playing fair?" said the other.

"Come on again. The two best out of three."

The trial began again. The veins stood out on Farrington's forehead, and the pallor of Weathers' complexion changed to peony. Their hands and arms trembled under the stress. After a long struggle Weathers again brought his opponent's hand slowly on to the table. There was a murmur of applause from the spectators. The curate, who was standing beside the table, nodded his red head towards the victor and said with stupid familiarity:

"Ah! that's the knack!"

"What the hell do you know about it?" said Farrington fiercely, turning on the man. "What do you put in your gab[15] for?"

"Sh, sh!" said O'Halloran, observing the violent expression of Farrington's face. "Pony up, boys. We'll have just one little smahan[16] more and then we'll be off."

A very sullen-faced man stood at the corner of O'Connell Bridge waiting for the little Sandymount tram to take him home. He was full of smouldering anger and revengefulness. He felt humiliated and discontented; he did not even feel drunk; and he had only twopence in his pocket. He cursed everything. He had done for himself in the office, pawned his watch, spent all his money; and he had not even got drunk. He began to feel thirsty again and he longed to be back again in the hot reeking public-house. He had lost his reputation as a strong man, having been defeated twice by a mere boy. His heart swelled with fury and, when he thought of the woman in the big hat who had brushed against him and said *Pardon!* his fury nearly choked him.

---

[14] Child.
[15] Nose.
[16] Swallow.

His tram let him down at Shelbourne Road and he steered his great body along in the shadow of the wall of the barracks. He loathed returning to his home. When he went in by the side-door he found the kitchen empty and the kitchen fire nearly out. He bawled upstairs:

"Ada! Ada!"

His wife was a little sharp-faced woman who bullied her husband when he was sober and was bullied by him when he was drunk. They had five children. A little boy came running down the stairs.

"Who is that?" said the man, peering through the darkness.

"Me, pa."

"Who are you? Charlie?"

"No, pa. Tom."

"Where's your mother?"

"She's out at the chapel."

"That's right... Did she think of leaving any dinner for me?"

"Yes, pa. I—"

"Light the lamp. What do you mean by having the place in darkness? Are the other children in bed?"

The man sat down heavily on one of the chairs while the little boy lit the lamp. He began to mimic his son's flat accent, saying half to himself: *"At the chapel. At the chapel, if you please!"* When the lamp was lit he banged his fist on the table and shouted:

"What's for my dinner?"

"I'm going... to cook it, pa," said the little boy.

The man jumped up furiously and pointed to the fire.

"On that fire! You let the fire out! By God, I'll teach you to do that again!"

He took a step to the door and seized the walking-stick which was standing behind it.

"I'll teach you to let the fire out!" he said, rolling up his sleeve in order to give his arm free play.

The little boy cried, *"O, pa!"* and ran whimpering round the table, but the man followed him and caught him by the coat. The little boy looked about him wildly but, seeing no way of escape, fell upon his knees.

"Now, you'll let the fire out the next time!" said the man striking at him vigorously with the stick. "Take that, you little whelp!"

The boy uttered a squeal of pain as the stick cut his thigh. He clasped his hands together in the air and his voice shook with fright.

"O, pa!" he cried. "Don't beat me, pa! And I'll... I'll say a *Hail Mary* for you... I'll say a *Hail Mary* for you, pa, if you don't beat me... I'll say a *Hail Mary*..."

CRAFT: COUNTERPARTS

Increasing Action, Tension and Conflict

When Mr. Alleyne calls Farrington into his office at the beginning of "Counterparts" and complains about Farrington's performance, Farrington, though clearly frustrated and angry, evidenced by his earlier muttering of "*Blast him!*" responds passively: "'Yes, sir.'" The tension in this scene comes from the disparity we see between what Farrington feels and what he says. He is angry, yet he takes the abuse.

Later in the story, after Mr. Alleyne complains about the two missing letters, and lays down a "tirade of abuse," Farrington replies passive-aggressively now, saying that he knows nothing of the lost letters. When Mr. Alleyne mocks Farrington and asks him, "Do you think me an utter fool?" Farrington's passivity from the beginning of the story escalates to aggression and he replies, "I don't think, sir ... that that's a fair question to put to me." As the others in the office admire Farrington's "witticism," Mr. Alleyne responds angrily—"You impertinent ruffian!"—and demands an apology.

This **increasing action** and **conflict** work to alter the source of the tension. While the tension centers on Farrington's passivity in the beginning of the story, it shifts to his attack on Mr. Alleyne. Farrington has questioned Mr. Alleyne's authority and his behavior, making Farrington vulnerable to his wrath.

As Farrington carouses in the pubs, he gets some pleasure out of repeating the story of his insult to his friends. However, the victory is short lived and he ends the night having spent too much money, having lost an arm wrestling contest, and having been rejected by a beautiful woman. His anger increases, and when he returns home the aggression mounts to violence when he beats his son.

By the end of "Counterparts" the **action** increases to the **climax**. The conflict rests on Farrington's failure not only as a clerk in his law office, but as a father, and the tension shifts from passivity to unleashed, violent aggression.

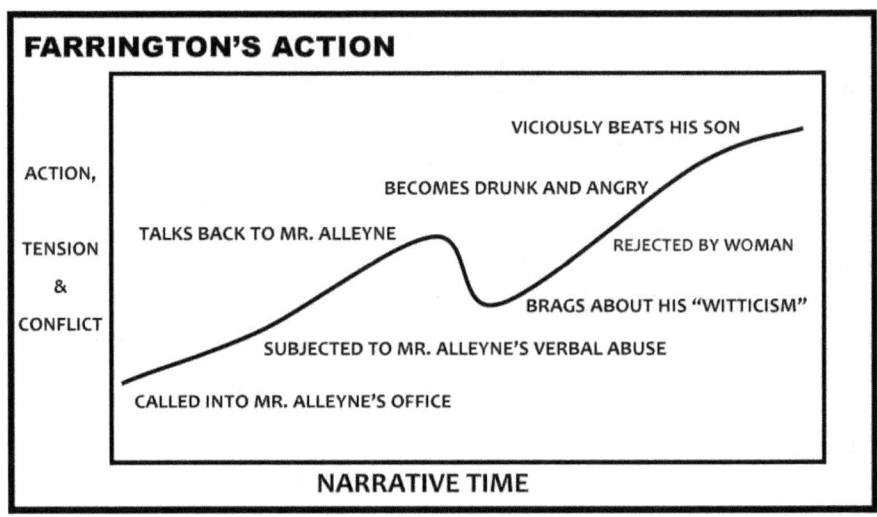

While the reasons for the tension and conflict change throughout the story, we can see from the illustration that they spend most of the story increasing. We get a brief respite in the middle after Farrington stands up to his boss and brags about his victory, but other than that, Joyce increases action, tension and conflict straight to the end.

Character versus Type

Joyce's use of the phrase "the man" to describe Farrington throughout the story—"The man muttered *Blast him!* under his breath and pushed back his chair to stand up"—indicates that Joyce has created a **type** (as in archetype). This "man" was created to comment on many men in Dublin, and suggests Joyce's **idea** about paralysis and his social argument about aggression, alcoholism, and domestic violence.

However, at the same time, Joyce individualizes Farrington with **details** and precise descriptions. Farrington has a "hanging face," "fair eyebrows and mustache," and eyes with dirty whites that bulge "forward slightly." Joyce describes him as being "tall and of great bulk" and often references Farrington's "great body" and his heavy walk. These particulars help to individualize a character who we know to be an archetype—one who embodies Joyce's social message. Even our disgust for Farrington by the end of the story individualizes his character. We feel strongly about him because we have come to understand him as an individual—both the oppressed and the oppressor. Joyce is therefore able to carry out a delicate balance between character and type, and this balance effectively works to put Farrington's character in conversation with Joyce's social comment and idea.

Character in Conflict with Setting

Throughout *Dubliners*, the sense of paralysis that so many of the characters feel comes from an insular conflict they experience inside the **setting**. Joyce's Dublin often acts like a trap. In "A Little Cloud" Chandler feels trapped in the unsophisticated prison that is both his life and the city of Dublin. In "Counterparts" Farrington's conflict with his setting parallels Chandler's. Farrington's paralysis is the result of alcoholism, pessimism, and passive-aggressiveness. It seems that everything in his environment causes frustration and acute anger. He dislikes his job and Mr. Alleyne. He is unhappy at home. He cannot fulfill his occupational duties. The only place that seems to give him any comfort is the pub, but even the pub leads him to poverty, humiliation, and anger. "He cursed everything."

Some writers, in their attempt to describe the conflict between character and setting, often mistakenly call the setting "a character" in a story like "Counterparts," because the setting becomes like an **antagonist**. While Farrington often appears at odds with his environment, the antagonism that writers often like to direct at the setting actually comes from the **protagonist** himself. The setting only incites or irritates an inner conflict. In Farrington's case, his conflict comes from what he knows is his failure. When he stands up to Mr.

Allenye's abuse, he is not justified in his cocky witticism. In fact, he is only covering up his own vocational ineptitude. While he should have been carrying out his job, he was out drinking a beer. His passive-aggressiveness, while it finds **tension** in the setting, results from Farrington himself—both the protagonist and the antagonist of this story.

While it often sounds interesting to call Dublin a character in *Dubliners*, it certainly doesn't help us understand much about how Joyce created conflict in the setting. In fact, it actually makes it far more difficult because it's such an ambiguous and generalized comparison. In both "A Little Cloud" and "Counterparts" the most effective way to describe the setting is to compare it to a prison. Both characters feel imprisoned in Dublin and their lives. That setting is not dynamic; it doesn't move or act. In fact, it's just the opposite. The conflict these characters feel in their setting comes from the lack of movement and change. When Joyce writes about Farrington near the end of "Counterparts" that he "loathed returning to his home," the conflict comes from his feelings of stagnancy. The setting helps create a conflicted character, not act as one.

Questions

1. We have discussed how Joyce **increases tension** and **conflict**, but we haven't discussed how he creates it in the first place. Because creating tension is such an important part of the writer's craft, how does Joyce create tension in "Counterparts"?

2. How does the title "Counterparts" operate in this story? What does this title imply and what does it add to your knowledge about the characters? Does it act a **symbol**? An **image**? The core **idea**? The **premise**?

3. Let's examine several characters from past stories: Mrs. Mooney and Mr. Doran from "The Boarding House," and Chandler from "A Little Cloud." Do you consider these characters individuals or **types**? What elements cause you to consider them one or the other?

Clay

The Matron had given her leave to go out as soon as the women's tea was over and Maria looked forward to her evening out. The kitchen was spick and span: the cook said you could see yourself in the big copper boilers. The fire was nice and bright and on one of the side-tables were four very big barmbracks.[1] These barmbracks seemed uncut; but if you went closer you would see that they had been cut into long thick even slices and were ready to be handed round at tea. Maria had cut them herself.

Maria was a very, very small person indeed but she had a very long nose and a very long chin. She talked a little through her nose, always soothingly: "*Yes, my dear,*" and "*No, my dear.*" She was always sent for when the women quarrelled over their tubs and always succeeded in making peace. One day the matron had said to her:

"Maria, you are a veritable peace-maker!"

And the sub-matron and two of the Board ladies had heard the compliment. And Ginger Mooney was always saying what she wouldn't do to the dummy who had charge of the irons if it wasn't for Maria. Everyone was so fond of Maria.

The women would have their tea at six o'clock and she would be able to get away before seven. From Ballsbridge to the Pillar, twenty minutes; from the Pillar to Drumcondra, twenty minutes; and twenty minutes to buy the things. She would be there before eight. She took out her purse with the silver clasps and read again the words *A Present from Belfast*. She was very fond of that purse because Joe had brought it to her five years before when he and Alphy had gone to Belfast on a Whit-Monday[2] trip. In the purse were two half-crowns and some coppers. She would have five shillings clear after paying tram fare. What a nice evening they would have, all the children singing! Only she hoped that Joe wouldn't come in drunk. He was so different when he took any drink.

Often he had wanted her to go and live with them; but she would have felt herself in the way (though Joe's wife was ever so nice with her) and she had become accustomed to the life of the laundry.

---

[1] Cakes.
[2] Holiday.

Joe was a good fellow. She had nursed him and Alphy too; and Joe used often say:

"Mamma is mamma but Maria is my proper mother."

After the break-up at home the boys had got her that position in the *Dublin by Lamplight* laundry, and she liked it. She used to have such a bad opinion of Protestants but now she thought they were very nice people, a little quiet and serious, but still very nice people to live with. Then she had her plants in the conservatory and she liked looking after them. She had lovely ferns and wax-plants and, whenever anyone came to visit her, she always gave the visitor one or two slips from her conservatory. There was one thing she didn't like and that was the tracts[3] on the walls; but the matron was such a nice person to deal with, so genteel.

When the cook told her everything was ready she went into the women's room and began to pull the big bell. In a few minutes the women began to come in by twos and threes, wiping their steaming hands in their petticoats and pulling down the sleeves of their blouses over their red steaming arms. They settled down before their huge mugs which the cook and the dummy filled up with hot tea, already mixed with milk and sugar in huge tin cans. Maria superintended the distribution of the barmbrack and saw that every woman got her four slices. There was a great deal of laughing and joking during the meal. Lizzie Fleming said Maria was sure to get the ring[4] and, though Fleming had said that for so many Hallow Eves, Maria had to laugh and say she didn't want any ring or man either; and when she laughed her grey-green eyes sparkled with disappointed shyness and the tip of her nose nearly met the tip of her chin. Then Ginger Mooney lifted her mug of tea and proposed Maria's health while all the other women clattered with their mugs on the table, and said she was sorry she hadn't a sup of porter to drink it in. And Maria laughed again till the tip of her nose nearly met the tip of her chin and till her minute body nearly shook itself asunder because she knew that Mooney meant well though, of course, she had the notions of a common woman.

But wasn't Maria glad when the women had finished their tea and the cook and the dummy had begun to clear away the tea-things! She went into her little bedroom and, remembering that the next morning was a mass morning, changed the hand of the alarm from

---

[3] Pamphlets.
[4] Meaning marriage.

seven to six. Then she took off her working skirt and her house-boots and laid her best skirt out on the bed and her tiny dress-boots beside the foot of the bed. She changed her blouse too and, as she stood before the mirror, she thought of how she used to dress for mass on Sunday morning when she was a young girl; and she looked with quaint affection at the diminutive body which she had so often adorned. In spite of its years she found it a nice tidy little body.

When she got outside the streets were shining with rain and she was glad of her old brown waterproof. The tram was full and she had to sit on the little stool at the end of the car, facing all the people, with her toes barely touching the floor. She arranged in her mind all she was going to do and thought how much better it was to be independent and to have your own money in your pocket. She hoped they would have a nice evening. She was sure they would but she could not help thinking what a pity it was Alphy and Joe were not speaking. They were always falling out now but when they were boys together they used to be the best of friends: but such was life.

She got out of her tram at the Pillar and ferreted her way quickly among the crowds. She went into Downes's cake-shop but the shop was so full of people that it was a long time before she could get herself attended to. She bought a dozen of mixed penny cakes, and at last came out of the shop laden with a big bag. Then she thought what else would she buy: she wanted to buy something really nice. They would be sure to have plenty of apples and nuts. It was hard to know what to buy and all she could think of was cake. She decided to buy some plumcake but Downes's plumcake had not enough almond icing on top of it so she went over to a shop on Henry Street. Here she was a long time in suiting herself and the stylish young lady behind the counter, who was evidently a little annoyed by her, asked her was it wedding-cake she wanted to buy. That made Maria blush and smile at the young lady; but the young lady took it all very seriously and finally cut a thick slice of plumcake, parcelled it up and said:

"Two-and-four, please."

She thought she would have to stand in the Drumcondra tram because none of the young men seemed to notice her but an elderly gentleman made room for her. He was a stout gentleman and he wore a brown hard hat; he had a square red face and a grayish moustache. Maria thought he was a colonel-looking gentleman and she reflected how much more polite he was than the young men who simply stared straight before them. The gentleman began to chat with her about Hallow Eve and the rainy weather. He supposed the bag was full of good things for the little ones and said it was only right that the youngsters should enjoy themselves while they were young. Maria agreed with him and favoured him with demure nods and hems. He was very nice with her, and when she was getting out at the Canal Bridge she thanked him and bowed, and he bowed to her and raised his hat and smiled agreeably, and while she was going up along the terrace, bending her tiny head under the rain, she thought how easy it was to know a gentleman even when he has a drop taken.[5]

Everybody said: *"O, here's Maria!"* when she came to Joe's house. Joe was there, having come home from business, and all the children had their Sunday dresses on. There were two big girls in from next door and games were going on. Maria gave the bag of cakes to the eldest boy, Alphy, to divide and Mrs Donnelly said it was too good of her to bring such a big bag of cakes and made all the children say:

"Thanks, Maria."

But Maria said she had brought something special for papa and mamma, something they would be sure to like, and she began to look for her plumcake. She tried in Downes's bag and then in the pockets of her waterproof and then on the hallstand but nowhere could she find it. Then she asked all the children had any of them eaten it—by mistake, of course—but the children all said no and looked as if they did not like to eat cakes if they were to be accused of stealing. Everybody had a solution for the mystery and Mrs Donnelly said it was plain that Maria had left it behind her in the tram. Maria, remembering how confused the gentleman with the greyish moustache had made her, coloured with shame and vexation and disappointment. At the thought of the failure of her little surprise and of the two and fourpence she had thrown away for nothing she nearly cried outright.

But Joe said it didn't matter and made her sit down by the fire. He was very nice with her. He told her all that went on in his office, repeating for her a smart answer which he had made to the manager. Maria did not understand why Joe laughed so much over the answer he had made but she said that the manager must have been a very overbearing person to deal with. Joe said he wasn't so

---

[5] Been drinking.

bad when you knew how to take him, that he was a decent sort so long as you didn't rub him the wrong way. Mrs Donnelly played the piano for the children and they danced and sang. Then the two next-door girls handed round the nuts. Nobody could find the nutcrackers and Joe was nearly getting cross over it and asked how did they expect Maria to crack nuts without a nutcracker. But Maria said she didn't like nuts and that they weren't to bother about her. Then Joe asked would she take a bottle of stout and Mrs Donnelly said there was port wine too in the house if she would prefer that. Maria said she would rather they didn't ask her to take anything: but Joe insisted.

So Maria let him have his way and they sat by the fire talking over old times and Maria thought she would put in a good word for Alphy. But Joe cried that God might strike him stone dead if ever he spoke a word to his brother again and Maria said she was sorry she had mentioned the matter. Mrs Donnelly told her husband it was a great shame for him to speak that way of his own flesh and blood but Joe said that Alphy was no brother of his and there was nearly being a row on the head of it. But Joe said he would not lose his temper on account of the night it was and asked his wife to open some more stout. The two next-door girls had arranged some Hallow Eve games and soon everything was merry again. Maria was delighted to see the children so merry and Joe and his wife in such good spirits. The next-door girls put some saucers on the table and then led the children up to the table, blindfold. One got the prayer-book and the other three got the water; and when one of the next-door girls got the ring Mrs Donnelly shook her finger at the blushing girl as much as to say: *O, I know all about it!* They insisted then on blindfolding Maria and leading her up to the table to see what she would get; and, while they were putting on the bandage, Maria laughed and laughed again till the tip of her nose nearly met the tip of her chin.

They led her up to the table amid laughing and joking and she put her hand out in the air as she was told to do. She moved her hand about here and there in the air and descended on one of the saucers. She felt a soft wet substance with her fingers and was surprised that nobody spoke or took off her bandage. There was a pause for a few seconds; and then a great deal of scuffling and whispering. Somebody said something about the garden, and at last Mrs Donnelly said something very cross to one of the next-door girls and told her to throw it out at once: that was no play. Maria understood that it was wrong that time and so she had to do it over again: and this time she got the prayer-book.

After that Mrs Donnelly played Miss McCloud's Reel for the children and Joe made Maria take a glass of wine. Soon they were all quite merry again and Mrs Donnelly said Maria would enter a convent before the year was out because she had got the prayer-book. Maria had never seen Joe so nice to her as he was that night, so full of pleasant talk and reminiscences. She said they were all very good to her.

At last the children grew tired and sleepy and Joe asked Maria would she not sing some little song before she went, one of the old songs. Mrs Donnelly said "Do, please, Maria!" and so Maria had to get up and stand beside the piano. Mrs Donnelly bade the children be quiet and listen to Maria's song. Then she played the prelude and said "Now, Maria!" and Maria, blushing very much began to sing in a tiny quavering voice. She sang *I Dreamt that I Dwelt*, and when she came to the second verse she sang again:

> I dreamt that I dwelt in marble halls
>   With vassals and serfs at my side,
> And of all who assembled within those walls
>   That I was the hope and the pride.
>
> I had riches too great to count; could boast
>   Of a high ancestral name,
> But I also dreamt, which pleased me most,
>   That you loved me still the same.

But no one tried to show her her mistake; and when she had ended her song Joe was very much moved. He said that there was no time like the long ago and no music for him like poor old Balfe, whatever other people might say; and his eyes filled up so much with tears that he could not find what he was looking for and in the end he had to ask his wife to tell him where the corkscrew was.

CRAFT: CLAY

Tone: Dramatic Irony

When a reader first begins "Clay," he or she immediately notices the change in **tone**, or the sound, color and feeling of the language from the previous stories. Let's compare the first sentences of "Counterparts" and "Clay."

> "Counterparts": "The bell rang furiously and, when Miss Parker went to the tube, a furious voice called out in a piercing North of Ireland accent: 'Send Farrington here!'"

> "Clay": "The matron had given her leave to go out as soon as the women's tea was over and Maria looked forward to her evening out."

The first thing you probably notice is the urgency and energy in "Counterparts" versus the lulling carefulness of "Clay." In "Counterparts," the phrases "ran furiously," "furious voice," and "piercing North of Ireland accent" all give the sentence a "furious" tone. In "Clay" the phrases "given her leave" and "looked forward" have a muted and cautious tone.

However, we should notice the difference between the points of view too. While both of these narrators are **third person narrators**, these first sentences have slightly different modes. In "Counterparts" the narrator describes the events only and remains **objective**. We have not yet entered Farrington's thoughts. In "Clay" the first sentence immediately plunges us into Maria's mind—"Maria looked forward to her evening out"—and is therefore **subjective**. The objective first sentence of "Counterparts" helps to give a sense of the franticness of the office, and plunges us into the **action** and setting. The subjective first sentence of "Clay" creates a tone that invites the reader into Maria's point of view from the very beginning.

In the first sentence of the second paragraph of "Clay" Joyce writes, "Maria was a very, very small person indeed but she had a very long nose and a very long chin." This sentence is charmingly simple and straightforward. The repetition of the modifier "very" may be unnecessary, but it immediately informs us of Maria's lack of sophistication. The sentence sounds nothing like James Joyce, and because the narrator actually narrates parts of the story in Maria's "voice" this is a case of **point of view inflection**.

This infusion of modifiers and proliferation of conjunctions create a lulling and quiet tone:

> Lizzie Fleming said Maria was sure to get the ring and, though Fleming had said that for so many Hallow Eves, Maria had to laugh and say she didn't want any ring or man either; and when she laughed her grey-green eyes sparkled with disappointed shyness and the tip of her nose nearly met the tip of her chin.

Joyce uses the word "and" four times in this sentence, and it acts to soothe the reader into this slowly progressing narrative. The tone of Maria's laughter and "disappointed shyness" create a sense of **pathos** in this story we haven't felt as readers yet in *Dubliners*.

When Maria plays the Halloween game, she is blindfolded and sticks her hand in "a soft wet substance." Clay, in this popular game of the time, represents an early death, and the silence that follows in the room indicates the awkwardness of the moment. This narrative twist comments on the tone of the story. It's as though somewhere in those lulling conjunctions and repeated modifiers lies Maria's death, and the story is much like a lullaby.

It's at this point in the narrative that readers may begin to sense that the tone results from **dramatic irony**, which occurs when the reader and/or the other characters understand what is happening to a character without that character understanding it for him- or herself.

Even the way characters speak about and to Maria in this story reflect the tone of the narration. To readers, their forced graciousness raises flags to which Maria seems wholly oblivious. The matron tells her, "Maria, you are a veritable peace-maker!" Joe says, "Mamma is mamma but Maria is my proper mother." Even the narrator says, "Everyone was so fond of Maria." The tone nears nostalgic and even patronizing, as though Maria is already dead. All of her faux pas are forgiven instantly. When she realizes that she left the plumcake she bought for Joe on the tram, they won't listen to her apology. When she brings up the touchy subject of Joe's brother Alphy, Joe simply changes the subject. When she places her hand in the clay during the Halloween game, "nobody spoke or took off her bandage" and she simply does it over again and gets "the prayer-book." When she sings a song at the end of the story, she misses a verse and repeats the first, but "no one tried to show her her mistake." In the end, the dramatic irony that creates the tone feels less lulling and more haunting, as though the pity that those around Maria obviously feel for her has something to do with her victimhood. She may not yet be dead, but she is disconnected from the intricacies of life and has only a partial understanding of the situation around her.

The tone and the characters' pandering to Maria, who had "never seen Joe so nice to her as he was that night" **foreshadow** the death symbolized by the clay. The tone that asks the reader to pity Maria also asks whether or not he or she will see her through the same patronizing lens through which most of the characters see her. In "Clay" Joyce demonstrates the fine line between pathos and condescension very well.

Questions

1. Critics have argued extensively about Maria's character in "Clay." Some critics claim she is a lost character, socially inept, and ignorant. Others say she is misunderstood and that, like many of the characters in the story, readers are quick to dismiss her as simple or even dumb. What is your interpretation of Joyce's **characterization** of Maria? What parts of the crafting of this narrative make her so perplexing?

2. In considering the **tone** of "Clay" versus the tone of "Counterparts" how do they compare? How does Joyce manipulate the tone? Isolate two key sentences in each of these stories that you believe communicate the overall tone of each story particularly well. How do they differ, and how do those differences affect your sense of the events or characters?

A Painful Case

Mr James Duffy lived in Chapelizod because he wished to live as far as possible from the city of which he was a citizen and because he found all the other suburbs of Dublin mean, modern and pretentious. He lived in an old sombre house and from his windows he could look into the disused distillery or upwards along the shallow river on which Dublin is built. The lofty walls of his uncarpeted room were free from pictures. He had himself bought every article of furniture in the room: a black iron bedstead, an iron washstand, four cane chairs, a clothes-rack, a coal-scuttle,[1] a fender and irons and a square table on which lay a double desk. A bookcase had been made in an alcove by means of shelves of white wood. The bed was clothed with white bedclothes and a black and scarlet rug covered the foot. A little hand-mirror hung above the washstand and during the day a white-shaded lamp stood as the sole ornament of the mantelpiece. The books on the white wooden shelves were arranged from below upwards according to bulk. A complete Wordsworth stood at one end of the lowest shelf and a copy of the *Maynooth Catechism*, sewn into the cloth cover of a notebook, stood at one end of the top shelf. Writing materials were always on the desk. In the desk lay a manuscript translation of Hauptmann's *Michael Kramer*, the stage directions of which were written in purple ink, and a little sheaf of papers held together by a brass pin. In these sheets a sentence was inscribed from time to time and, in an ironical moment, the headline of an advertisement for *Bile Beans* had been pasted on to the first sheet. On lifting the lid of the desk a faint fragrance escaped—the fragrance of new cedarwood pencils or of a bottle of gum[2] or of an overripe apple which might have been left there and forgotten.

Mr Duffy abhorred anything which betokened physical or mental disorder. A medieval doctor would have called him saturnine. His face, which carried the entire tale of his years, was of the brown tint of Dublin streets. On his long and rather large head grew dry black hair and a tawny moustache did not quite cover an unamiable mouth. His cheekbones also gave his face a harsh character; but there

---

[1] Container for coal.
[2] Glue.

was no harshness in the eyes which, looking at the world from under their tawny eyebrows, gave the impression of a man ever alert to greet a redeeming instinct in others but often disappointed. He lived at a little distance from his body, regarding his own acts with doubtful side-glasses. He had an odd autobiographical habit which led him to compose in his mind from time to time a short sentence about himself containing a subject in the third person and a predicate in the past tense. He never gave alms to beggars and walked firmly, carrying a stout hazel.[3]

He had been for many years cashier of a private bank in Baggot Street. Every morning he came in from Chapelizod by tram. At midday he went to Dan Burke's and took his lunch—a bottle of lager beer and a small trayful of arrowroot biscuits. At four o'clock he was set free. He dined in an eatinghouse in George's Street where he felt himself safe from the society of Dublin's gilded youth and where there was a certain plain honesty in the bill of fare. His evenings were spent either before his landlady's piano or roaming about the outskirts of the city. His liking for Mozart's music brought him sometimes to an opera or a concert: these were the only dissipations of his life.

He had neither companions nor friends, church nor creed. He lived his spiritual life without any communion with others, visiting his relatives at Christmas and escorting them to the cemetery when they died. He performed these two social duties for old dignity's sake but conceded nothing further to the conventions which regulate the civic life. He allowed himself to think that in certain circumstances he would rob his bank but, as these circumstances never arose, his life rolled out evenly—an adventureless tale.

One evening he found himself sitting beside two ladies in the Rotunda. The house, thinly peopled and silent, gave distressing prophecy of failure. The lady who sat next him looked round at the deserted house once or twice and then said:

"What a pity there is such a poor house to-night! It's so hard on people to have to sing to empty benches."

He took the remark as an invitation to talk. He was surprised that she seemed so little awkward. While they talked he tried to fix her permanently in his memory. When he learned that the young girl beside her was her daughter he judged her to be a year or so younger

---

[3] Cane or stick.

than himself. Her face, which must have been handsome, had remained intelligent. It was an oval face with strongly marked features. The eyes were very dark blue and steady. Their gaze began with a defiant note but was confused by what seemed a deliberate swoon of the pupil into the iris, revealing for an instant a temperament of great sensibility. The pupil reasserted itself quickly, this half-disclosed nature fell again under the reign of prudence, and her astrakhan jacket, moulding a bosom of a certain fullness, struck the note of defiance more definitely.

He met her again a few weeks afterwards at a concert in Earlsfort Terrace and seized the moments when her daughter's attention was diverted to become intimate. She alluded once or twice to her husband but her tone was not such as to make the allusion a warning. Her name was Mrs Sinico. Her husband's great-great-grandfather had come from Leghorn. Her husband was captain of a mercantile boat plying between Dublin and Holland; and they had one child.

Meeting her a third time by accident he found courage to make an appointment. She came. This was the first of many meetings; they met always in the evening and chose the most quiet quarters for their walks together. Mr Duffy, however, had a distaste for underhand ways and, finding that they were compelled to meet stealthily, he forced her to ask him to her house. Captain Sinico encouraged his visits, thinking that his daughter's hand was in question. He had dismissed his wife so sincerely from his gallery of pleasures that he did not suspect that anyone else would take an interest in her. As the husband was often away and the daughter out giving music lessons Mr Duffy had many opportunities of enjoying the lady's society. Neither he nor she had had any such adventure before and neither was conscious of any incongruity. Little by little he entangled his thoughts with hers. He lent her books, provided her with ideas, shared his intellectual life with her. She listened to all.

Sometimes in return for his theories she gave out some fact of her own life. With almost maternal solicitude she urged him to let his nature open to the full: she became his confessor. He told her that for some time he had assisted at the meetings of an Irish Socialist Party where he had felt himself a unique figure amidst a score of sober workmen in a garret lit by an inefficient oil-lamp. When the party had divided into three sections, each under its own leader and in its own garret, he had discontinued his attendances. The workmen's discussions, he said, were too timorous; the interest they took in the question of wages was inordinate. He felt that they were hard-featured realists and that they resented an exactitude which was the product of a leisure not within their reach. No social revolution, he told her, would be likely to strike Dublin for some centuries.

She asked him why did he not write out his thoughts. For what, he asked her, with careful scorn. To compete with phrasemongers, incapable of thinking consecutively for sixty seconds? To submit himself to the criticisms of an obtuse middle class which entrusted its morality to policemen and its fine arts to impresarios?

He went often to her little cottage outside Dublin; often they spent their evenings alone. Little by little, as their thoughts entangled, they spoke of subjects less remote. Her companionship was like a warm soil about an exotic. Many times she allowed the dark to fall upon them, refraining from lighting the lamp. The dark discreet room, their isolation, the music that still vibrated in their ears united them. This union exalted him, wore away the rough edges of his character, emotionalised his mental life. Sometimes he caught himself listening to the sound of his own voice. He thought that in her eyes he would ascend to an angelical stature; and, as he attached the fervent nature of his companion more and more closely to him, he heard the strange impersonal voice which he recognised as his own, insisting on the soul's incurable loneliness. We cannot give ourselves, it said: we are our own. The end of these discourses was that one night during which she had shown every sign of unusual excitement, Mrs Sinico caught up his hand passionately and pressed it to her cheek.

Mr Duffy was very much surprised. Her interpretation of his words disillusioned him. He did not visit her for a week, then he wrote to her asking her to meet him. As he did not wish their last interview to be troubled by the influence of their ruined confessional they meet in a little cake shop near the Park gate. It was cold autumn weather but in spite of the cold they wandered up and down the roads of the Park for nearly three hours. They agreed to break off their intercourse: every bond, he said, is a bond to sorrow. When they came out of the Park they walked in silence towards the tram; but here she began to tremble so violently that, fearing another collapse on her part, he bade her good-bye quickly and left her. A few days later he received a parcel containing his books and music.

Four years passed. Mr Duffy returned to his even way of life. His room still bore witness of the orderliness of his mind. Some new pieces of music encumbered the music-stand in the lower room and on his shelves stood two volumes by Nietzsche: Thus *Spake Zarathustra* and *The Gay Science*. He wrote seldom in the sheaf of papers which lay in his desk. One of his sentences, written two months after his last interview with Mrs Sinico, read: Love between man and man is impossible because there must not be sexual intercourse and friendship between man and woman is impossible because there must be sexual intercourse. He kept away from concerts lest he should meet her. His father died; the junior partner of the bank retired. And still every morning he went into the city by tram and every evening walked home from the city after having dined moderately in George's Street and read the evening paper for dessert.

One evening as he was about to put a morsel of corned beef and cabbage into his mouth his hand stopped. His eyes fixed themselves on a paragraph in the evening paper which he had propped against the water-carafe. He replaced the morsel of food on his plate and read the paragraph attentively. Then he drank a glass of water, pushed his plate to one side, doubled the paper down before him between his elbows and read the paragraph over and over again. The cabbage began to deposit a cold white grease on his plate. The girl came over to him to ask was his dinner not properly cooked. He said it was very good and ate a few mouthfuls of it with difficulty. Then he paid his bill and went out.

He walked along quickly through the November twilight, his stout hazel stick striking the ground regularly, the fringe of the buff *Mail* peeping out of a side-pocket of his tight reefer[4] overcoat. On the lonely road which leads from the Park gate to Chapelizod he slackened his pace. His stick struck the ground less emphatically and his breath, issuing irregularly, almost with a sighing sound, condensed in the wintry air. When he reached his house he went up at once to his bedroom and, taking the paper from his pocket, read the paragraph again by the failing light of the window. He read it not

---

[4] Short, heavy coat.

aloud, but moving his lips as a priest does when he reads the prayers *In Secreto*. This was the paragraph:

DEATH OF A LADY AT SYDNEY PARADE
A PAINFUL CASE

To-day at the City of Dublin Hospital the Deputy Coroner (in the absence of Mr Leverett) held an inquest on the body of Mrs Emily Sinico, aged forty-three years, who was killed at Sydney Parade Station yesterday evening. The evidence showed that the deceased lady, while attempting to cross the line, was knocked down by the engine of the ten o'clock slow train from Kingstown, thereby sustaining injuries of the head and right side which led to her death.

James Lennon, driver of the engine, stated that he had been in the employment of the railway company for fifteen years. On hearing the guard's whistle he set the train in motion and a second or two afterwards brought it to rest in response to loud cries. The train was going slowly.

P. Dunne, railway porter, stated that as the train was about to start he observed a woman attempting to cross the lines. He ran towards her and shouted, but, before he could reach her, she was caught by the buffer of the engine and fell to the ground.

A juror: "You saw the lady fall?"

Witness: "Yes."

Police Sergeant Croly deposed that when he arrived he found the deceased lying on the platform apparently dead. He had the body taken to the waiting-room pending the arrival of the ambulance.

Constable 57E corroborated.

Dr. Halpin, assistant house surgeon of the City of Dublin Hospital, stated that the deceased had two lower ribs fractured and had sustained severe contusions of the right shoulder. The right side of the head had been injured in the fall. The injuries were not sufficient to have caused death in a normal person. Death, in his opinion, had been probably due to shock and sudden failure of the heart's action.

Mr H. B. Patterson Finlay, on behalf of the railway company, expressed his deep regret at the accident. The company had always taken every precaution to prevent people crossing the lines except by the bridges, both by placing notices in every station and by the use of patent spring gates at level crossings. The deceased had been in the habit of crossing the lines late at night from platform to platform and, in view of certain other circumstances of the case, he did not think the railway officials were to blame.

Captain Sinico, of Leoville, Sydney Parade, husband of the deceased, also gave evidence. He stated that the deceased was his wife. He was not in Dublin at the time of the accident as he had arrived only that morning from Rotterdam. They had been married for twenty-two years and had lived happily until about two years ago when his wife began to be rather intemperate in her habits.

Miss Mary Sinico said that of late her mother had been in the habit of going out at night to buy spirits. She, witness, had often tried to reason with her mother and had induced her to join a League. She was not at home until an hour after the accident. The jury returned a verdict in accordance with the medical evidence and exonerated Lennon from all blame.

The Deputy Coroner said it was a most painful case, and expressed great sympathy with Captain Sinico and his daughter. He urged on the railway company to take strong measures to prevent the possibility of similar accidents in the future. No blame attached to anyone.

Mr Duffy raised his eyes from the paper and gazed out of his window on the cheerless evening landscape. The river lay quiet beside the empty distillery and from time to time a light appeared in some house on the Lucan road. What an end! The whole narrative of her death revolted him and it revolted him to think that he had ever spoken to her of what he held sacred. The threadbare phrases, the inane expressions of sympathy, the cautious words of a reporter won over to conceal the details of a commonplace vulgar death attacked his stomach. Not merely had she degraded herself; she had degraded him. He saw the squalid tract of her vice, miserable and malodorous. His soul's companion! He thought of the hobbling wretches whom he had seen carrying cans and bottles to be filled by the barman. Just God, what an end! Evidently she had been unfit to live, without any strength of purpose, an easy prey to habits, one of the wrecks on which civilisation has been reared. But that she could have sunk so low! Was it possible he had deceived himself so utterly about her? He remembered her outburst of that night and interpreted it in a harsher sense than he had ever done. He had no difficulty now in approving of the course he had taken.

As the light failed and his memory began to wander he thought her hand touched his. The shock which had first attacked his stomach was now attacking his nerves. He put on his overcoat and hat quickly and went out. The cold air met him on the threshold; it crept into the sleeves of his coat. When he came to the public-house at Chapelizod Bridge he went in and ordered a hot punch.

The proprietor served him obsequiously but did not venture to talk. There were five or six workingmen in the shop discussing the value of a gentleman's estate in County Kildare. They drank at intervals from their huge pint tumblers and smoked, spitting often on the floor and sometimes dragging the sawdust over their spits with their heavy boots. Mr Duffy sat on his stool and gazed at them, without seeing or hearing them. After a while they went out and he called for another punch. He sat a long time over it. The shop was very quiet. The proprietor sprawled on the counter reading the *Herald* and yawning. Now and again a tram was heard swishing along the lonely road outside.

As he sat there, living over his life with her and evoking alternately the two images in which he now conceived her, he realised that she was dead, that she had ceased to exist, that she had become a memory. He began to feel ill at ease. He asked himself what else could he have done. He could not have carried on a comedy of deception with her; he could not have lived with her openly. He had done what seemed to him best. How was he to blame? Now that she was gone he understood how lonely her life must have been, sitting night after night alone in that room. His life would be lonely too until he, too, died, ceased to exist, became a memory—if anyone remembered him.

It was after nine o'clock when he left the shop. The night was cold and gloomy. He entered the Park by the first gate and walked along under the gaunt trees. He walked through the bleak alleys where they had walked four years before. She seemed to be near him in the darkness. At moments he seemed to feel her voice touch his ear, her hand touch his. He stood still to listen. Why had he withheld life from her? Why had he sentenced her to death? He felt his moral nature falling to pieces.

When he gained the crest of the Magazine Hill he halted and looked along the river towards Dublin, the lights of which burned redly and hospitably in the cold night. He looked down the slope and, at the base, in the shadow of the wall of the Park, he saw some human figures lying. Those venal and furtive loves filled him with despair. He gnawed the rectitude of his life; he felt that he had been outcast from life's feast. One human being had seemed to love him and he had denied her life and happiness: he had sentenced her to ignominy, a death of shame. He knew that the prostrate creatures down by the wall were watching him and wished him gone. No one wanted him; he was outcast from life's feast. He turned his eyes to the grey gleaming river, winding along towards Dublin. Beyond the river he saw a goods train winding out of Kingsbridge Station, like a worm with a fiery head winding through the darkness, obstinately and laboriously. It passed slowly out of sight; but still he heard in his ears the laborious drone of the engine reiterating the syllables of her name.

    He turned back the way he had come, the rhythm of the engine pounding in his ears. He began to doubt the reality of what memory told him. He halted under a tree and allowed the rhythm to die away. He could not feel her near him in the darkness nor her voice touch his ear. He waited for some minutes listening. He could hear nothing: the night was perfectly silent. He listened again: perfectly silent. He felt that he was alone.

CRAFT: A PAINFUL CASE

Metafiction

Like in "A Little Cloud," "Counterparts," and "Clay" Joyce employs the **close third person point of view** in "A Painful Case." However, unlike Maria in "Clay," Joyce remains at a greater narrative **distance** from this story's **protagonist**, Mr. Duffy. Because the narrator still has access to Mr. Duffy's thoughts, we would not call this an **objective** narrator. But the narrator is far more objective in "A Painful Case" than in "Clay." The reader feels a greater distance between the narrator and the character in this story.

Joyce even goes so far as to subtly comment on the narration while he describes Mr. Duffy's character: "He lived at a little distance from his body, regarding his own acts with doubtful side-glances." This witty sentence has two meanings. The first is to describe Mr. Duffy's discomfort when it comes to the way he sees and considers himself. The second subtextual meaning comments on the narrator—the narrator being third person is also "at a little distance" from Mr. Duffy, and Joyce suggests that this narrator regards the character with a bit of doubt.

If readers find that subtextual meaning dubious, Joyce takes it a step further in the remainder of the paragraph. "He had an odd autobiographical habit which led him to compose in his mind from time to time a short sentence about himself containing a subject in third person and a predicate in the past tense." This playful, complex sentence reflects itself. On one level, Joyce is describing Mr. Duffy, and on another level he is commenting on the fiction. It's almost as if Joyce is suggesting that the close third person narrator of this story is actually Mr. Duffy himself.

This **trope** is called **metafiction**—a self-conscious device that surfaces the fictional artifice and comments on the act of creating fiction. For many, metafictional tropes take readers out of the fiction and remind them that they are reading a story. Some find it irritating and distracting. Many critics have suggested that Joyce's self-consciousness at the beginning of this story shows his inability to connect with Mr. Duffy's character—a connection that he only manages to make later in the story. Other readers, however, find it deeply meaningful. Here, for example, Joyce is pointing out that long and empty space that exists between us, the narrator, and the character. Like Mr. Duffy, we as readers are attempting to get to know this man. If he is a solitary man with "neither companions nor friends," who barely understands himself, how are we to understand him?

Verisimilitude

Consider this presentation of narrative information: *A lonely man meets a married woman and they get along great, but then she brings his hand to her cheek and he gets uncomfortable, so they agree to never see one another again. But before he realizes that he loves this woman, she gets hit by a train and dies.*

It sounds absurd, **hyperbolized**, melodramatic, and unbelievable. Why would he get uncomfortable when this woman brings his hand to her cheek? And, come on, she gets hit by a train! And yet, this is the story of "A Painful Case."

One of the writer's core objectives when constructing a story is to make it believable. **Verisimilitude** is the quality of appearing plausible and believable. It is narrative persuasiveness. Some suggest that verisimilitude indicates "truth" or "reality," but to a fiction writer, the project of verisimilitude is more complex. Readers often know that the story is untrue and unreal, and yet they find it plausible and believable and therefore **suspend their disbelief**.

Most people would never categorize a fictional story as a persuasive piece of writing, but it is. Verisimilitude is all about persuading readers to believe.

Let's focus on three ways that Joyce uses verisimilitude to make the above summary of this story come to life and appear plausible: details, **jargon**, and source texts.

Why would a man who is clearly attracted to a woman break up the relationship when she brings his hand to her cheek? Joyce makes this odd act plausible by constructing a detailed, intellectual relationship between Mr. Duffy and Mrs. Sinico. While they may be physically attracted to one another, Joyce instead sexualizes their intellectual relationship with details. As they argue and discuss social issues, their "thoughts entangled." "Her companionship was like a warm soil about an exotic." As they sit alone together in a dark room talking and listening to music, "this union exalted him, wore away the rough edges of his character, emotionalised his mental life." Notice how his mental life, rather than his sexual or spiritual life becomes emotionalized. Joyce even refers to their relationship, one that has been strictly a friendship, as "their intercourse." Therefore, when Mrs. Sinico shows "unusual excitement" and catches "up his hand passionately" pressing "it to her cheek," Mr. Duffy becomes disillusioned and disturbed by what he thinks is her misinterpretation of his intent.

This reaction from Mr. Duffy would surely seem unbelievable if Joyce had focused the sensual descriptions on their physicality. If Mr. Duffy had desired Mrs. Sinico sexually, it would seem absurd that he would react in such a way to her touch. But the fact that Joyce has, using detailed descriptions, sexualized their intellectual relationship, helps the reader understand the shift and disillusionment that Mr. Duffy feels when Mrs. Sinico attempts to translate that intellectual stimulation into physical stimulation. Therefore, the reader "believes" Mr. Duffy's reaction, and Joyce has maintained verisimilitude in an event that could easily seem implausible (many readers may still find it implausible, and may be rolling their eyes right now).

The verisimilitude of Mrs. Sinico's death begins with Joyce teasing us by withholding the information. When Mr. Duffy eats corned beef and cabbage in a restaurant, "his eyes fixed themselves on a paragraph in the evening paper" that he reads "over and over again."

After he leaves the restaurant, the reader remains in the dark about what he has read. "When he reached his house he went up at once to his bedroom and, taking the paper from his pocket, read the paragraph again by the failing light of the window." By this time, the reader is anxious to know what has troubled him so much.

However, instead of summarizing what Mr. Duffy has read in the paper, Joyce inserts the article into the story, which explains that the "Deputy Coroner held an inquest on the body of Mrs Emily Sinico, aged forty-three years, who was killed at Sydney Parade Station yesterday evening." Because the article is believably written, there's no reason for the reader to doubt the believability of the death or the coincidence of Mr. Duffy stumbling upon the article in the evening paper. Joyce's detailed command of the exact kind of **jargon** that might appear in such an article—"Police Sergeant Corly deposed," "contusions of the right shoulder," "sudden failure of the heart's action"—all allow the reader to accept this tragic and sudden death as plausible.

If, however, a reader is not convinced of Mrs. Sinico's death and finds Mr. Duffy's discovery of it and the article unconvincing, he or she will be immediately removed from the story, unable to connect with Mr. Duffy's following reaction to the news, which should suggest the importance of verisimilitude. It's one of the few things in fiction that disappears completely on the page when a writer does it well. Only when a writer fails to make a story believable do we notice and question verisimilitude.

Epiphany and Peripeteia

We have covered **epiphany**—or a character's realization—briefly in both "Two Gallants" and "A Little Cloud." Mr. Duffy has a significant epiphany at the end of "A Painful Case," where he realizes that he squandered love and happiness with Mrs. Sinico and has been "outcast from life's feast." He feels this realization so strongly that the narrator repeats it several sentences later in an instance of **point of view inflection**: "No one wanted him; he was outcast from life's feast."

And yet, Mr. Duffy's epiphany is bigger than just a realization; it concludes a large shift that occurs in both his life and the environment around him—a shift that includes the "painful case" of Mrs. Sinoco's death. A **peripeteia** is often referred to as a reversal or an alteration. The classic example of peripeteia occurs in *Oedipus Rex*, when the prophecy that Oedipus will sleep with his mother and kill his father proves true and he finally realizes that he has failed to prevent it and cannot escape his fate. Therefore, peripeteia not only involves a character's realization or epiphany, but a shift in the world around that character—a shift that usually gives rise to the epiphany.

The narrative structure of "A Painful Case" follows typically. The **setup** involves a solitary man whose life is "rolled out evenly" and has been an "adventurless tale." That immediately communicates to the reader that **action** will rise into **conflict**—that this character will be thrown into an adventure that will test his ability to adapt, grow and perhaps change. Here, of course, after Mr. Duffy experiences the conflicts that accompany his relationship with Mrs. Sinico, he fails to change in the **climax** of this story, when Mrs. Sinico touches his face, and the **resolution** or **dénouement** is a long and "painful case" that contains the peripeteia and the epiphany that Mr. Duffy failed to capture the adventure that his life always lacked. The knowledge that he failed to change becomes the resolution.

Mrs. Sinico's death creates a change or reversal in the environment that makes it impossible for Mr. Duffy to act on his epiphany. This creates a sense of sympathy or **pathos** for Mr. Duffy, because, like Oedipus, his failure cannot be "fixed."

Questions

1. If you've never examined a story for **verisimilitude,** start now. In fact, keep verisimilitude in mind as you read the next story, "Ivy Day in the Committee Room," and we'll return to a question about it after our analysis of that story. For now, consider the idea more broadly. Have you found the stories in *Dubliners* believable? If so, how has Joyce made them believable to you? Details? Setting? Characters? Prose style? If not, where has Joyce's verisimilitude failed?

2. Joyce is known for his almost obsessive interest in character **epiphany.** Some readers may find epiphanies contrived, especially if they don't seem motivated by previous events in the **plot.** How does Joyce lead up to Mr. Duffy's epiphany in this narrative? What motivates this character to have such an epiphany? How does Joyce's plotting of this story create a causal relationship between events that attempt to add **verisimilitude** to Mr. Duffy's epiphany?

Ivy Day in the Committee Room

Old Jack raked the cinders together with a piece of cardboard and spread them judiciously over the whitening dome of coals. When the dome was thinly covered his face lapsed into darkness but, as he set himself to fan the fire again, his crouching shadow ascended the opposite wall and his face slowly reemerged into light. It was an old man's face, very bony and hairy. The moist blue eyes blinked at the fire and the moist mouth fell open at times, munching once or twice mechanically when it closed. When the cinders had caught he laid the piece of cardboard against the wall, sighed and said:

"That's better now, Mr O'Connor."

Mr O'Connor, a grey-haired young man, whose face was disfigured by many blotches and pimples, had just brought the tobacco for a cigarette into a shapely cylinder but when spoken to he undid his handiwork meditatively. Then he began to roll the tobacco again meditatively and after a moment's thought decided to lick the paper.

"Did Mr Tierney say when he'd be back?" he asked in a sky falsetto.

"He didn't say."

Mr O'Connor put his cigarette into his mouth and began to search his pockets. He took out a pack of thin pasteboard cards.

"I'll get you a match," said the old man.

"Never mind, this'll do," said Mr O'Connor.

He selected one of the cards and read what was printed on it:

Municipal Elections

Royal Exchange Ward

Mr Richard J. Tierney, P.L.G.,[1] respectfully solicits the favour of your vote and influence at the coming election in the Royal Exchange Ward.

Mr O'Connor had been engaged by Tierney's agent to canvass one part of the ward but, as the weather was inclement and his boots let in the wet, he spent a great part of the day sitting by the fire in the Committee Room in Wicklow Street with Jack, the old caretaker. They had been sitting thus since the short day had grown dark. It was the sixth of October, dismal and cold out of doors.

Mr O'Connor tore a strip off the card and, lighting it, lit his cigarette. As he did so the flame lit up a leaf of dark glossy ivy in the lapel of his coat. The old man watched him attentively and then, taking up the piece of cardboard again, began to fan the fire slowly while his companion smoked.

"Ah, yes," he said, continuing, "it's hard to know what way to bring up children. Now who'd think he'd turn out like that! I sent him to the Christian Brothers and I done what I could for him, and there he goes boosing about. I tried to make him someway decent."

He replaced the cardboard wearily.

"Only I'm an old man now I'd change his tune for him. I'd take the stick to his back and beat him while I could stand over him—as I done many a time before. The mother, you know, she cocks him up[2] with this and that…"

---

[1] Poor Law Guardian.
[2] Flatters him.

"That's what ruins children," said Mr O'Connor.

"To be sure it is," said the old man. "And little thanks you get for it, only impudence. He takes th'upper hand of me whenever he sees I've a sup taken. What's the world coming to when sons speaks that way to their fathers?"

"What age is he?" said Mr O'Connor.

"Nineteen," said the old man.

"Why don't you put him to something?"

"Sure, amn't I never done at the drunken bowsy[3] ever since he left school? 'I won't keep you,' I says. 'You must get a job for yourself.' But, sure, it's worse whenever he gets a job; he drinks it all."

Mr O'Connor shook his head in sympathy, and the old man fell silent, gazing into the fire. Someone opened the door of the room and called out:

"Hello! Is this a Freemason's meeting?"

"Who's that?" said the old man.

"What are you doing in the dark?" asked a voice.

"Is that you, Hynes?" asked Mr O'Connor.

"Yes. What are you doing in the dark?" said Mr Hynes. advancing into the light of the fire.

He was a tall, slender young man with a light brown moustache. Imminent little drops of rain hung at the brim of his hat and the collar of his jacket-coat was turned up.

"Well, Mat," he said to Mr O'Connor, "how goes it?"

Mr O'Connor shook his head. The old man left the hearth and after stumbling about the room returned with two candlesticks which he thrust one after the other into the fire and carried to the table. A denuded room came into view and the fire lost all its cheerful colour. The walls of the room were bare except for a copy of an election address. In the middle of the room was a small table on which papers were heaped.

Mr Hynes leaned against the mantelpiece and asked:

"Has he paid you yet?"

"Not yet," said Mr O'Connor. "I hope to God he'll not leave us in the lurch tonight."

Mr Hynes laughed.

"O, he'll pay you. Never fear," he said.

---

[3] Idiot.

"I hope he'll look smart about it if he means business," said Mr O'Connor.

"What do you think, Jack?" said Mr Hynes satirically to the old man.

The old man returned to his seat by the fire, saying:

"It isn't but he has it, anyway. Not like the other tinker.[4]"

"What other tinker?" said Mr Hynes.

"Colgan," said the old man scornfully.

"It is because Colgan's a working-man you say that? What's the difference between a good honest bricklayer and a publican—eh? Hasn't the working-man as good a right to be in the Corporation[5] as anyone else—ay, and a better right than those shoneens[6] that are always hat in hand before any fellow with a handle[7] to his name? Isn't that so, Mat?" said Mr Hynes, addressing Mr O'Connor.

"I think you're right," said Mr O'Connor.

"One man is a plain honest man with no hunker-sliding[8] about him. He goes in to represent the labour classes. This fellow you're working for only wants to get some job or other."

"Of course, the working-classes should be represented," said the old man.

"The working-man," said Mr Hynes, "gets all kicks and no ha'pence[9]. But it's labour produces everything. The working-man is not looking for fat jobs for his sons and nephews and cousins. The working-man is not going to drag the honour of Dublin in the mud to please a German monarch."

"How's that?" said the old man.

"Don't you know they want to present an address of welcome to Edward Rex if he comes here next year? What do we want kowtowing to a foreign king?"

"Our man won't vote for the address," said Mr O'Connor. "He goes in on the Nationalist ticket."

"Won't he?" said Mr Hynes. "Wait till you see whether he will or not. I know him. Is it Tricky Dicky Tierney?"

---

[4] Beggar.
[5] Government.
[6] Phony politicians.
[7] Aristocratic sound.
[8] Dishonesty.
[9] Halfpence.

"By God! Perhaps you're right, Joe," said Mr O'Connor. "Anyway, I wish he'd turn up with the spondulics[10]."

The three men fell silent. The old man began to rake more cinders together. Mr Hynes took off his hat, shook it and then turned down the collar of his coat, displaying, as he did so, an ivy leaf in the lapel.

"If this man was alive," he said, pointing to the leaf, "we'd have no talk of an address of welcome."

"That's true," said Mr O'Connor.

"Musha[11], God be with them times!" said the old man. "There was some life in it then."

The room was silent again. Then a bustling little man with a snuffling nose and very cold ears pushed in the door. He walked over quickly to the fire, rubbing his hands as if he intended to produce a spark from them.

"No money, boys," he said.

"Sit down here, Mr Henchy," said the old man, offering him his chair.

"O, don't stir, Jack, don't stir," said Mr Henchy.

He nodded curtly to Mr Hynes and sat down on the chair which the old man vacated.

"Did you serve Aungier Street?" he asked Mr O'Connor.

"Yes," said Mr O'Connor, beginning to search his pockets for memoranda.

"Did you call on Grimes?"

"I did."

"Well? How does he stand?"

"He wouldn't promise. He said: 'I won't tell anyone what way I'm going to vote.' But I think he'll be all right."

"Why so?"

"He asked me who the nominators were; and I told him. I mentioned Father Burke's name. I think it'll be all right."

Mr Henchy began to snuffle and to rub his hands over the fire at a terrific speed. Then he said:

"For the love of God, Jack, bring us a bit of coal. There must be some left."

The old man went out of the room.

---

[10] Money.
[11] Gosh!

"It's no go," said Mr Henchy, shaking his head. "I asked the little shoeboy, but he said: 'Oh, now, Mr Henchy, when I see work going on properly I won't forget you, you may be sure.' Mean little tinker! 'Usha, how could he be anything else?"

"What did I tell you, Mat?" said Mr Hynes. "Tricky Dicky Tierney."

"O, he's as tricky as they make 'em," said Mr Henchy. "He hasn't got those little pigs' eyes for nothing. Blast his soul! Couldn't he pay up like a man instead of: 'O, now, Mr Henchy, I must speak to Mr Fanning... I've spent a lot of money'? Mean little schoolboy of hell! I suppose he forgets the time his little old father kept the hand-me-down shop in Mary's Lane."

"But is that a fact?" asked Mr O'Connor.

"God, yes," said Mr Henchy. "Did you never hear that? And the men used to go in on Sunday morning before the houses[12] were open to buy a waistcoat or a trousers—moya! But Tricky Dicky's little old father always had a tricky little black bottle up in a corner. Do you mind now? That's that. That's where he first saw the light."

The old man returned with a few lumps of coal which he placed here and there on the fire.

"That's a nice how-do-you-do," said Mr O'Connor. "How does he expect us to work for him if he won't stump up?"

"I can't help it," said Mr Henchy. "I expect to find the bailiffs in the hall when I go home."

Mr Hynes laughed and, shoving himself away from the mantelpiece with the aid of his shoulders, made ready to leave.

"It'll be all right when King Eddie comes," he said. "Well boys, I'm off for the present. See you later. 'Bye, 'bye."

He went out of the room slowly. Neither Mr Henchy nor the old man said anything, but, just as the door was closing, Mr O'Connor, who had been staring moodily into the fire, called out suddenly:

" 'Bye, Joe."

Mr Henchy waited a few moments and then nodded in the direction of the door.

"Tell me," he said across the fire, "what brings our friend in here? What does he want?"

" 'Usha, poor Joe!" said Mr O'Connor, throwing the end of his cigarette into the fire, "he's hard up, like the rest of us."

---

[12] Public-houses, pubs.

Mr Henchy snuffled vigorously and spat so copiously that he nearly put out the fire, which uttered a hissing protest.

"To tell you my private and candid opinion," he said, "I think he's a man from the other camp. He's a spy of Colgan's, if you ask me. Just go round and try and find out how they're getting on. They won't suspect you. Do you twig?[13]"

"Ah, poor Joe is a decent skin," said Mr O'Connor.

"His father was a decent, respectable man," Mr Henchy admitted. "Poor old Larry Hynes! Many a good turn he did in his day! But I'm greatly afraid our friend is not nineteen carat. Damn it, I can understand a fellow being hard up, but what I can't understand is a fellow sponging. Couldn't he have some spark of manhood about him?"

"He doesn't get a warm welcome from me when he comes," said the old man. "Let him work for his own side and not come spying around here."

"I don't know," said Mr O'Connor dubiously, as he took out cigarette-papers and tobacco. "I think Joe Hynes is a straight man. He's a clever chap, too, with the pen. Do you remember that thing he wrote...?"

"Some of these hillsiders[14] and fenians[15] are a bit too clever if ask me," said Mr Henchy. "Do you know what my private and candid opinion is about some of those little jokers? I believe half of them are in the pay of the Castle.[16]"

"There's no knowing," said the old man.

"O, but I know it for a fact," said Mr Henchy. "They're Castle hacks... I don't say Hynes... No, damn it, I think he's a stroke above that... But there's a certain little nobleman with a cock-eye—you know the patriot I'm alluding to?"

Mr O'Connor nodded.

"There's a lineal descendant of Major Sirr[17] for you if you like! O, the heart's blood of a patriot! That's a fellow now that'd sell his country for fourpence—ay—and go down on his bended knees and thank the Almighty Christ he had a country to sell."

---

[13] Understand?
[14] Country folk.
[15] The Fenian Brotherhood or Irish Republican Brotherhood.
[16] In reference to the British government, which had its headquarters at Dublin Castle.
[17] In reference to Henry Charles Sirr.

There was a knock at the door.

"Come in!" said Mr Henchy.

A person resembling a poor clergyman or a poor actor appeared in the doorway. His black clothes were tightly buttoned on his short body and it was impossible to say whether he wore a clergyman's collar or a layman's, because the collar of his shabby frock-coat, the uncovered buttons of which reflected the candlelight, was turned up about his neck. He wore a round hat of hard black felt. His face, shining with raindrops, had the appearance of damp yellow cheese save where two rosy spots indicated the cheekbones. He opened his very long mouth suddenly to express disappointment and at the same time opened wide his very bright blue eyes to express pleasure and surprise.

"O Father Keon!" said Mr Henchy, jumping up from his chair. "Is that you? Come in!"

"O, no, no, no!" said Father Keon quickly, pursing his lips as if he were addressing a child.

"Won't you come in and sit down?"

"No, no, no!" said Father Keon, speaking in a discreet, indulgent, velvety voice. "Don't let me disturb you now! I'm just looking for Mr Fanning..."

"He's round at the *Black Eagle*," said Mr Henchy. "But won't you come in and sit down a minute?"

"No, no, thank you. It was just a little business matter," said Father Keon. "Thank you, indeed."

He retreated from the doorway and Mr Henchy, seizing one of the candlesticks, went to the door to light him downstairs.

"O, don't trouble, I beg!"

"No, but the stairs is so dark."

"No, no, I can see... Thank you, indeed."

"Are you right now?"

"All right, thanks... Thanks."

Mr Henchy returned with the candlestick and put it on the table. He sat down again at the fire. There was silence for a few moments.

"Tell me, John," said Mr O'Connor, lighting his cigarette with another pasteboard card.

"Hm?"

"What he is exactly?"

"Ask me an easier one," said Mr Henchy.

"Fanning and himself seem to me very thick. They're often in Kavanagh's together. Is he a priest at all?"

"Mmm yes, I believe so... I think he's what you call a black sheep. We haven't many of them, thank God! But we have a few... He's an unfortunate man of some kind..."

"And how does he knock it out?[18]" asked Mr O'Connor.

"That's another mystery."

"Is he attached to any chapel or church or institution or——"

"No," said Mr Henchy, "I think he's travelling on his own account... God forgive me," he added, "I thought he was the dozen of stout."

"Is there any chance of a drink itself?" asked Mr O'Connor.

"I'm dry too," said the old man.

"I asked that little shoeboy three times," said Mr Henchy, "would he send up a dozen of stout. I asked him again now, but he was leaning on the counter in his shirt-sleeves having a deep goster[19] with Alderman Cowley."

"Why didn't you remind him?" said Mr O'Connor.

"Well, I couldn't go over while he was talking to Alderman Cowley. I just waited till I caught his eye, and said: 'About that little matter I was speaking to you about...' 'That'll be all right, Mr H.,' he said. Yerra,[20] sure the little hop-o'-my-thumb[21] has forgotten all about it."

"There's some deal on in that quarter," said Mr O'Connor thoughtfully. "I saw the three of them hard at it yesterday at Suffolk Street corner."

"I think I know the little game they're at," said Mr Henchy. "You must owe the City Fathers money nowadays if you want to be made Lord Mayor. Then they'll make you Lord Mayor. By God! I'm thinking seriously of becoming a City Father myself. What do you think? Would I do for the job?"

Mr O'Connor laughed.

"So far as owing money goes..."

"Driving out of the Mansion House," said Mr Henchy, "in all my vermin, with Jack here standing up behind me in a powdered wig—eh?"

---

[18] Make money.
[19] Discussion.
[20] Really.
[21] Small person.

"And make me your private secretary, John."

"Yes. And I'll make Father Keon my private chaplain. We'll have a family party."

"Faith, Mr Henchy," said the old man, "you'd keep up better style than some of them. I was talking one day to old Keegan, the porter. 'And how do you like your new master, Pat?' says I to him. 'You haven't much entertaining now,' says I. 'Entertaining!' says he. 'He'd live on the smell of an oil-rag.' And do you know what he told me? Now, I declare to God I didn't believe him."

"What?" said Mr Henchy and Mr O'Connor.

"He told me: 'What do you think of a Lord Mayor of Dublin sending out for a pound of chops for his dinner? How's that for high living?' says he. 'Wisha! wisha,'[22] says I. 'A pound of chops,' says he, 'coming into the Mansion House.' 'Wisha!' says I. 'What kind of people is going at all now?'"

At this point there was a knock at the door, and a boy put in his head.

"What is it?" said the old man.

"From the *Black Eagle*," said the boy, walking in sideways and depositing a basket on the floor with a noise of shaken bottles.

The old man helped the boy to transfer the bottles from the basket to the table and counted the full tally. After the transfer the boy put his basket on his arm and asked:

"Any bottles?"

"What bottles?" said the old man.

"Won't you let us drink them first?" said Mr Henchy.

"I was told to ask for the bottles."

"Come back to-morrow," said the old man.

"Here, boy!" said Mr Henchy, "will you run over to O'Farrell's and ask him to lend us a corkscrew—for Mr Henchy, say. Tell him we won't keep it a minute. Leave the basket there."

The boy went out and Mr Henchy began to rub his hands cheerfully, saying:

"Ah, well, he's not so bad after all. He's as good as his word, anyhow."

"There's no tumblers," said the old man.

"O, don't let that trouble you, Jack," said Mr Henchy. "Many's the good man before now drank out of the bottle."

---

[22] Wow!

"Anyway, it's better than nothing," said Mr O'Connor.

"He's not a bad sort," said Mr Henchy, "only Fanning has such a loan of[23] him. He means well, you know, in his own tinpot[24] way."

The boy came back with the corkscrew. The old man opened three bottles and was handing back the corkscrew when Mr Henchy said to the boy:

"Would you like a drink, boy?"

"If you please, sir," said the boy.

The old man opened another bottle grudgingly, and handed it to the boy.

"What age are you?" he asked.

"Seventeen," said the boy.

As the old man said nothing further, the boy took the bottle, said: "Here's my best respects, sir, to Mr Henchy," drank the contents, put the bottle back on the table and wiped his mouth with his sleeve. Then he took up the corkscrew and went out of the door sideways, muttering some form of salutation.

"That's the way it begins," said the old man.

"The thin edge of the wedge," said Mr Henchy.

The old man distributed the three bottles which he had opened and the men drank from them simultaneously. After having drank each placed his bottle on the mantelpiece within hand's reach and drew in a long breath of satisfaction.

"Well, I did a good day's work to-day," said Mr Henchy, after a pause.

"That so, John?"

"Yes. I got him one or two sure things in Dawson Street, Crofton and myself. Between ourselves, you know, Crofton (he's a decent chap, of course), but he's not worth a damn as a canvasser. He hasn't a word to throw to a dog. He stands and looks at the people while I do the talking."

Here two men entered the room. One of them was a very fat man whose blue serge clothes seemed to be in danger of falling from his sloping figure. He had a big face which resembled a young ox's face in expression, staring blue eyes and a grizzled moustache. The other man, who was much younger and frailer, had a thin, clean-shaven face. He wore a very high double collar and a wide-brimmed bowler hat.

---

[23] Impact on.
[24] Shoddy.

"Hello, Crofton!" said Mr Henchy to the fat man. "Talk of the devil…"

"Where did the boose come from?" asked the young man. "Did the cow calve?"

"O, of course, Lyons spots the drink first thing!" said Mr O'Connor, laughing.

"Is that the way you chaps canvass," said Mr Lyons, "and Crofton and I out in the cold and rain looking for votes?"

"Why, blast your soul," said Mr Henchy, "I'd get more votes in five minutes than you two'd get in a week."

"Open two bottles of stout, Jack," said Mr O'Connor.

"How can I?" said the old man, "when there's no corkscrew?"

"Wait now, wait now!" said Mr Henchy, getting up quickly. "Did you ever see this little trick?"

He took two bottles from the table and, carrying them to the fire, put them on the hob.[25] Then he sat down again by the fire and took another drink from his bottle. Mr Lyons sat on the edge of the table, pushed his hat towards the nape of his neck and began to swing his legs.

"Which is my bottle?" he asked.

"This, lad," said Mr Henchy.

Mr Crofton sat down on a box and looked fixedly at the other bottle on the hob. He was silent for two reasons. The first reason, sufficient in itself, was that he had nothing to say; the second reason was that he considered his companions beneath him. He had been a canvasser for Wilkins, the Conservative, but when the Conservatives had withdrawn their man and, choosing the lesser of two evils, given their support to the Nationalist candidate, he had been engaged to work for Mr Tierney.

In a few minutes an apologetic "Pok!" was heard as the cork flew out of Mr Lyons' bottle. Mr Lyons jumped off the table, went to the fire, took his bottle and carried it back to the table.

"I was just telling them, Crofton," said Mr Henchy, "that we got a good few votes to-day."

"Who did you get?" asked Mr Lyons.

"Well, I got Parkes for one, and I got Atkinson for two, and got Ward of Dawson Street. Fine old chap he is, too—regular old toff,[26] old Conservative! 'But isn't your candidate a Nationalist?' said

---

[25] Fireplace shelf.
[26] Gentleman.

he. 'He's a respectable man,' said I. 'He's in favour of whatever will benefit this country. He's a big ratepayer,'[27] I said. 'He has extensive house property in the city and three places of business and isn't it to his own advantage to keep down the rates? He's a prominent and respected citizen,' said I, 'and a Poor Law Guardian, and he doesn't belong to any party, good, bad, or indifferent.' That's the way to talk to 'em."

"And what about the address to the King?" said Mr Lyons, after drinking and smacking his lips.

"Listen to me," said Mr Henchy. "What we want in this country, as I said to old Ward, is capital. The King's coming here will mean an influx of money into this country. The citizens of Dublin will benefit by it. Look at all the factories down by the quays there, idle! Look at all the money there is in the country if we only worked the old industries, the mills, the shipbuilding yards and factories. It's capital we want."

"But look here, John," said Mr O'Connor. "Why should we welcome the King of England? Didn't Parnell himself..."

"Parnell," said Mr Henchy, "is dead. Now, here's the way I look at it. Here's this chap come to the throne after his old mother keeping him out of it till the man was grey. He's a man of the world, and he means well by us. He's a jolly fine decent fellow, if you ask me, and no damn nonsense about him. He just says to himself: 'The old one never went to see these wild Irish. By Christ, I'll go myself and see what they're like.' And are we going to insult the man when he comes over here on a friendly visit? Eh? Isn't that right, Crofton?"

Mr Crofton nodded his head.

"But after all now," said Mr Lyons argumentatively, "King Edward's life, you know, is not the very..."

"Let bygones be bygones," said Mr Henchy." I admire the man personally. He's just an ordinary knockabout like you and me. He's fond of his glass of grog and he's a bit of a rake, perhaps, and he's a good sportsman. Damn it, can't we Irish play fair?"

"That's all very fine," said Mr Lyons. " But look at the case of Parnell now."

"In the name of God," said Mr Henchy, "where's the analogy between the two cases?"

---

[27] Taxpayer.

"What I mean," said Mr Lyons, "is we have our ideals. Why, now, would we welcome a man like that? Do you think now after what he did Parnell was a fit man to lead us? And why, then, would we do it for Edward the Seventh?"

"This is Parnell's anniversary," said Mr O'Connor, "and don't let us stir up any bad blood. We all respect him now that he's dead and gone—even the Conservatives," he added, turning to Mr Crofton.

Pok! The tardy cork flew out of Mr Crofton's bottle. Mr Crofton got up from his box and went to the fire. As he returned with his capture he said in a deep voice:

"Our side of the house respects him, because he was a gentleman."

"Right you are, Crofton!" said Mr Henchy fiercely. "He was the only man that could keep that bag of cats in order. 'Down, ye dogs! Lie down, ye curs!'[28] That's the way he treated them. Come in, Joe! Come in!" he called out, catching sight of Mr Hynes in the doorway.

Mr Hynes came in slowly.

"Open another bottle of stout, Jack," said Mr Henchy. "O, I forgot there's no corkscrew! Here, show me one here and I'll put it at the fire."

The old man handed him another bottle and he placed it on the hob.

"Sit down, Joe," said Mr O'Connor, "we're just talking about the Chief."[29]

"Ay, ay!" said Mr Henchy.

Mr Hynes sat on the side of the table near Mr Lyons but said nothing.

"There's one of them, anyhow," said Mr Henchy, "that didn't renege him. By God, I'll say for you, Joe! No, by God, you stuck to him like a man!"

"O, Joe," said Mr O'Connor suddenly. "Give us that thing you wrote— do you remember? Have you got it on you?"

"O, ay!" said Mr Henchy. "Give us that. Did you ever hear that. Crofton? Listen to this now: splendid thing."

"Go on," said Mr O'Connor. "Fire away, Joe."

---

[28] Cowards.
[29] Parnell.

Mr Hynes did not seem to remember at once the piece to which they were alluding, but, after reflecting a while, he said:

"O, that thing is it... Sure, that's old now."

"Out with it, man!" said Mr O'Connor.

" 'Sh, 'sh," said Mr Henchy. "Now, Joe!"

Mr Hynes hesitated a little longer. Then amid the silence he took off his hat, laid it on the table and stood up. He seemed to be rehearsing the piece in his mind. After a rather long pause he announced:

THE DEATH OF PARNELL
6th October, 1891

He cleared his throat once or twice and then began to recite:

He is dead. Our Uncrowned King is dead.
O, Erin, mourn with grief and woe
For he lies dead whom the fell gang
Of modern hypocrites laid low.

He lies slain by the coward hounds
He raised to glory from the mire;
And Erin's hopes and Erin's dreams
Perish upon her monarch's pyre.

In palace, cabin or in cot
The Irish heart where'er it be
Is bowed with woe—for he is gone
Who would have wrought her destiny.

He would have had his Erin famed,
The green flag gloriously unfurled,
Her statesmen, bards and warriors raised
Before the nations of the World.

He dreamed (alas, 'twas but a dream!)
Of Liberty: but as he strove
To clutch that idol, treachery
Sundered him from the thing he loved.

> *Shame on the coward, caitiff hands*
> *That smote their Lord or with a kiss*
> *Betrayed him to the rabble-rout*
> *Of fawning priests—no friends of his.*
>
> *May everlasting shame consume*
> *The memory of those who tried*
> *To befoul and smear the exalted name*
> *Of one who spurned them in his pride.*
>
> *He fell as fall the mighty ones,*
> *Nobly undaunted to the last,*
> *And death has now united him*
> *With Erin's heroes of the past.*
>
> *No sound of strife disturb his sleep!*
> *Calmly he rests: no human pain*
> *Or high ambition spurs him now*
> *The peaks of glory to attain.*
>
> *They had their way: they laid him low.*
> *But Erin, list, his spirit may*
> *Rise, like the Phoenix from the flames,*
> *When breaks the dawning of the day,*
>
> *The day that brings us Freedom's reign.*
> *And on that day may Erin well*
> *Pledge in the cup she lifts to Joy*
> *One grief—the memory of Parnell.*

Mr Hynes sat down again on the table. When he had finished his recitation there was a silence and then a burst of clapping: even Mr Lyons clapped. The applause continued for a little time. When it had ceased all the auditors drank from their bottles in silence.

Pok! The cork flew out of Mr Hynes' bottle, but Mr Hynes remained sitting flushed and bare-headed on the table. He did not seem to have heard the invitation.

"Good man, Joe!" said Mr O'Connor, taking out his cigarette papers and pouch the better to hide his emotion.

"What do you think of that, Crofton?" cried Mr Henchy. "Isn't that fine? What?"

Crofton said that it was a very fine piece of writing.

CRAFT: IVY DAY IN THE COMMITTEE ROOM

The Objective Correlative

When analyzing craft, it seems that we have many different words and phrases that mean the exact same thing. Yet, more often than not, there are subtle differences between terms. **Peripeteia**, though it includes **epiphany** (which may seem like just a synonym of "realization), also requires a change or reversal in the environment that surrounds the character. Likewise, although the objective correlative is certainly a symbol, not every symbol is an objective correlative.

We have defined a **symbol** as something that represents something else—most often an object that represents something incorporeal. The **objective correlative** is a type of symbol—one in which an object specifically represents and incites an emotion. T.S. Eliot went so far as to say that the "only way of expressing emotion in the form of art is by finding an 'objective correlative.'"[1]

In "Araby" the narrator goes to the bazaar to look for an object to buy for Mangan's sister. What he is essentially looking for is an objective correlative—an object that correlates to his desire for her. He wants to buy her something that represents his adoration. His inability to find that object represents his inability to turn a childhood crush into a more mature relationship. Joyce deprives not only this character, but also the reader of the objective correlative in "Araby," creating **increasing tension and conflict** throughout the story as the narrator struggles to find it and attain it. Because the objective correlative in "Araby" exists only as an idea, so does the narrator's

---

[1] T.S. Eliot, *Selected Essay 1917 – 1932* (New York: Harcourt, Brace and Company, Inc., 1932), 124.

love of Mangan's sister. It's a young, idealized, and abstract love that works as a fantasy, but not a reality.

Throughout *Dubliners*, Joyce has used alcohol to suggest the problems, depravations, violence, and failures of many of his characters. Little Chandler's drunkenness leads him to scream at his infant son in "A Little Cloud," which sends the child into a fit of crying. Similarly, Farrington's drunkenness leads him to beat his son viciously with a stick at the end of "Counterparts." By the time we reach "Ivy Day in the Committee Room" Joyce has correlated alcohol with apprehension in his readers and hostility and failure in his characters.

But even without the previous stories, Joyce makes sure to create a complete **objective correlative** of the stout bottle in "Ivy Day in the Committee Room." When we first read the title of this story, we might imagine a bright and happy day of celebration. We know it's a political holiday—Ivy Day—and we're going to be in a political setting—a committee room. The green and shining associations we make when we read the title are then reversed as we're plunged into a dark room, where an old man rakes "the cinders together with a piece of cardboard." Our first indication of the objective correlative of alcohol or "the bottle" comes from the old man, Old Jack, who complains to Mr. O'Connor of his nineteen year old son "boosing about." This introduces the apprehension and danger that is associated with alcohol and it **foreshadows** the **tension** involving alcohol that follows. As fellow canvassers arrive in the room, the conversation slowly creeps from politics to the subject of booze, or the characters' lack of it.

It begins when Mr. Henchy suggests that Mr. Tierney, who owns a pub called the Black Eagle, "first saw the light" when he saw his father had "a tricky little black bottle up there in the corner" of his hand-me-down shop. In fact, Mr. Henchy later reveals that he supposed that Father Keon, the priest that stops in looking for Mr. Fanning, had arrived to deliver stout to the room, as though all these men are hanging around waiting for beer to show up from the provider—the pub owner and candidate for Lord Mayor.

Finally, a seventeen year old boy shows up from the Black Eagle, "depositing a basket on the floor with a noise of shaken bottles."

Before he leaves, Mr. Henchy asks him if he'd like a drink. The boy drinks a bottle, and after he's gone, Old Joe—who does nothing to stop it—says, "That's the way it begins." Mr. Henchy, who offered the boy the drink in the first place, says, "The thin edge of the wedge." We question Old Joe's silence when Mr. Henchy gives the seventeen year old beer, especially after his admission early in the story that his own son has been corrupted by alcohol. Mr. Henchy disaffectedly admits that he has inserted the first part of the "wedge" into the boy, but seems not to care, or views it as inevitable.

Shortly after, when another canvasser enterers the room, he says, "Where did the boose come from?" and Mr. O'Connor, as though he is aware of the group's preoccupation with alcohol says, "O, of course, Lyons spots the drink first thing!" On the one hand, you have a group of guys drinking some stout, joking around, and having a good time. But on the other hand, Joyce imbues these moments with tension—even the jokes are correlated to that dangerous object that may or may not doom these characters.

The objective correlative establishes itself by the end of the story, as the characters, who have no corkscrew to open the bottles, are forced to lay them on the hob of the fire and wait for them to heat up so that the tops blast off the bottles. Joyce signifies this with a "Pok!" This image of men sitting around in a dark room, gossiping about their employer in a disaffected manner, no corkscrew, but so desperate for stout that they heat their beers in the fire to open them, correlates directly to the uneasiness readers may feel about these characters.

After Mr. Hynes recites his poem about Parnell, the bottle he placed in the fire blows its top—"Pok!"—but he doesn't move to retrieve it. Here, the reader may wonder if this suggests hope for Mr. Hynes—a rejection of that object that brings failure, hostility, and corruption to so many men.

Allusion or Reference

Mr. Hynes refers to the Phoenix in his poem about Parnell—an **allusion** that may comment on the bottle of stout that erupts in the fire immediately after he reads this poem. The Phoenix, in mythology, dies in the fire and then rises from the ashes, and this **allusion** helps to reinforce some sense of hope or rebirth in Hynes's refusal to retrieve the alcohol that has doomed so many men.

Writers often use allusions to bring a sense of artistic "bigness" to their work. By referring to well-known artists or classic mythology, allusions often function to suggest connections between celebrated work and the author's own work. Readers may often roll their eyes at the pompousness of a writer's forced allusions. But allusions can work to entice and intrigue readers too. They can attract readers' curiosity, incite them to investigate, or connect a character, event, object, or idea to something ubiquitous or universal outside of the narrative. At the very least, allusions suggest that the small and seemingly isolated world of the narrative is bigger than the reader previously thought—informing readers' understandings of individual characters and specific events with comparisons outward.

Questions

1. Do you find the characters and the situations believable in this story? Does Joyce achieve **verisimilitude**? If so, how does he accomplish this? What details help you **suspend your disbelief**? How does the dialogue operate? What makes it believable or contrived?

2. What objects stick out in your memory after reading these stories? First, why do those particular objects stick out? Do you remember them because Joyce described them as **images** or do you remember them because they were associated with an **idea**, character, or emotion? Investigate those objects in the text and decide how Joyce managed to work them into your memory. Are those objects **objective correlatives**? Do you associate them with a particular emotion?

3. How has Joyce used **allusions** so far? Would you consider these stories filled with allusions or short on allusions? Why might Joyce use allusions or avoid them in *Dubliners*?

A Mother

Mr Holohan, assistant secretary of the *Eire Abu* Society, had been walking up and down Dublin for nearly a month, with his hands and pockets full of dirty pieces of paper, arranging about the series of concerts. He had a game leg and for this his friends called him Hoppy Holohan. He walked up and down constantly, stood by the hour at street corners arguing the point and made notes; but in the end it was Mrs Kearney who arranged everything.

Miss Devlin had become Mrs Kearney out of spite. She had been educated in a high-class convent, where she had learned French and music. As she was naturally pale and unbending in manner she made few friends at school. When she came to the age of marriage she was sent out to many houses, where her playing and ivory manners were much admired. She sat amid the chilly circle of her accomplishments, waiting for some suitor to brave it and offer her a brilliant life. But the young men whom she met were ordinary and she gave them no encouragement, trying to console her romantic desires by eating a great deal of Turkish Delight in secret. However, when she drew near the limit and her friends began to loosen their tongues about her, she silenced them by marrying Mr Kearney, who was a bootmaker on Ormond Quay.

He was much older than she. His conversation, which was serious, took place at intervals in his great brown beard. After the first year of married life, Mrs Kearney perceived that such a man would wear better than a romantic person, but she never put her own romantic ideas away. He was sober, thrifty and pious; he went to the altar every first Friday, sometimes with her, oftener by himself. But she never weakened in her religion and was a good wife to him. At some party in a strange house when she lifted her eyebrow ever so slightly he stood up to take his leave and, when his cough troubled him, she put the eider-down quilt over his feet and made a strong rum punch. For his part, he was a model father. By paying a small sum every week into a society, he ensured for both his daughters a dowry of one hundred pounds each when they came to the age of twenty-four. He sent the older daughter, Kathleen, to a good convent, where she learned French and music, and afterward paid her fees at the

Academy. Every year in the month of July Mrs Kearney found occasion to say to some friend:

"My good man is packing us off to Skerries for a few weeks."

If it was not Skerries it was Howth or Greystones.

When the Irish Revival began to be appreciable Mrs Kearney determined to take advantage of her daughter's name and brought an Irish teacher to the house. Kathleen and her sister sent Irish picture postcards to their friends and these friends sent back other Irish picture postcards. On special Sundays, when Mr Kearney went with his family to the pro-cathedral, a little crowd of people would assemble after mass at the corner of Cathedral Street. They were all friends of the Kearneys—musical friends or Nationalist friends; and, when they had played every little counter of gossip, they shook hands with one another all together, laughing at the crossing of so many hands, and said good-bye to one another in Irish. Soon the name of Miss Kathleen Kearney began to be heard often on people's lips. People said that she was very clever at music and a very nice girl and, moreover, that she was a believer in the language movement. Mrs Kearney was well content at this. Therefore she was not surprised when one day Mr Holohan came to her and proposed that her daughter should be the accompanist at a series of four grand concerts which his Society was going to give in the Antient Concert Rooms. She brought him into the drawing-room, made him sit down and brought out the decanter and the silver biscuit-barrel. She entered heart and soul into the details of the enterprise, advised and dissuaded: and finally a contract was drawn up by which Kathleen was to receive eight guineas for her services as accompanist at the four grand concerts.

As Mr Holohan was a novice in such delicate matters as the wording of bills and the disposing of items for a programme, Mrs Kearney helped him. She had tact. She knew what *artistes* should go into capitals and what *artistes* should go into small type. She knew that the first tenor would not like to come on after Mr Meade's comic turn. To keep the audience continually diverted she slipped the doubtful items in between the old favourites. Mr Holohan called to see her every day to have her advice on some point. She was invariably friendly and advising—homely, in fact. She pushed the decanter towards him, saying:

"Now, help yourself, Mr Holohan!"

And while he was helping himself she said:

"Don't be afraid! Don't be afraid of it!"

Everything went on smoothly. Mrs Kearney bought some lovely blushpink charmeuse in Brown Thomas's to let into the front of Kathleen's dress. It cost a pretty penny; but there are occasions when a little expense is justifiable. She took a dozen of two-shilling tickets for the final concert and sent them to those friends who could not be trusted to come otherwise. She forgot nothing, and, thanks to her, everything that was to be done was done.

The concerts were to be on Wednesday, Thursday, Friday and Saturday. When Mrs Kearney arrived with her daughter at the Antient Concert Rooms on Wednesday night she did not like the look of things. A few young men, wearing bright blue badges in their coats, stood idle in the vestibule; none of them wore evening dress. She passed by with her daughter and a quick glance through the open door of the hall showed her the cause of the stewards' idleness. At first she wondered had she mistaken the hour. No, it was twenty minutes to eight.

In the dressing-room behind the stage she was introduced to the secretary of the Society, Mr Fitzpatrick. She smiled and shook his hand. He was a little man, with a white, vacant face. She noticed that he wore his soft brown hat carelessly on the side of his head and that his accent was flat. He held a programme in his hand, and, while he was talking to her, he chewed one end of it into a moist pulp. He seemed to bear disappointments lightly. Mr Holohan came into the dressing room every few minutes with reports from the box-office. The *artistes* talked among themselves nervously, glanced from time to time at the mirror and rolled and unrolled their music. When it was nearly half-past eight, the few people in the hall began to express their desire to be entertained. Mr Fitzpatrick came in, smiled vacantly at the room, and said:

"Well now, ladies and gentlemen. I suppose we'd better open the ball."

Mrs Kearney rewarded his very flat final syllable with a quick stare of contempt, and then said to her daughter encouragingly:

"Are you ready, dear?"

When she had an opportunity, she called Mr Holohan aside and asked him to tell her what it meant. Mr Holohan did not know what it meant. He said that the committee had made a mistake in arranging for four concerts: four was too many.

"And the *artistes!*" said Mrs Kearney. "Of course they are doing their best, but really they are not good."

Mr Holohan admitted that the *artistes* were no good but the committee, he said, had decided to let the first three concerts go as they pleased and reserve all the talent for Saturday night. Mrs Kearney said nothing, but, as the mediocre items followed one another on the platform and the few people in the hall grew fewer and fewer, she began to regret that she had put herself to any expense for such a concert. There was something she didn't like in the look of things and Mr Fitzpatrick's vacant smile irritated her very much. However, she said nothing and waited to see how it would end. The concert expired shortly before ten, and everyone went home quickly.

The concert on Thursday night was better attended, but Mrs Kearney saw at once that the house was filled with paper.[1] The audience behaved indecorously, as if the concert were an informal dress rehearsal. Mr Fitzpatrick seemed to enjoy himself; he was quite unconscious that Mrs Kearney was taking angry note of his conduct. He stood at the edge of the screen, from time to time jutting out his head and exchanging a laugh with two friends in the corner of the balcony. In the course of the evening, Mrs Kearney learned that the Friday concert was to be abandoned and that the committee was going to move heaven and earth to secure a bumper house on Saturday night. When she heard this, she sought out Mr Holohan. She buttonholed him as he was limping out quickly with a glass of lemonade for a young lady and asked him was it true. Yes, it was true.

"But, of course, that doesn't alter the contract," she said. "The contract was for four concerts."

Mr Holohan seemed to be in a hurry; he advised her to speak to Mr Fitzpatrick. Mrs Kearney was now beginning to be alarmed. She called Mr Fitzpatrick away from his screen and told him that her daughter had signed for four concerts and that, of course, according to the terms of the contract, she should receive the sum originally stipulated for, whether the society gave the four concerts or not. Mr Fitzpatrick, who did not catch the point at issue very quickly, seemed unable to resolve the difficulty and said that he would bring the matter before the committee. Mrs Kearney's anger began to flutter in her cheek and she had all she could do to keep from asking:

---

[1] As in people with complimentary tickets.

"And who is the *cometty* pray?"

But she knew that it would not be ladylike to do that: so she was silent.

Little boys were sent out into the principal streets of Dublin early on Friday morning with bundles of handbills. Special puffs[2] appeared in all the evening papers, reminding the music loving public of the treat which was in store for it on the following evening. Mrs Kearney was somewhat reassured, but thought well to tell her husband part of her suspicions. He listened carefully and said that perhaps it would be better if he went with her on Saturday night. She agreed. She respected her husband in the same way as she respected the General Post Office, as something large, secure and fixed; and though she knew the small number of his talents she appreciated his abstract value as a male. She was glad that he had suggested coming with her. She thought her plans over.

The night of the grand concert came. Mrs Kearney, with her husband and daughter, arrived at the Antient Concert Rooms three-quarters of an hour before the time at which the concert was to begin. By ill luck it was a rainy evening. Mrs Kearney placed her daughter's clothes and music in charge of her husband and went all over the building looking for Mr Holohan or Mr Fitzpatrick. She could find neither. She asked the stewards was any member of the committee in the hall and, after a great deal of trouble, a steward brought out a little woman named Miss Beirne to whom Mrs Kearney explained that she wanted to see one of the secretaries. Miss Beirne expected them any minute and asked could she do anything. Mrs Kearney looked searchingly at the oldish face which was screwed into an expression of trustfulness and enthusiasm and answered:

"No, thank you!"

The little woman hoped they would have a good house. She looked out at the rain until the melancholy of the wet street effaced all the trustfulness and enthusiasm from her twisted features. Then she gave a little sigh and said:

"Ah, well! We did our best, the dear knows."

Mrs Kearney had to go back to the dressing-room.

The *artistes* were arriving. The bass and the second tenor had already come. The bass, Mr Duggan, was a slender young man with a scattered black moustache. He was the son of a hall porter in an

---

[2] Puff pieces.

office in the city and, as a boy, he had sung prolonged bass notes in the resounding hall. From this humble state he had raised himself until he had become a first-rate *artiste*. He had appeared in grand opera. One night, when an operatic *artiste* had fallen ill, he had undertaken the part of the king in the opera of *Maritana* at the Queen's Theatre. He sang his music with great feeling and volume and was warmly welcomed by the gallery; but, unfortunately, he marred the good impression by wiping his nose in his gloved hand once or twice out of thoughtlessness. He was unassuming and spoke little. He said *yous* so softly that it passed unnoticed and he never drank anything stronger than milk for his voice's sake. Mr Bell, the second tenor, was a fair-haired little man who competed every year for prizes at the Feis Ceoil. On his fourth trial he had been awarded a bronze medal. He was extremely nervous and extremely jealous of other tenors and he covered his nervous jealousy with an ebullient friendliness. It was his humour to have people know what an ordeal a concert was to him. Therefore when he saw Mr Duggan he went over to him and asked:

"Are you in it too?"

"Yes," said Mr Duggan.

Mr Bell laughed at his fellow-sufferer, held out his hand and said:

"Shake!"

Mrs Kearney passed by these two young men and went to the edge of the screen to view the house. The seats were being filled up rapidly and a pleasant noise circulated in the auditorium. She came back and spoke to her husband privately. Their conversation was evidently about Kathleen for they both glanced at her often as she stood chatting to one of her Nationalist friends, Miss Healy, the contralto. An unknown solitary woman with a pale face walked through the room. The women followed with keen eyes the faded blue dress which was stretched upon a meagre body. Someone said that she was Madam Glynn, the soprano.

"I wonder where did they dig her up," said Kathleen to Miss Healy. "I'm sure I never heard of her."

Miss Healy had to smile. Mr Holohan limped into the dressing-room at that moment and the two young ladies asked him who was the unknown woman. Mr Holohan said that she was Madam Glynn from London. Madam Glynn took her stand in a corner of the room, holding a roll of music stiffly before her and from time to time changing the direction of her startled gaze. The shadow took her faded dress into shelter but fell revengefully into the little cup behind her collar-bone. The noise of the hall became more audible. The first tenor and the baritone arrived together. They were both well dressed, stout and complacent and they brought a breath of opulence among the company.

Mrs Kearney brought her daughter over to them, and talked to them amiably. She wanted to be on good terms with them but, while she strove to be polite, her eyes followed Mr Holohan in his limping and devious courses. As soon as she could she excused herself and went out after him.

"Mr Holohan, I want to speak to you for a moment," she said.

They went down to a discreet part of the corridor. Mrs Kearney asked him when was her daughter going to be paid. Mr Holohan said that Mr Fitzpatrick had charge of that. Mrs Kearney said that she didn't know anything about Mr Fitzpatrick. Her daughter had signed a contract for eight guineas and she would have to be paid. Mr Holohan said that it wasn't his business.

"Why isn't it your business?" asked Mrs Kearney. "Didn't you yourself bring her the contract? Anyway, if it's not your business it's my business and I mean to see to it."

"You'd better speak to Mr Fitzpatrick," said Mr Holohan distantly.

"I don't know anything about Mr Fitzpatrick," repeated Mrs Kearney. "I have my contract, and I intend to see that it is carried out."

When she came back to the dressing-room her cheeks were slightly suffused. The room was lively. Two men in outdoor dress had taken possession of the fireplace and were chatting familiarly with Miss Healy and the baritone. They were the *Freeman* man and Mr O'Madden Burke. The *Freeman* man had come in to say that he could not wait for the concert as he had to report the lecture which an American priest was giving in the Mansion House. He said they were to leave the report for him at the *Freeman* office and he would see that it went in. He was a grey-haired man, with a plausible voice and careful manners. He held an extinguished cigar in his hand and the aroma of cigar smoke floated near him. He had not intended to stay a moment because concerts and *artistes* bored him considerably but he remained leaning against the mantelpiece. Miss Healy stood in front of him, talking and laughing. He was old enough to suspect one reason for her politeness but young enough in spirit to turn the moment to account. The warmth, fragrance and colour of her body appealed to his senses. He was pleasantly conscious that the bosom which he saw rise and fall slowly beneath him rose and fell at that moment for him, that the laughter and fragrance and wilful glances were his tribute. When he could stay no longer he took leave of her regretfully.

"O'Madden Burke will write the notice," he explained to Mr Holohan, "and I'll see it in."

"Thank you very much, Mr Hendrick," said Mr Holohan. You'll see it in, I know. Now, won't you have a little something before you go?"

"I don't mind," said Mr Hendrick.

The two men went along some tortuous passages and up a dark staircase and came to a secluded room where one of the stewards was uncorking bottles for a few gentlemen. One of these gentlemen was Mr O'Madden Burke, who had found out the room by instinct. He was a suave, elderly man who balanced his imposing body, when at rest, upon a large silk umbrella. His magniloquent western name was the moral umbrella upon which he balanced the fine problem of his finances. He was widely respected.

While Mr Holohan was entertaining the *Freeman* man Mrs Kearney was speaking so animatedly to her husband that he had to ask her to lower her voice. The conversation of the others in the dressing-room had become strained. Mr Bell, the first item, stood ready with his music but the accompanist made no sign. Evidently something was wrong. Mr Kearney looked straight before him, stroking his beard, while Mrs Kearney spoke into Kathleen's ear with subdued emphasis. From the hall came sounds of encouragement, clapping and stamping of feet. The first tenor and the baritone and Miss Healy stood together, waiting tranquilly, but Mr Bell's nerves were greatly agitated because he was afraid the audience would think that he had come late.

Mr Holohan and Mr O'Madden Burke came into the room. In a moment Mr Holohan perceived the hush. He went over to Mrs Kearney and spoke with her earnestly. While they were speaking the noise in the hall grew louder. Mr Holohan became very red and excited. He spoke volubly, but Mrs Kearney said curtly at intervals:

"She won't go on. She must get her eight guineas."

Mr Holohan pointed desperately towards the hall where the audience was clapping and stamping. He appealed to Mr Kearney and to Kathleen. But Mr Kearney continued to stroke his beard and Kathleen looked down, moving the point of her new shoe: it was not her fault. Mrs Kearney repeated:

"She won't go on without her money."

After a swift struggle of tongues Mr Holohan hobbled out in haste. The room was silent. When the strain of the silence had become somewhat painful Miss Healy said to the baritone:

"Have you seen Mrs Pat Campbell this week?"

The baritone had not seen her but he had been told that she was very fine. The conversation went no further. The first tenor bent his head and began to count the links of the gold chain which was extended across his waist, smiling and humming random notes to observe the effect on the frontal sinus. From time to time everyone glanced at Mrs Kearney.

The noise in the auditorium had risen to a clamour when Mr Fitzpatrick burst into the room, followed by Mr Holohan who was panting. The clapping and stamping in the hall were punctuated by whistling. Mr Fitzpatrick held a few banknotes in his hand. He counted out four into Mrs Kearney's hand and said she would get the other half at the interval. Mrs Kearney said:

"This is four shillings short."

But Kathleen gathered in her skirt and said: "Now. Mr Bell," to the first item, who was shaking like an aspen. The singer and the accompanist went out together. The noise in hall died away. There was a pause of a few seconds: and then the piano was heard.

The first part of the concert was very successful except for Madam Glynn's item. The poor lady sang *Killarney* in a bodiless gasping voice, with all the old-fashioned mannerisms of intonation and pronunciation which she believed lent elegance to her singing. She looked as if she had been resurrected from an old stage-wardrobe and the cheaper parts of the hall made fun of her high wailing notes. The first tenor and the contralto, however, brought down the house. Kathleen played a selection of Irish airs which was generously applauded. The first part closed with a stirring patriotic recitation delivered by a young lady who arranged amateur theatricals. It was deservedly applauded; and, when it was ended, the men went out for the interval, content.

All this time the dressing-room was a hive of excitement. In one corner were Mr Holohan, Mr Fitzpatrick, Miss Beirne, two of the stewards, the baritone, the bass, and Mr O'Madden Burke. Mr O'Madden Burke said it was the most scandalous exhibition he had ever witnessed. Miss Kathleen Kearney's musical career was ended in Dublin after that, he said. The baritone was asked what did he think of Mrs Kearney's conduct. He did not like to say anything. He had been paid his money and wished to be at peace with men. However, he said that Mrs Kearney might have taken the *artistes* into consideration. The stewards and the secretaries debated hotly as to what should be done when the interval came.

"I agree with Miss Beirne," said Mr O'Madden Burke. "Pay her nothing."

In another corner of the room were Mrs Kearney and her husband, Mr Bell, Miss Healy and the young lady who had to recite the patriotic piece. Mrs Kearney said that the Committee had treated her scandalously. She had spared neither trouble nor expense and this was how she was repaid.

They thought they had only a girl to deal with and that therefore, they could ride roughshod over her. But she would show them their mistake. They wouldn't have dared to have treated her like that if she had been a man. But she would see that her daughter got her rights: she wouldn't be fooled. If they didn't pay her to the last farthing she would make Dublin ring. Of course she was sorry for the sake of the *artistes*. But what else could she do? She appealed to the second tenor who said he thought she had not been well treated. Then she appealed to Miss Healy. Miss Healy wanted to join the other group but she did not like to do so because she was a great friend of Kathleen's and the Kearneys had often invited her to their house.

As soon as the first part was ended Mr Fitzpatrick and Mr Holohan went over to Mrs Kearney and told her that the other four guineas would be paid after the committee meeting on the following Tuesday and that, in case her daughter did not play for the second part, the committee would consider the contract broken and would pay nothing.

"I haven't seen any committee," said Mrs Kearney angrily. "My daughter has her contract. She will get four pounds eight into her hand or a foot she won't put on that platform."

"I'm surprised at you, Mrs Kearney," said Mr Holohan. "I never thought you would treat us this way."

"And what way did you treat me?" asked Mrs Kearney.

Her face was inundated with an angry colour and she looked as if she would attack someone with her hands.

"I'm asking for my rights." she said.

"You might have some sense of decency," said Mr Holohan.

"Might I, indeed?...And when I ask when my daughter is going to be paid I can't get a civil answer."

She tossed her head and assumed a haughty voice:

"You must speak to the secretary. It's not my business. I'm a great fellow fol-the-diddle-I-do."

"I thought you were a lady," said Mr Holohan, walking away from her abruptly.

After that Mrs Kearney's conduct was condemned on all hands: everyone approved of what the committee had done. She stood at the door, haggard with rage, arguing with her husband and daughter, gesticulating with them. She waited until it was time for the second part to begin in the hope that the secretaries would approach her. But Miss Healy had kindly consented to play one or two accompaniments. Mrs Kearney had to stand aside to allow the baritone and his accompanist to pass up to the platform. She stood still for an instant like an angry stone image and, when the first notes of the song struck her ear, she caught up her daughter's cloak and said to her husband:

"Get a cab!"

He went out at once. Mrs Kearney wrapped the cloak round her daughter and followed him. As she passed through the doorway she stopped and glared into Mr Holohan's face.

"I'm not done with you yet," she said.

"But I'm done with you," said Mr Holohan.

Kathleen followed her mother meekly. Mr Holohan began to pace up and down the room, in order to cool himself for he felt his skin on fire.

"That's a nice lady!" he said. "O, she's a nice lady!"

"You did the proper thing, Holohan," said Mr O'Madden Burke, poised upon his umbrella in approval.

CRAFT: A MOTHER

Satire

While I wouldn't categorize the story of "A Mother" as a satire (though I do think one could argue that point), I would categorize Mrs. Kearney as a satirical character. In terms of craft, a satirical character embedded in a realistic story provides a compelling examination of how a writer can use elements of satire in a story that otherwise remains realistic. In effect, the satirical rendering of Mrs. Kearney's character becomes the very thing that creates tension between her and the other characters in this story, especially Mr. Holohan and Mr. Fitzpatrick.

While many writers might consider a satirical character a caricature, **satire** suggests that the follies of a character are manifested for ridicule, while a **caricature** suggests that the traits of a character are **hyperbolized** for comic effect. Caricature usually relies on clichés or stereotypes, exaggerating them to achieve comedy. Although satire often achieves comic effect, it is not fundamental to its definition. We might easily consider Farrington a satirical character in "Counterparts" because his follies of alcoholism and domestic violence are manifested for ridicule. However, there's nothing comic about Farrington.

It might seem unusual that Joyce begins the story with Mr. Holohan. Joyce devotes the first paragraph to introducing him, providing **exposition** about his role as "assistant secretary of the *Eire Abu* Society" and telling us that, when it comes to the concerts, Mrs. Kearney "arranged everything." In the second paragraph, Joyce thrusts us into satire: "Mrs Devlin had become Mrs Kearney out of spite." Joyce holds Mrs. Kearney up for ridicule by suggesting that she married her husband simply because she did not want to face the loose tongues of her friends. As we come to understand Mrs. Kearney, it becomes clear why Joyce began the story with Mr. Holohan. Because the story itself is not a satire, starting with Mrs. Kearney would suggest that the narrative be considered a satire. While readers accept Mrs. Kearney as a satirical character, they would have a much harder time accepting Mr. Holohan as a realistic character if they were first introduced to Mrs. Kearney. It would, in fact, disrupt Joyce's narrative **premise**, which has less to do with satire, and more to do with pitting a strong and aggressive woman character in opposition to weak and passive-aggressive male characters.

As we get to know Mrs. Kearney, we understand that her privilege—"she had been educated in a high-class convent"—and her unreasonably high expectations are the things that get her into trouble. She makes sure to find occasion to boast to her friends. She harshly judges the other artists in the concerts and dislikes Mr. Fitzpatrick's "white vacant face." When she gets angry about her daughter's payment, her impulse is to mock Mr. Fitzpatrick's accent and his unsophisticated pronunciation of the word "committee." Joyce even brings up her regard for her husband for further ridicule when he writes, "She respected her husband in the same way as she respected the General Post Office, as something large, secure and fixed." Worse still, Joyce points out that Mrs. Kearney "appreciated his abstract value as a male."

It's not until only minutes before the last concert begins that Mrs. Kearney decides to exert her power in full. She demands money, threatening to hold her daughter back from performing as the audience claps and anticipates the concert's start. She fails to take the other artists into consideration because she has already judged and trivialized their talents. She fails to take her daughter into consideration, who is without a voice and completely under the thumb of her mother throughout the entire story. When Mrs. Kearney suggests that "the committee has treated her scandalously" the reader is hard-pressed to sympathize with her because Joyce has made such deliberate attempts to satirize her.

Up to the end, there is no indication that Joyce or the **omniscient narrator** of this story sympathizes with Mrs. Kearney's behavior or complaints. And yet Mr. Holohan and Mr. Fitzpatrick are both lackadaisical and inefficient in their roles. Mr. Holohan continually defers to a largely absent Mr. Fitzpatrick, forcing Mrs. Kearney to go in circles in order to get an answer to a very straightforward question. Not only that, but Mr. Fitzpatrick and Mr. Holohan are liars. After they agree to pay the rest of the money to Mrs. Kearney at intermission, they then tell her at intermission that "the other four guineas would be paid after the committee meeting on the following Tuesday." Although Mrs. Kearney makes a fool of herself by the end of the story, it's Mr. Holohan and Mr. Fitzpatrick who are comfortable in their smug, male roles. Mrs. Kearney is probably right when she suggests that they "wouldn't have dared to have treated her like that if she had been a man." At the end of the story, Mr. Holohan goes so far as to bring her womanhood into question: "I thought you were a lady."

Joyce pulls the satirical rug out from under the reader and exposes Mr. Holohan for the sexist and incompetent man he truly is. For the first time, the reader understands that, despite the satirical portrayal, Mrs. Kearney has been abused and victimized too. Joyce transports this satirical character into a sympathetic character who has been wronged, and who has acted badly because of it. When Mr. O'Madden Burke suggests to Mr. Holohan at the very end that he "did the proper thing," we, perhaps for the first time, understand it's not true at all. In fact, one could easily argue that, by the end of the story, there has been a kind of **chiasmus** or reversal in which Mr. Holohan becomes the satirical character.

Both writers and readers often expect simple explanations of art. A satire is a satire. A tragedy is a tragedy. A comedy is ha, ha, ha. Categories, categories. But "A Mother" shows us how writers use many different techniques and categories to create art. A critic might easily just say, "It's realism" or "It's satire," but those of us interested in craft must go deeper and see how writers intersect many different techniques and categories to create something that, in the end, is difficult to categorize simply.

Dynamic versus Static & Round versus Flat

At times, Joyce's dialogue crackles and sparks, and he creates characters that take each other apart or "undo" each other. In "Ivy Day in the Committee Room" Joyce presents most of the narrative through dialogue. It's a difficult task to tell so much of the story through the words spoken by characters without it sounding like the writer is forcing **exposition** into conversation.

In "A Mother" Joyce's choice at what dialogue to summarize and what dialogue to provide may perplex and frustrate many readers. When Mrs. Kearney holds her daughter back from the stage until Mr. Holohan produces payment, the narrator states:

> Mr Holohan pointed desperately towards the hall where the audience was clapping and stamping. He appealed to Mr Kearney and to Kathleen. But Mr Kearney continued to stroke his beard and Kathleen looked down, moving the point of her new shoe: it was not her fault. Mrs. Kearney repeated: "She won't go on without her money."

The tension in this scene comes from Mr. Holohan's panic and the tight spot Mrs. Kearney has put him in. Therefore, with more direct access to that panic the readers would more acutely feel the **tension** and the **crisis**. We know that Mrs. Kearney won't let Kathleen go on without the money, so the repetition of that in dialogue, while it continues to satirize her by reinforcing her stubbornness and showing she's not going to relent, deadens the scene, making it **static**. Hearing Mr. Holohan's desperate "appeal" to Mrs. Kearney in dialogue would dramatize the scene, making the exchange and crisis **dynamic**, revealing how Mrs. Kearney has undone him.

When we use the word **"dynamic"** to describe a scene in literature, we refer to the "movement" or the "activity" of the scene. As an antonym we use **"static"** to indicate that a scene has no movement or activity. When we apply those to a character, they become much broader. A dynamic or **round** character is one who changes in a story and shows a range of actions and reactions to events and characters. A static or **flat** character is one who does not change and who shows a limited range of actions and reactions. Mrs. Kearney's dynamism as a character comes from her change from enthusiastic and engaged in the concerts to skeptical, judgmental, and then irrational. We might argue that Mr. Holohan's character remains static or flat—that he maintains that same level, smug, and disaffected manner throughout the story.

Questions

1. Would you consider Mr. Holohan a **satirical character**? How about Mr. Fitzpatrick? Why or why not? Specifically, where does Joyce either hold these characters up for ridicule or cause you to sympathize with them? If you find all the characters held up for ridicule, does that mean that this story is a satire? If so, what is Joyce satirizing?

2. Let's think back to "Two Gallants." Would you call the characters of Corley and Lenehan **round** or **flat**? Would you call their dialogue **dynamic** or **static**? If one character seems rounder than the other, how and why does Joyce create that effect?

3. What characters in *Dubliners* stick out in your mind as particularly **round**? Oppositely, what characters seem **flat**? What reasons might Joyce have for creating a flat character or a **static** moment or situation? Can you find instances of flat characters and static moments that you would describe as adding something to the narrative? Oppositely, can you find flat characters and static moments that detract from the narrative's effectiveness or **verisimilitude**?

Grace

Two gentlemen who were in the lavatory at the time tried to lift him up: but he was quite helpless. He lay curled up at the foot of the stairs down which he had fallen. They succeeded in turning him over. His hat had rolled a few yards away and his clothes were smeared with the filth and ooze of the floor on which he had lain, face downwards. His eyes were closed and he breathed with a grunting noise. A thin stream of blood trickled from the corner of his mouth.

These two gentlemen and one of the curates carried him up the stairs and laid him down again on the floor of the bar. In two minutes he was surrounded by a ring of men. The manager of the bar asked everyone who he was and who was with him. No one knew who he was but one of the curates said he had served the gentleman with a small rum.

"Was he by himself?" asked the manager.

"No, sir. There was two gentlemen with him."

"And where are they?"

No one knew; a voice said:

"Give him air. He's fainted."

The ring of onlookers distended and closed again elastically. A dark medal of blood had formed itself near the man's head on the tessellated floor. The manager, alarmed by the grey pallor of the man's face, sent for a policeman.

His collar was unfastened and his necktie undone. He opened his eyes for an instant, sighed and closed them again. One of the gentlemen who had carried him upstairs held a dinged silk hat in his hand. The manager asked repeatedly did no one know who the injured man was or where had his friends gone. The door of the bar opened and an immense constable entered. A crowd which had followed him down the laneway collected outside the door, struggling to look in through the glass panels.

The manager at once began to narrate what he knew. The constable, a young man with thick immobile features, listened. He moved his head slowly to right and left and from the manager to the person on the floor, as if he feared to be the victim of some delusion. Then he drew off his glove, produced a small book from his waist, licked the lead of his pencil and made ready to indite. He asked in a suspicious provincial accent:

"Who is the man? What's his name and address?"

A young man in a cycling-suit cleared his way through the ring of bystanders. He knelt down promptly beside the injured man and called for water. The constable knelt down also to help. The young man washed the blood from the injured man's mouth and then called for some brandy. The constable repeated the order in an authoritative voice until a curate came running with the glass. The brandy was forced down the man's throat. In a few seconds he opened his eyes and looked about him. He looked at the circle of faces and then, understanding, strove to rise to his feet.

"You're all right now?" asked the young man in the cycling-suit.

"Sha, 's nothing," said the injured man, trying to stand up.

He was helped to his feet. The manager said something about a hospital and some of the bystanders gave advice. The battered silk hat was placed on the man's head. The constable asked:

"Where do you live?"

The man, without answering, began to twirl the ends of his moustache. He made light of his accident. "It was nothing," he said: "only a little accident." He spoke very thickly.

"Where do you live?" repeated the constable.

The man said they were to get a cab for him. While the point was being debated a tall agile gentleman of fair complexion, wearing a long yellow ulster, came from the far end of the bar. Seeing the spectacle, he called out:

"Hallo, Tom, old man! What's the trouble?"

"Sha, 's nothing," said the man.

The new-comer surveyed the deplorable figure before him and then turned to the constable, saying:

"It's all right, constable. I'll see him home."

The constable touched his helmet and answered:

"All right, Mr Power!"

"Come now, Tom," said Mr Power, taking his friend by the arm. "No bones broken. What? Can you walk?"

The young man in the cycling-suit took the man by the other arm and the crowd divided.

"How did you get yourself into this mess?" asked Mr Power.

"The gentleman fell down the stairs," said the young man.

"I' 'ery 'uch o'liged to you, sir," said the injured man.

"Not at all."

" 'ant we have a little…?"

"Not now. Not now."

The three men left the bar and the crowd sifted through the doors in to the laneway. The manager brought the constable to the stairs to inspect the scene of the accident. They agreed that the gentleman must have missed his footing. The customers returned to the counter and a curate set about removing the traces of blood from the floor.

When they came out into Grafton Street, Mr Power whistled for an outsider.[1] The injured man said again as well as he could.

"I' 'ery 'uch o'liged to you, sir. I hope we'll 'eet again. 'y na'e is Kernan."

The shock and the incipient pain had partly sobered him.

"Don't mention it," said the young man.

They shook hands. Mr Kernan was hoisted on to the car and, while Mr Power was giving directions to the carman, he expressed his gratitude to the young man and regretted that they could not have a little drink together.

"Another time," said the young man.

The car drove off towards Westmoreland Street. As it passed Ballast Office the clock showed half-past nine. A keen east wind hit them, blowing from the mouth of the river. Mr Kernan was huddled together with cold. His friend asked him to tell how the accident had happened.

"I 'an't 'an," he answered, " 'y 'ongue is hurt."

"Show."

The other leaned over the well of the car and peered into Mr Kernan's mouth but he could not see. He struck a match and, sheltering it in the shell of his hands, peered again into the mouth which Mr Kernan opened obediently. The swaying movement of the car brought the match to and from the opened mouth. The lower teeth and gums were covered with clotted blood and a minute piece of the tongue seemed to have been bitten off. The match was blown out.

"That's ugly," said Mr Power.

---

[1] Carriage taxi.

"Sha, 's nothing," said Mr Kernan, closing his mouth and pulling the collar of his filthy coat across his neck.

Mr Kernan was a commercial traveller of the old school which believed in the dignity of its calling. He had never been seen in the city without a silk hat of some decency and a pair of gaiters. By grace of these two articles of clothing, he said, a man could always pass muster. He carried on the tradition of his Napoleon, the great Blackwhite, whose memory he evoked at times by legend and mimicry. Modern business methods had spared him only so far as to allow him a little office in Crowe Street, on the window blind of which was written the name of his firm with the address—London, E.C.[2] On the mantelpiece of this little office a little leaden battalion of canisters was drawn up and on the table before the window stood four or five china bowls which were usually half full of a black liquid. From these bowls Mr Kernan tasted tea. He took a mouthful, drew it up, saturated his palate with it and then spat it forth into the grate. Then he paused to judge.

Mr Power, a much younger man, was employed in the Royal Irish Constabulary Office in Dublin Castle. The arc of his social rise intersected the arc of his friend's decline, but Mr Kernan's decline was mitigated by the fact that certain of those friends who had known him at his highest point of success still esteemed him as a character. Mr Power was one of these friends. His inexplicable debts were a byword in his circle; he was a debonair young man.

The car halted before a small house on the Glasnevin Road and Mr Kernan was helped into the house. His wife put him to bed while Mr Power sat downstairs in the kitchen asking the children where they went to school and what book they were in. The children—two girls and a boy, conscious of their father's helplessness and of their mother's absence, began some horseplay with him. He was surprised at their manners and at their accents, and his brow grew thoughtful. After a while Mrs Kernan entered the kitchen, exclaiming:

"Such a sight! O, he'll do for himself one day and that's the holy alls of it. He's been drinking since Friday."

Mr Power was careful to explain to her that he was not responsible, that he had come on the scene by the merest accident.

---

[2] East Central.

Mrs Kernan, remembering Mr Power's good offices during domestic quarrels, as well as many small, but opportune loans, said:

"O, you needn't tell me that, Mr Power. I know you're a friend of his, not like some of the others he does be with. They're all right so long as he has money in his pocket to keep him out from his wife and family. Nice friends! Who was he with tonight, I'd like to know?"

Mr Power shook his head but said nothing.

"I'm so sorry," she continued, "that I've nothing in the house to offer you. But if you wait a minute I'll send round to Fogarty's, at the corner."

Mr Power stood up.

"We were waiting for him to come home with the money. He never seems to think he has a home at all."

"O, now, Mrs Kernan," said Mr Power, "we'll make him turn over a new leaf. I'll talk to Martin. He's the man. We'll come here one of these nights and talk it over."

She saw him to the door. The carman was stamping up and down the footpath, and swinging his arms to warm himself.

"It's very kind of you to bring him home," she said.

"Not at all," said Mr Power.

He got up on the car. As it drove off he raised his hat to her gaily.

"We'll make a new man of him," he said. "Good-night, Mrs Kernan."

*****

Mrs Kernan's puzzled eyes watched the car till it was out of sight. Then she withdrew them, went into the house and emptied her husband's pockets.

She was an active, practical woman of middle age. Not long before she had celebrated her silver wedding[3] and renewed her intimacy with her husband by waltzing with him to Mr Power's accompaniment. In her days of courtship, Mr Kernan had seemed to her a not ungallant figure: and she still hurried to the chapel door whenever a wedding was reported and, seeing the bridal pair, recalled with vivid pleasure how she had passed out of the Star of the Sea Church in Sandymount, leaning on the arm of a jovial wellfed

---

[3] Twenty-fifth anniversary.

man, who was dressed smartly in a frock-coat and lavender trousers and carried a silk hat gracefully balanced upon his other arm. After three weeks she had found a wife's life irksome and, later on, when she was beginning to find it unbearable, she had become a mother. The part of mother presented to her no insuperable difficulties and for twenty-five years she had kept house shrewdly for her husband. Her two eldest sons were launched. One was in a draper's shop in Glasgow and the other was clerk to a tea-merchant in Belfast. They were good sons, wrote regularly and sometimes sent home money. The other children were still at school.

Mr Kernan sent a letter to his office next day and remained in bed. She made beef-tea for him and scolded him roundly. She accepted his frequent intemperance as part of the climate, healed him dutifully whenever he was sick and always tried to make him eat a breakfast. There were worse husbands. He had never been violent since the boys had grown up, and she knew that he would walk to the end of Thomas Street and back again to book even a small order.

Two nights after, his friends came to see him. She brought them up to his bedroom, the air of which was impregnated with a personal odour, and gave them chairs at the fire. Mr Kernan's tongue, the occasional stinging pain of which had made him somewhat irritable during the day, became more polite. He sat propped up in the bed by pillows and the little colour in his puffy cheeks made them resemble warm cinders. He apologised to his guests for the disorder of the room, but at the same time looked at them a little proudly, with a veteran's pride.

He was quite unconscious that he was the victim of a plot which his friends, Mr Cunningham, Mr M'Coy and Mr Power had disclosed to Mrs Kernan in the parlour. The idea been Mr Power's, but its development was entrusted to Mr Cunningham. Mr Kernan came of Protestant stock and, though he had been converted to the Catholic faith at the time of his marriage, he had not been in the pale of the Church for twenty years. He was fond, moreover, of giving side-thrusts at Catholicism.

Mr Cunningham was the very man for such a case. He was an elder colleague of Mr Power. His own domestic life was not very happy. People had great sympathy with him, for it was known that he had married an unpresentable woman who was an incurable drunkard. He had set up house for her six times; and each time she had pawned the furniture on him.

Everyone had respect for poor Martin Cunningham. He was a thoroughly sensible man, influential and intelligent. His blade of human knowledge, natural astuteness particularised by long association with cases in the police courts, had been tempered by brief immersions in the waters of general philosophy. He was well informed. His friends bowed to his opinions and considered that his face was like Shakespeare's.

When the plot had been disclosed to her, Mrs Kernan had said:

"I leave it all in your hands, Mr Cunningham."

After a quarter of a century of married life, she had very few illusions left. Religion for her was a habit, and she suspected that a man of her husband's age would not change greatly before death. She was tempted to see a curious appropriateness in his accident and, but that she did not wish to seem bloody-minded, would have told the gentlemen that Mr Kernan's tongue would not suffer by being shortened. However, Mr Cunningham was a capable man; and religion was religion. The scheme might do good and, at least, it could do no harm. Her beliefs were not extravagant. She believed steadily in the Sacred Heart as the most generally useful of all Catholic devotions and approved of the sacraments. Her faith was bounded by her kitchen, but, if she was put to it, she could believe also in the banshee and in the Holy Ghost.

The gentlemen began to talk of the accident. Mr Cunningham said that he had once known a similar case. A man of seventy had bitten off a piece of his tongue during an epileptic fit and the tongue had filled in again, so that no one could see a trace of the bite.

"Well, I'm not seventy," said the invalid.

"God forbid," said Mr Cunningham.

"It doesn't pain you now?" asked Mr M'Coy.

Mr M'Coy had been at one time a tenor of some reputation. His wife, who had been a soprano, still taught young children to play the piano at low terms. His line of life had not been the shortest distance between two points and for short periods he had been driven to live by his wits. He had been a clerk in the Midland Railway, a canvasser for advertisements for *The Irish Times* and for *The Freeman's Journal*, a town traveller for a coal firm on commission, a private inquiry agent,[4] a clerk in the office of the Sub-Sheriff, and he

---

[4] Private detective.

had recently become secretary to the City Coroner. His new office made him professionally interested in Mr Kernan's case.

"Pain? Not much," answered Mr Kernan. "But it's so sickening. I feel as if I wanted to retch off."

"That's the boose," said Mr Cunningham firmly.

"No," said Mr Kernan. "I think I caught cold on the car. There's something keeps coming into my throat, phlegm or——"

"Mucus." said Mr M'Coy.

"It keeps coming like from down in my throat; sickening thing."

"Yes, yes," said Mr M'Coy, "that's the thorax."

He looked at Mr Cunningham and Mr Power at the same time with an air of challenge. Mr Cunningham nodded his head rapidly and Mr Power said:

"Ah, well, all's well that ends well."

"I'm very much obliged to you, old man," said the invalid.

Mr Power waved his hand.

"Those other two fellows I was with——"

"Who were you with?" asked Mr Cunningham.

"A chap. I don't know his name. Damn it now, what's his name? Little chap with sandy hair..."

"And who else?"

"Harford."

"Hm," said Mr Cunningham.

When Mr Cunningham made that remark, people were silent. It was known that the speaker had secret sources of information. In this case the monosyllable had a moral intention. Mr Harford sometimes formed one of a little detachment which left the city shortly after noon on Sunday with the purpose of arriving as soon as possible at some public-house on the outskirts of the city where its members duly qualified themselves as bona fide travellers. But his fellow-travellers had never consented to overlook his origin. He had begun life as an obscure financier by lending small sums of money to workmen at usurious interest. Later on he had become the partner of a very fat, short gentleman, Mr Goldberg, in the Liffey Loan Bank. Though he had never embraced more than the Jewish ethical code, his fellow-Catholics, whenever they had smarted in person or by proxy under his exactions, spoke of him bitterly as an Irish Jew and an illiterate, and saw divine disapproval of usury made manifest through the person of his idiot son. At other times they remembered his good points.

"I wonder where did he go to," said Mr Kernan.

He wished the details of the incident to remain vague. He wished his friends to think there had been some mistake, that Mr Harford and he had missed each other. His friends, who knew quite well Mr Harford's manners in drinking were silent. Mr Power said again:

"All's well that ends well."

Mr Kernan changed the subject at once.

"That was a decent young chap, that medical fellow," he said. "Only for him——"

"O, only for him," said Mr Power, "it might have been a case of seven days, without the option of a fine."

"Yes, yes," said Mr Kernan, trying to remember. "I remember now there was a policeman. Decent young fellow, he seemed. How did it happen at all?"

"It happened that you were peloothered,[5] Tom," said Mr Cunningham gravely.

"True bill," said Mr Kernan, equally gravely.

"I suppose you squared[6] the constable, Jack," said Mr M'Coy.

Mr Power did not relish the use of his Christian name. He was not straight-laced, but he could not forget that Mr M'Coy had recently made a crusade in search of valises and portmanteaus to enable Mrs M'Coy to fulfill imaginary engagements in the country. More than he resented the fact that he had been victimised he resented such low playing of the game. He answered the question, therefore, as if Mr Kernan had asked it.

The narrative made Mr Kernan indignant. He was keenly conscious of his citizenship, wished to live with his city on terms mutually honourable and resented any affront put upon him by those whom he called country bumpkins.

"Is this what we pay rates for?" he asked. "To feed and clothe these ignorant bostoons[7]... and they're nothing else."

Mr Cunningham laughed. He was a Castle official only during office hours.

"How could they be anything else, Tom?" he said.

---

[5] Drunk.
[6] Squared with or came to an agreement.
[7] Buffoons.

He assumed a thick, provincial accent and said in a tone of command:

"65, catch your cabbage!"

Everyone laughed. Mr M'Coy, who wanted to enter the conversation by any door, pretended that he had never heard the story. Mr Cunningham said:

"It is supposed—they say, you know—to take place in the depot where they get these thundering big country fellows, omadhauns,[8] you know, to drill. The sergeant makes them stand in a row against the wall and hold up their plates."

He illustrated the story by grotesque gestures.

"At dinner, you know. Then he has a bloody big bowl of cabbage before him on the table and a bloody big spoon like a shovel. He takes up a wad of cabbage on the spoon and pegs it across the room and the poor devils have to try and catch it on their plates: *65, catch your cabbage.*"

Everyone laughed again: but Mr Kernan was somewhat indignant still. He talked of writing a letter to the papers.

"These yahoos coming up here," he said, "think they can boss the people. I needn't tell you, Martin, what kind of men they are."

Mr Cunningham gave a qualified assent.

"It's like everything else in this world," he said. "You get some bad ones and you get some good ones."

"O yes, you get some good ones, I admit," said Mr Kernan, satisfied.

"It's better to have nothing to say to them," said Mr M'Coy. "That's my opinion!"

Mrs Kernan entered the room and, placing a tray on the table, said:

"Help yourselves, gentlemen."

Mr Power stood up to officiate, offering her his chair. She declined it, saying she was ironing downstairs, and, after having exchanged a nod with Mr Cunningham behind Mr Power's back, prepared to leave the room. Her husband called out to her:

"And have you nothing for me, duckie?"

"O, you! The back of my hand to you!" said Mrs Kernan tartly.

Her husband called after her:

"Nothing for poor little hubby!"

---

[8] Idiots.

He assumed such a comical face and voice that the distribution of the bottles of stout took place amid general merriment.

The gentlemen drank from their glasses, set the glasses again on the table and paused. Then Mr Cunningham turned towards Mr Power and said casually:

"On Thursday night, you said, Jack?"

"Thursday, yes," said Mr Power.

"Righto!" said Mr Cunningham promptly.

"We can meet in M'Auley's," said Mr M'Coy. "That'll be the most convenient place."

"But we mustn't be late," said Mr Power earnestly, "because it is sure to be crammed to the doors."

"We can meet at half-seven," said Mr M'Coy.

"Righto!" said Mr Cunningham.

"Half-seven at M'Auley's be it!"

There was a short silence. Mr Kernan waited to see whether he would be taken into his friends' confidence. Then he asked:

"What's in the wind?"

"O, it's nothing," said Mr Cunningham. "It's only a little matter that we're arranging about for Thursday."

"The opera, is it?" said Mr Kernan.

"No, no," said Mr Cunningham in an evasive tone, "it's just a little… spiritual matter."

"O," said Mr Kernan.

There was silence again. Then Mr Power said, point blank:

"To tell you the truth, Tom, we're going to make a retreat."

"Yes, that's it," said Mr Cunningham, "Jack and I and M'Coy here— we're all going to wash the pot.[9]"

He uttered the metaphor with a certain homely energy and, encouraged by his own voice, proceeded:

"You see, we may as well all admit we're a nice collection of scoundrels, one and all. I say, one and all," he added with gruff charity and turning to Mr Power. "Own up now!"

"I own up," said Mr Power.

"And I own up," said Mr M'Coy.

"So we're going to wash the pot together," said Mr Cunningham.

---

[9] Clear the conscience.

A thought seemed to strike him. He turned suddenly to the invalid and said:

"D'ye know what, Tom, has just occurred to me? You might join in and we'd have a four-handed reel."

"Good idea," said Mr Power. "The four of us together."

Mr Kernan was silent. The proposal conveyed very little meaning to his mind, but, understanding that some spiritual agencies were about to concern themselves on his behalf, he thought he owed it to his dignity to show a stiff neck. He took no part in the conversation for a long while, but listened, with an air of calm enmity, while his friends discussed the Jesuits.

"I haven't such a bad opinion of the Jesuits," he said, intervening at length. "They're an educated order. I believe they mean well, too."

"They're the grandest order in the Church, Tom," said Mr Cunningham, with enthusiasm. "The General of the Jesuits stands next to the Pope."

"There's no mistake about it," said Mr M'Coy, "if you want a thing well done and no flies about, you go to a Jesuit. They're the boyos have influence. I'll tell you a case in point... "

"The Jesuits are a fine body of men," said Mr Power.

"It's a curious thing," said Mr Cunningham, "about the Jesuit Order. Every other order of the Church had to be reformed at some time or other but the Jesuit Order was never once reformed. It never fell away."

"Is that so?" asked Mr M'Coy.

"That's a fact," said Mr Cunningham. "That's history."

"Look at their church, too," said Mr Power. "Look at the congregation they have."

"The Jesuits cater for the upper classes," said Mr M'Coy.

"Of course," said Mr Power.

"Yes," said Mr Kernan. "That's why I have a feeling for them. It's some of those secular priests, ignorant, bumptious——"

"They're all good men," said Mr Cunningham, "each in his own way. The Irish priesthood is honoured all the world over."

"O yes," said Mr Power.

"Not like some of the other priesthoods on the continent," said Mr M'Coy, "unworthy of the name."

"Perhaps you're right," said Mr Kernan, relenting.

"Of course I'm right," said Mr Cunningham. "I haven't been in the world all this time and seen most sides of it without being a judge of character."

The gentlemen drank again, one following another's example. Mr Kernan seemed to be weighing something in his mind. He was impressed. He had a high opinion of Mr Cunningham as a judge of character and as a reader of faces. He asked for particulars.

"O, it's just a retreat, you know," said Mr Cunningham. "Father Purdon is giving it. It's for business men, you know."

"He won't be too hard on us, Tom," said Mr Power persuasively.

"Father Purdon? Father Purdon?" said the invalid.

"O, you must know him, Tom," said Mr Cunningham stoutly. "Fine, jolly fellow! He's a man of the world like ourselves."

"Ah,... yes. I think I know him. Rather red face; tall."

"That's the man."

"And tell me, Martin... Is he a good preacher?"

"Munno... It's not exactly a sermon, you know. It's just kind of a friendly talk, you know, in a common-sense way."

Mr Kernan deliberated. Mr M'Coy said:

"Father Tom Burke, that was the boy!"

"O, Father Tom Burke," said Mr Cunningham, "that was a born orator. Did you ever hear him, Tom?"

"Did I ever hear him!" said the invalid, nettled. "Rather! I heard him..."

"And yet they say he wasn't much of a theologian," said Mr Cunningham.

"Is that so?" said Mr M'Coy.

"O, of course, nothing wrong, you know. Only sometimes, they say, he didn't preach what was quite orthodox."

"Ah!... he was a splendid man," said Mr M'Coy.

"I heard him once," Mr Kernan continued. "I forget the subject of his discourse now. Crofton and I were in the back of the... pit, you know... the———"

"The body," said Mr Cunningham.

"Yes, in the back near the door. I forget now what... O yes, it was on the Pope, the late Pope. I remember it well. Upon my word it was magnificent, the style of the oratory. And his voice! God! Hadn't he a voice! *The Prisoner of the Vatican*, he called him. I remember Crofton saying to me when we came out———"

"But he's an Orangeman, Crofton, isn't he?" said Mr Power.

" 'Course he is," said Mr Kernan, "and a damned decent Orangeman too. We went into Butler's in Moore Street—faith, was genuinely moved, tell you the God's truth—and I remember well his very words. *Kernan*, he said, *we worship at different altars*, he said, *but our belief is the same*. Struck me as very well put."

"There's a good deal in that," said Mr Power. "There used always be crowds of Protestants in the chapel where Father Tom was preaching."

"There's not much difference between us," said Mr M'Coy.

"We both believe in——"

He hesitated for a moment.

"...in the Redeemer. Only they don't believe in the Pope and in the mother of God."

"But, of course," said Mr Cunningham quietly and effectively, "our religion is *the* religion, the old, original faith."

"Not a doubt of it," said Mr Kernan warmly.

Mrs Kernan came to the door of the bedroom and announced:

"Here's a visitor for you!"

"Who is it?"

"Mr Fogarty."

"O, come in! come in!"

A pale, oval face came forward into the light. The arch of its fair trailing moustache was repeated in the fair eyebrows looped above pleasantly astonished eyes. Mr Fogarty was a modest grocer. He had failed in business in a licensed house in the city because his financial condition had constrained him to tie himself to second-class distillers and brewers. He had opened a small shop on Glasnevin Road where, he flattered himself, his manners would ingratiate him with the housewives of the district. He bore himself with a certain grace, complimented little children and spoke with a neat enunciation. He was not without culture.

Mr Fogarty brought a gift with him, a half-pint of special whisky. He inquired politely for Mr Kernan, placed his gift on the table and sat down with the company on equal terms. Mr Kernan appreciated the gift all the more since he was aware that there was a small account for groceries unsettled between him and Mr Fogarty. He said:

"I wouldn't doubt you, old man. Open that, Jack, will you?"

Mr Power again officiated. Glasses were rinsed and five small measures of whisky were poured out. This new influence enlivened the conversation. Mr Fogarty, sitting on a small area of the chair, was specially interested.

"Pope Leo XIII," said Mr Cunningham, "was one of the lights of the age. His great idea, you know, was the union of the Latin and Greek Churches. That was the aim of his life."

"I often heard he was one of the most intellectual men in Europe," said Mr Power. "I mean, apart from his being Pope."

"So he was," said Mr Cunningham, "if not *the* most so. His motto, you know, as Pope, was *Lux upon Lux—Light upon Light.*"

"No, no," said Mr Fogarty eagerly. "I think you're wrong there. It was *Lux in Tenebris,* I think—*Light in Darkness.*"

"O yes," said Mr M'Coy, "*Tenebrae.*"

"Allow me," said Mr Cunningham positively, "it was *Lux upon Lux.* And Pius IX his predecessor's motto was *Crux upon Crux*—that is, Cross upon Cross—to show the difference between their two pontificates."

The inference was allowed. Mr Cunningham continued.

"Pope Leo, you know, was a great scholar and a poet."

"He had a strong face," said Mr Kernan.

"Yes," said Mr Cunningham. "He wrote Latin poetry."

"Is that so?" said Mr Fogarty.

Mr M'Coy tasted his whisky contentedly and shook his head with a double intention, saying:

"That's no joke, I can tell you."

"We didn't learn that, Tom," said Mr Power, following Mr M'Coy's example, "when we went to the penny-a-week school."

"There was many a good man went to the penny-a-week school with a sod of turf under his oxter," said Mr Kernan sententiously. "The old system was the best: plain honest education. None of your modern trumpery..."

"Quite right," said Mr Power.

"No superfluities," said Mr Fogarty.

He enunciated the word and then drank gravely.

"I remember reading," said Mr Cunningham, "that one of Pope Leo's poems was on the invention of the photograph—in Latin, of course."

"On the photograph!" exclaimed Mr Kernan.

"Yes," said Mr Cunningham.

He also drank from his glass.

"Well, you know," said Mr M'Coy, "isn't the photograph wonderful when you come to think of it?"

"O, of course," said Mr Power, "great minds can see things."

"As the poet says: *Great minds are very near to madness*," said Mr Fogarty.

Mr Kernan seemed to be troubled in mind. He made an effort to recall the Protestant theology on some thorny points and in the end addressed Mr Cunningham.

"Tell me, Martin," he said. "Weren't some of the popes—of course, not our present man, or his predecessor, but some of the old popes—not exactly... you know... up to the knocker?[10]"

There was a silence. Mr Cunningham said:

"O, of course, there were some bad lots... But the astonishing thing is this. Not one of them, not the biggest drunkard, not the most... out-and-out ruffian, not one of them ever preached *ex cathedra* a word of false doctrine. Now isn't that an astonishing thing?"

"That is," said Mr Kernan.

"Yes, because when the Pope speaks *ex cathedra*," Mr Fogarty explained, "he is infallible."

"Yes," said Mr Cunningham.

"O, I know about the infallibility of the Pope. I remember I was younger then... Or was it that——?"

Mr Fogarty interrupted. He took up the bottle and helped the others to a little more. Mr M'Coy, seeing that there was not enough to go round, pleaded that he had not finished his first measure. The others accepted under protest. The light music of whisky falling into glasses made an agreeable interlude.

"What's that you were saying, Tom?" asked Mr M'Coy.

"Papal infallibility," said Mr Cunningham, "that was the greatest scene in the whole history of the Church."

"How was that, Martin?" asked Mr Power.

Mr Cunningham held up two thick fingers.

"In the sacred college, you know, of cardinals and archbishops and bishops there were two men who held out against it while the others were all for it. The whole conclave except these two was unanimous. No! They wouldn't have it!"

---

[10] Up to snuff, on the ball.

"Ha!" said Mr M'Coy.

"And they were a German cardinal by the name of Dolling... or Dowling... or——"

"Dowling was no German, and that's a sure five,[11]" said Mr Power, laughing.

"Well, this great German cardinal, whatever his name was, was one; and the other was John MacHale."

"What?" cried Mr Kernan. "Is it John of Tuam?"

"Are you sure of that now?" asked Mr Fogarty dubiously. "I thought it was some Italian or American."

"John of Tuam," repeated Mr Cunningham, "was the man."

He drank and the other gentlemen followed his lead. Then he resumed:

"There they were at it, all the cardinals and bishops and archbishops from all the ends of the earth and these two fighting dog and devil until at last the Pope himself stood up and declared infallibility a dogma of the Church *ex cathedra*. On the very moment John MacHale, who had been arguing and arguing against it, stood up and shouted out with the voice of a lion: '*Credo!*'"

"*I believe!*" said Mr Fogarty.

"*Credo!*" said Mr Cunningham "That showed the faith he had. He submitted the moment the Pope spoke."

"And what about Dowling?" asked Mr M'Coy.

"The German cardinal wouldn't submit. He left the church."

Mr Cunningham's words had built up the vast image of the church in the minds of his hearers. His deep, raucous voice had thrilled them as it uttered the word of belief and submission. When Mrs Kernan came into the room, drying her hands she came into a solemn company. She did not disturb the silence, but leaned over the rail at the foot of the bed.

"I once saw John MacHale," said Mr Kernan, "and I'll never forget it as long as I live."

He turned towards his wife to be confirmed.

"I often told you that?"

Mrs Kernan nodded.

"It was at the unveiling of Sir John Gray's statue. Edmund Dwyer Gray was speaking, blathering away, and here was this old

---

[11] Sure thing.

fellow, crabbed-looking old chap, looking at him from under his bushy eyebrows."

Mr Kernan knitted his brows and, lowering his head like an angry bull, glared at his wife.

"God!" he exclaimed, resuming his natural face, "I never saw such an eye in a man's head. It was as much as to say: *I have you properly taped, my lad*. He had an eye like a hawk."

"None of the Grays was any good," said Mr Power.

There was a pause again. Mr Power turned to Mrs Kernan and said with abrupt joviality:

"Well, Mrs Kernan, we're going to make your man here a good holy pious and God-fearing Roman Catholic."

He swept his arm round the company inclusively.

"We're all going to make a retreat together and confess our sins—and God knows we want it badly."

"I don't mind," said Mr Kernan, smiling a little nervously.

Mrs Kernan thought it would be wiser to conceal her satisfaction. So she said:

"I pity the poor priest that has to listen to your tale."

Mr Kernan's expression changed.

"If he doesn't like it," he said bluntly, "he can…do the other thing. I'll just tell him my little tale of woe. I'm not such a bad fellow——"

Mr Cunningham intervened promptly.

"We'll all renounce the devil," he said, "together, not forgetting his works and pomps."

"Get behind me, Satan!" said Mr Fogarty, laughing and looking at the others.

Mr Power said nothing. He felt completely out-generalled. But a pleased expression flickered across his face.

"All we have to do," said Mr Cunningham, "is to stand up with lighted candles in our hands and renew our baptismal vows."

"O, don't forget the candle, Tom," said Mr M'Coy, "whatever you do."

"What?" said Mr Kernan. "Must I have a candle?"

"O yes," said Mr Cunningham.

"No, damn it all," said Mr Kernan sensibly, "I draw the line there. I'll do the job right enough. I'll do the retreat business and confession, and…all that business. But…no candles! No, damn it all, I bar the candles!"

He shook his head with farcical gravity.

"Listen to that!" said his wife.

"I bar the candles," said Mr Kernan, conscious of having created an effect on his audience and continuing to shake his head to and fro. "I bar the magic-lantern business."

Everyone laughed heartily.

"There's a nice Catholic for you!" said his wife.

"No candles!" repeated Mr Kernan obdurately. "That's off!"

*****

The transept of the Jesuit Church in Gardiner Street was almost full; and still at every moment gentlemen entered from the side door and, directed by the lay-brother, walked on tiptoe along the aisles until they found seating accommodation. The gentlemen were all well dressed and orderly. The light of the lamps of the church fell upon an assembly of black clothes and white collars, relieved here and there by tweeds, on dark mottled pillars of green marble and on lugubrious canvases. The gentlemen sat in the benches, having hitched their trousers slightly above their knees and laid their hats in security. They sat well back and gazed formally at the distant speck of red light which was suspended before the high altar.

In one of the benches near the pulpit sat Mr Cunningham and Mr Kernan. In the bench behind sat Mr M'Coy alone: and in the bench behind him sat Mr Power and Mr Fogarty. Mr M'Coy had tried unsuccessfully to find a place in the bench with the others, and, when the party had settled down in the form of a quincunx, he had tried unsuccessfully to make comic remarks. As these had not been well received, he had desisted. Even he was sensible of the decorous atmosphere and even he began to respond to the religious stimulus. In a whisper, Mr Cunningham drew Mr Kernan's attention to Mr Harford, the moneylender, who sat some distance off, and to Mr Fanning, the registration agent and mayor maker of the city, who was sitting immediately under the pulpit beside one of the newly elected councillors of the ward. To the right sat old Michael Grimes, the owner of three pawnbroker's shops, and Dan Hogan's nephew, who was up for the job in the Town Clerk's office. Farther in front sat Mr Hendrick, the chief reporter of *The Freeman's Journal*, and poor O'Carroll, an old friend of Mr Kernan's, who had been at one time a considerable commercial figure. Gradually, as he recognised familiar faces, Mr Kernan began to feel more at home. His hat, which had been rehabilitated by his wife, rested upon his knees. Once or twice he pulled down his cuffs with one hand while he held the brim of his hat lightly, but firmly, with the other hand.

A powerful-looking figure, the upper part of which was draped with a white surplice, was observed to be struggling into the pulpit. Simultaneously the congregation unsettled, produced handkerchiefs and knelt upon them with care. Mr Kernan followed the general example. The priest's figure now stood upright in the pulpit, two-thirds of its bulk, crowned by a massive red face, appearing above the balustrade.

Father Purdon knelt down, turned towards the red speck of light and, covering his face with his hands, prayed. After an interval, he uncovered his face and rose. The congregation rose also and settled again on its benches. Mr Kernan restored his hat to its original position on his knee and presented an attentive face to the preacher. The preacher turned back each wide sleeve of his surplice with an elaborate large gesture and slowly surveyed the array of faces. Then he said:

"For the children of this world are wiser in their generation than the children of light. Wherefore make unto yourselves friends out of the mammon of iniquity so that when you die they may receive you into everlasting dwellings."

Father Purdon developed the text with resonant assurance. It was one of the most difficult texts in all the Scriptures, he said, to interpret properly. It was a text which might seem to the casual observer at variance with the lofty morality elsewhere preached by Jesus Christ. But, he told his hearers, the text had seemed to him specially adapted for the guidance of those whose lot it was to lead the life of the world and who yet wished to lead that life not in the manner of worldlings. It was a text for business men and professional men. Jesus Christ with His divine understanding of every cranny of our human nature, understood that all men were not called to the religious life, that by far the vast majority were forced to live in the world, and, to a certain extent, for the world: and in this sentence He designed to give them a word of counsel, setting before them as exemplars in the religious life those very worshippers of Mammon who were of all men the least solicitous in matters religious.

He told his hearers that he was there that evening for no terrifying, no extravagant purpose; but as a man of the world speaking to his fellow-men. He came to speak to business men and he would speak to them in a businesslike way. If he might use the metaphor, he said, he was their spiritual accountant; and he wished each and every one of his hearers to open his books, the books of his spiritual life, and see if they tallied accurately with conscience.

Jesus Christ was not a hard taskmaster. He understood our little failings, understood the weakness of our poor fallen nature, understood the temptations of this life. We might have had, we all had from time to time, our temptations: we might have, we all had, our failings. But one thing only, he said, he would ask of his hearers. And that was: to be straight and manly with God. If their accounts tallied in every point to say:

"Well, I have verified my accounts. I find all well."

But if, as might happen, there were some discrepancies, to admit the truth, to be frank and say like a man:

"Well, I have looked into my accounts. I find this wrong and this wrong. But, with God's grace, I will rectify this and this. I will set right my accounts."

CRAFT: GRACE

Parody versus Allegory: Which is it?

Both Warren Beck and Epifanio San Juan Jr., in their analyses of *Dubliners* bring up Stanislaus Joyce's suggestion that the three part structure of "Grace" was in reference to Dante's *Divine Comedy*. Under this interpretation by James Joyce's brother, we might understand "Grace" as a **parody**—imitating and commenting on both Dante's original work and the story itself. Kernan's fall in the beginning of the story reflects Dante's journey into hell in the *Inferno*. His domestic isolation in his bedroom as his tongue heals compares to Dante's experience in *Purgatorio*—the mountain island. Kernan's subsequent arrival at the "retreat" into the hands of Father Purdon is his final arrival in *Paradiso* or heaven.

However, Epifanio San Juan Jr. finds that, "superimposing this abstract scheme is to reduce our complex emotional response into one-dimensional concepts."[1] But it's also important to note that a **parody** is a far different form than an **allegory**. The *Divine Comedy* itself is an allegory of the Christian religious experience and the individual's quest toward God. While a parody imitates an artistic work in order to offer some interpretation or comment on it, an allegory creates characters and situations that represent abstract ideas. A **parody** is literal. An **allegory** is symbolic.

If you were to argue that "Grace" works as a parody, you would point out the obvious connections to Dante, especially the three part structure that represents Dante's descent into hell, the successes and faults of his Christian life, and his ascent to heaven. Alternatively, if you were to argue that "Grace" works as an allegory, you would point

---

[1] Epifanio San Juan, Jr., *James Joyce and the Craft of Fiction* (New Jersey: Associated University Presses, Inc., 1972), 192.

out that Mr. Kernan's accident represents a man's fall, his time in the bedroom represents his religious conversion, and his arrival in the church represents his redemption. This then becomes an allegory for religious salvation.

Therefore, as literary critics we may be far more interested in the allegorical interpretation than we are in the parodic interpretation because it is an abstract **idea** and symbolically diverse—wide open for a range of interpretations. As analyzers of craft, we're interested in both. As a parody of the *Divine Comedy*, this shows us how Joyce may have created his **plot** and **narrative structure**. As an allegory, this shows us how Joyce created the **symbolic architecture** of "Grace." The parodic interpretation about structure may only be a simple point, while the crafting of "Grace" as an allegory leads us deeply into the idea of the story and reflects on the **pathos** and motivations of the characters.

Joyce reveals in the second sentence of this story that the protagonist has literally fallen: "He lay curled up at the foot of the stairs down which he had fallen." Mr. Kernan's embarrassment and the following revelations about his drunkenness indicate this wasn't just a freak accident. We have just witnessed the failure of a man. His wife tells us as much when she reveals to Mr. Power that he has "'been drinking since Friday.'" Furthermore, Joyce reveals that the "arc of [Mr. Power's] social rise intersected the arc of his friend's decline." This shows us parody and allegory together. The parody is Mr. Kernan's fall—Joyce has taken Dante's metaphorical fall in the *Inferno* and turned it into a literal fall here. The allegory, however, stretches deeply into Mr. Kernan's life, and it appears that the literal fall actually represents "the arc" of Mr. Kernan's decline.

Mr. Power tells Mrs. Kernan that "We'll make a new man of him," but she's skeptical. He converted to Catholicism for marriage and she "suspected that a man of her husband's age would not change greatly before death." Her doubt brings tension to this allegorical, religious conversion. The reader wonders if Mr. Kernan's friends will be able to pull it off. As a parody, Joyce suggests that domestic life is a kind of purgatory—a place of purification and judgment.

When they succeed, Joyce provides us with Father Purdon, who instead of offering a difficult challenge on the road to redemption suggests that Jesus Christ "was not a hard taskmaster" and that he "understood our little failings." His message comes down to being "straight and manly with God" and to "set right" one's "accounts." Salvation, it seems, is not a hard road. Redemption is a business exchange with God, and as long we're honest in our accounting, God puts up with our sins.

Just as Joyce creates a dramatic and **dynamic** situation between the **satirical** character of Mrs. Kearney and the realistic character of Mr. Holohan in "A Mother," Joyce creates **tension** and drama between interpretations in "Grace." On the one hand we have both the allegorical and parodic interpretations of this story that suggest that Mr. Kernan finds paradise or salvation at the end of the narrative. However, many readers might find themselves doubting that Mr. Kernan is, in fact, saved. These contrasting interpretations are then thrown into conversation for the reader. Do we have a case of salvation here or a case of **ironic** salvation?

Understatement

It seems apropos to discuss understatement in a story in which the main character bites off part of his tongue and is unable to speak correctly. Understatement is another craft element that often goes under the radar, whereas overstatement sticks out on the page like an expletive thrown into Keats. Writers often call overstatement **"sentimentality,"** or the exaggeration of emotion in a character or a scene in order to force emotion or catharsis in readers.

Joyce is well-known for his understated prose. "The Sisters" offers an interesting example of **understatement** when it comes to emotion. When the narrator's uncle informs him that his "friend is gone," the narrator continues "eating as if the news had not interested" him. Not only do his actions understate his emotions to Old Cotter and his uncle, they understate his emotions to the reader. This narrator seems, at this moment, more interested in guarding his feelings than expressing them.

In "Grace" Mr. Kernan offers a classic understatement about his fall in the pub: " 'Sha, 's nothing.'" First of all, he has bitten off part of his tongue, which explains the broken speech. Second of all, we know it's not nothing the second we read his insistence that it is. Therefore, not only is it an understatement, it's an instance of **verbal irony**. Had he managed to explain that he was drunk and fell down the stairs, the truth would seem less troublesome than his ironic understatement, which indicates his embarrassment and denial.

Mr. Kernan continues to understate the seriousness of his mishap, repeating "'Sha, 's nothing'" to Mr. Power when he comments on the ugliness of his tongue. Even later in the story, when Mr. Cunningham suggests that Mr. Kernan's feeling of sickness is due to the booze, Mr. Kernan responds, "'I think I caught a cold on the car.'" It's not until later that Mr. Kernan finally agrees with Mr. Cunningham that he was "peloothered," or extremely drunk. And, in fact, it's when his understatement ends that he becomes more open to the suggestions of his friends. At that point, the tension shifts away from his denial and into whether or not he will change his ways.

Chiasmus

There are two ways to understand **chiasmus** when considering fiction. The first is as a figure of speech, where a writer constructs a sentence or a series of sentences with a reversal of grammatical structures.

The second involves a broader definition of reversal, in which words, images, characters, or events reverse or intersect. Here, I will focus on this second definition, as it more aptly applies to the fiction writer's craft.

It may help to understand **chiasmus** with its Greek root, which means "to follow in the shape of an X." On the most basic sentence level, we can achieve chiasmus with words. Nietzsche's famous quote about the abyss shows us a chiasmus of words: "…if you gaze into the abyss, the abyss gazes also into you." Here, Nietzsche has reversed the order of the words "you," "gaze," and "abyss" into an ABCCBA structure:

A - You
B - Gaze
C - Abyss
C - Abyss
B - Gaze
A – You

"You" and "gaze" intersect at "abyss":

In "After the Race" Joyce provides an ABCCBA chiasmus of images in his description of the car race:

> In what style they had come careering along the country roads! The journey laid a magical finger on the genuine pulse of life and gallantly the machinery of human nerves strove to answer the bounding courses of the swift blue animal.

Joyce doesn't reverse actual words, but reverses the images he describes with his series of metaphors and descriptive phrases:

A - Careering cars (Car)
B – Magical Finger (Journey)
C - Human nerves (Life)
C – Pulse of life (Life)
B – Bounding courses (Journey)
A – Swift blue animal (Car)

After we associate the metaphors and descriptive phrases with what they represent, we see that he intersects the racing car with the journey. With this chiasmus, this intersection, he suggests that the car and journey intersect at life.

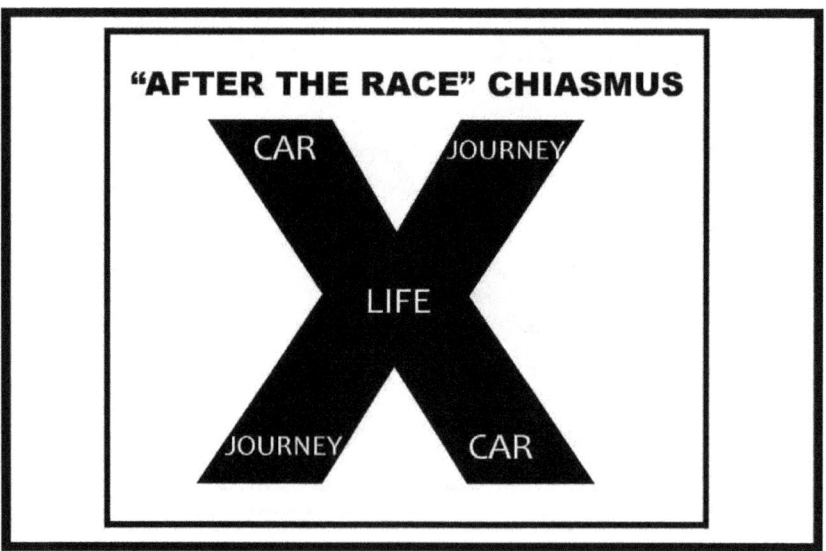

Because the car represents the traveler ("swift blue animal") we might further develop this chiasmus by saying that the journey and the traveler intersect at life, and that this "race" of life is all about the adventure of our journeys (if this sounds hokey or trite, you might understand why Joyce embedded it so deeply in a figurative chiasmus).

I like this example of chiasmus from "After the Race" because it demonstrates both the challenges a writer faces when constructing them, and the feats a writer can achieve. In earlier analysis, I pointed out the awkwardness of the sentence. While some readers may roll their eyes at such a sentence and call it an instance of stretched and mixed **metaphors**, others might argue that mixing is the point—that's the chiasmus: the intersection. Its effect as a chiasmus suggests Joyce's comparison of the journey of the race with a person's journey through life. In fact, it manages to be simultaneously clunky and elegant.

In "Grace," Joyce writes, "The arc of [Mr. Power's] social rise intersected the arc of his friend's decline but Mr Kernan's decline was mitigated by the fact that certain of those friends who had known him at his highest point of success still esteemed him as a character." By now you'll notice the chiasmus that Joyce suggests among these two characters. He even uses the word "intersected," and we can envision the rise of Mr. Power and the fall of Mr. Kernan like this:

This chiasmus that Joyce suggests between Mr. Power and Mr. Kernan reflects a similar chiasmus that occurs between Mr. Kernan and all the men who are trying to "save" him by recruiting him to the Catholic retreat. If readers interpret Mr. Kernan's salvation as **ironic** (suggesting that his fall is only truly complete when he sits down in that church at the end to be saved), a chiasmus occurs between the men and Mr. Kernan. Mr. Kernan loses all the power and esteem he once had and the men succeed in their overpowering of him.

On the other hand, if we read the end as though Mr. Kernan has indeed been saved, it's the other men who gradually lose their dignity throughout the story. As Mr. Kernan spiritually and physically heals, the men, who begin as concerned friends, begin to manipulate and taunt him. They drink in front of him in his bedroom, and their exaggerations about the history of the church indicate that they are cheats.

A reader could easily support either of these interpretations of chiasmus in "Grace," and that may have been Joyce's purpose—for us to question the allegory. After all, the intersection point between all these characters—the very center of that X—is not the pub, but the church.

Questions:

1. If we read this story as an **allegory** for religious salvation, how might we interpret Father Purdon's message at the end of the story? Does Joyce feel that his character has been saved and is now in the hands of those who will help him, or does Joyce indicate that, in fact, Mr. Kernan is in a new kind of trouble? Avoid making assumptions when answering this question. Instead, use craft elements to explain. What allegorical meanings in the story help us interpret moral implications at the end?

2. Can you isolate an instance when the narrator of "Grace" uses **understatement**? How does the understatement work to either increase the reader's curiosity and/or knowledge about a character or event or pass over the poignancy of an event?

3. How does the **chiasmus** between Mr. Power and Mr. Kernan play out in the narrative? What is the effect of this chiasmus on the reader's perception of their relationship?

The Dead

Lily, the caretaker's daughter, was literally run off her feet. Hardly had she brought one gentleman into the little pantry behind the office on the ground floor and helped him off with his overcoat than the wheezy hall-door bell clanged again and she had to scamper along the bare hallway to let in another guest. It was well for her she had not to attend to the ladies also. But Miss Kate and Miss Julia had thought of that and had converted the bathroom upstairs into a ladies' dressing-room. Miss Kate and Miss Julia were there, gossiping and laughing and fussing, walking after each other to the head of the stairs, peering down over the banisters and calling down to Lily to ask her who had come.

It was always a great affair, the Misses Morkan's annual dance. Everybody who knew them came to it, members of the family, old friends of the family, the members of Julia's choir, any of Kate's pupils that were grown up enough, and even some of Mary Jane's pupils too. Never once had it fallen flat. For years and years it had gone off in splendid style, as long as anyone could remember; ever since Kate and Julia, after the death of their brother Pat, had left the house in Stoney Batter and taken Mary Jane, their only niece, to live with them in the dark, gaunt house on Usher's Island, the upper part of which they had rented from Mr Fulham, the corn-factor on the ground floor. That was a good thirty years ago if it was a day. Mary Jane, who was then a little girl in short clothes, was now the main prop of the household, for she had the organ in Haddington Road. She had been through the Academy and gave a pupils' concert every year in the upper room of the Antient Concert Rooms. Many of her pupils belonged to the better-class families on the Kingstown and Dalkey line. Old as they were, her aunts also did their share. Julia, though she was quite grey, was still the leading soprano in Adam and Eve's, and Kate, being too feeble to go about much, gave music lessons to beginners on the old square piano in the back room. Lily, the caretaker's daughter, did housemaid's work for them. Though their life was modest, they believed in eating well; the best of everything: diamond-bone sirloins, three-shilling tea and the best bottled stout. But Lily seldom made a mistake in the orders, so that she got on well with her three mistresses. They were fussy, that was all. But the only thing they would not stand was back answers.[1]

Of course, they had good reason to be fussy on such a night. And then it was long after ten o'clock and yet there was no sign of Gabriel and his wife. Besides they were dreadfully afraid that Freddy Malins might turn up screwed.[2] They would not wish for worlds that any of Mary Jane's pupils should see him under the influence; and when he was like that it was sometimes very hard to manage him. Freddy Malins always came late, but they wondered what could be keeping Gabriel: and that was what brought them every two minutes to the banisters to ask Lily had Gabriel or Freddy come.

"O, Mr Conroy," said Lily to Gabriel when she opened the door for him, "Miss Kate and Miss Julia thought you were never coming. Good-night, Mrs Conroy."

"I'll engage they did," said Gabriel, "but they forget that my wife here takes three mortal hours to dress herself."

He stood on the mat, scraping the snow from his galoshes, while Lily led his wife to the foot of the stairs and called out:

"Miss Kate, here's Mrs Conroy."

Kate and Julia came toddling down the dark stairs at once. Both of them kissed Gabriel's wife, said she must be perished alive, and asked was Gabriel with her.

"Here I am as right as the mail, Aunt Kate! Go on up. I'll follow," called out Gabriel from the dark.

He continued scraping his feet vigorously while the three women went upstairs, laughing, to the ladies' dressing-room. A light fringe of snow lay like a cape on the shoulders of his overcoat and like toecaps on the toes of his galoshes; and, as the buttons of his overcoat slipped with a squeaking noise through the snow-stiffened frieze, a cold, fragrant air from out-of-doors escaped from crevices and folds.

"Is it snowing again, Mr Conroy?" asked Lily.

She had preceded him into the pantry to help him off with his overcoat. Gabriel smiled at the three syllables she had given his surname and glanced at her. She was a slim; growing girl, pale in complexion and with hay-coloured hair. The gas in the pantry made her look still paler. Gabriel had known her when she was a child and used to sit on the lowest step nursing a rag doll.

---

[1] Back talk.
[2] Drunk.

"Yes, Lily," he answered, "and I think we're in for a night of it."

He looked up at the pantry ceiling, which was shaking with the stamping and shuffling of feet on the floor above, listened for a moment to the piano and then glanced at the girl, who was folding his overcoat carefully at the end of a shelf.

"Tell me. Lily," he said in a friendly tone, "do you still go to school?"

"O no, sir," she answered. "I'm done schooling this year and more."

"O, then," said Gabriel gaily, "I suppose we'll be going to your wedding one of these fine days with your young man, eh?"

The girl glanced back at him over her shoulder and said with great bitterness:

"The men that is now is only all palaver[3] and what they can get out of you."

Gabriel coloured, as if he felt he had made a mistake and, without looking at her, kicked off his galoshes and flicked actively with his muffler[4] at his patent-leather shoes.

He was a stout, tallish young man. The high colour of his cheeks pushed upwards even to his forehead, where it scattered itself in a few formless patches of pale red; and on his hairless face there scintillated restlessly the polished lenses and the bright gilt rims of the glasses which screened his delicate and restless eyes. His glossy black hair was parted in the middle and brushed in a long curve behind his ears where it curled slightly beneath the groove left by his hat.

When he had flicked lustre into his shoes he stood up and pulled his waistcoat down more tightly on his plump body. Then he took a coin rapidly from his pocket.

"O Lily," he said, thrusting it into her hands, "it's Christmas-time, isn't it? Just... here's a little..."

He walked rapidly towards the door.

"O no, sir!" cried the girl, following him. "Really, sir, I wouldn't take it."

"Christmas-time! Christmas-time!" said Gabriel, almost trotting to the stairs and waving his hand to her in deprecation.

---

[3] Talk.
[4] Scarf.

The girl, seeing that he had gained the stairs, called out after him:

"Well, thank you, sir."

He waited outside the drawing-room door until the waltz should finish, listening to the skirts that swept against it and to the shuffling of feet. He was still discomposed by the girl's bitter and sudden retort. It had cast a gloom over him which he tried to dispel by arranging his cuffs and the bows of his tie. He then took from his waistcoat pocket a little paper and glanced at the headings he had made for his speech. He was undecided about the lines from Robert Browning, for he feared they would be above the heads of his hearers. Some quotation that they would recognise from Shakespeare or from the Melodies would be better. The indelicate clacking of the men's heels and the shuffling of their soles reminded him that their grade of culture differed from his. He would only make himself ridiculous by quoting poetry to them which they could not understand. They would think that he was airing his superior education. He would fail with them just as he had failed with the girl in the pantry. He had taken up a wrong tone. His whole speech was a mistake from first to last, an utter failure.

Just then his aunts and his wife came out of the ladies' dressing-room. His aunts were two small, plainly dressed old women. Aunt Julia was an inch or so the taller. Her hair, drawn low over the tops of her ears, was grey; and grey also, with darker shadows, was her large flaccid face. Though she was stout in build and stood erect, her slow eyes and parted lips gave her the appearance of a woman who did not know where she was or where she was going. Aunt Kate was more vivacious. Her face, healthier than her sister's, was all puckers and creases, like a shrivelled red apple, and her hair, braided in the same old-fashioned way, had not lost its ripe nut colour.

They both kissed Gabriel frankly. He was their favourite nephew, the son of their dead elder sister, Ellen, who had married T. J. Conroy of the Port and Docks.

"Gretta tells me you're not going to take a cab back to Monkstown tonight, Gabriel," said Aunt Kate.

"No," said Gabriel, turning to his wife, "we had quite enough of that last year, hadn't we? Don't you remember, Aunt Kate, what a cold Gretta got out of it? Cab windows rattling all the way, and the east wind blowing in after we passed Merrion. Very jolly it was. Gretta caught a dreadful cold."

Aunt Kate frowned severely and nodded her head at every word.

"Quite right, Gabriel, quite right," she said. "You can't be too careful."

"But as for Gretta there," said Gabriel, "she'd walk home in the snow if she were let."

Mrs Conroy laughed.

"Don't mind him, Aunt Kate," she said. "He's really an awful bother, what with green shades for Tom's eyes at night and making him do the dumb-bells, and forcing Eva to eat the stirabout. The poor child! And she simply hates the sight of it!... O, but you'll never guess what he makes me wear now!"

She broke out into a peal of laughter and glanced at her husband, whose admiring and happy eyes had been wandering from her dress to her face and hair. The two aunts laughed heartily, too, for Gabriel's solicitude was a standing joke with them.

"Galoshes!" said Mrs Conroy. "That's the latest. Whenever it's wet underfoot I must put on my galoshes. Tonight even, he wanted me to put them on, but I wouldn't. The next thing he'll buy me will be a diving suit."

Gabriel laughed nervously and patted his tie reassuringly, while Aunt Kate nearly doubled herself, so heartily did she enjoy the joke. The smile soon faded from Aunt Julia's face and her mirthless eyes were directed towards her nephew's face. After a pause she asked:

"And what are galoshes, Gabriel?"

"Galoshes, Julia!" exclaimed her sister "Goodness me, don't you know what galoshes are? You wear them over your... over your boots, Gretta, isn't it?"

"Yes," said Mrs Conroy. "Guttapercha[5] things. We both have a pair now. Gabriel says everyone wears them on the Continent."

"O, on the Continent," murmured Aunt Julia, nodding her head slowly.

Gabriel knitted his brows and said, as if he were slightly angered:

"It's nothing very wonderful, but Gretta thinks it very funny because she says the word reminds her of Christy Minstrels."

---

[5] Rubbery.

"But tell me, Gabriel," said Aunt Kate, with brisk tact. "Of course, you've seen about the room. Gretta was saying…"

"O, the room is all right," replied Gabriel. "I've taken one in the Gresham."

"To be sure," said Aunt Kate, "by far the best thing to do. And the children, Gretta, you're not anxious about them?"

"O, for one night," said Mrs Conroy. "Besides, Bessie will look after them."

"To be sure," said Aunt Kate again. "What a comfort it is to have a girl like that, one you can depend on! There's that Lily, I'm sure I don't know what has come over her lately. She's not the girl she was at all."

Gabriel was about to ask his aunt some questions on this point, but she broke off suddenly to gaze after her sister, who had wandered down the stairs and was craning her neck over the banisters.

"Now, I ask you," she said almost testily, "where is Julia going? Julia! Julia! Where are you going?"

Julia, who had gone half way down one flight, came back and announced blandly:

"Here's Freddy."

At the same moment a clapping of hands and a final flourish of the pianist told that the waltz had ended. The drawing-room door was opened from within and some couples came out. Aunt Kate drew Gabriel aside hurriedly and whispered into his ear:

"Slip down, Gabriel, like a good fellow and see if he's all right, and don't let him up if he's screwed. I'm sure he's screwed. I'm sure he is."

Gabriel went to the stairs and listened over the banisters. He could hear two persons talking in the pantry. Then he recognised Freddy Malins' laugh. He went down the stairs noisily.

"It's such a relief," said Aunt Kate to Mrs Conroy, "that Gabriel is here. I always feel easier in my mind when he's here… Julia, there's Miss Daly and Miss Power will take some refreshment. Thanks for your beautiful waltz, Miss Daly. It made lovely time."

A tall wizen-faced man, with a stiff grizzled moustache and swarthy skin, who was passing out with his partner, said:

"And may we have some refreshment, too, Miss Morkan?"

"Julia," said Aunt Kate summarily, "and here's Mr Browne and Miss Furlong. Take them in, Julia, with Miss Daly and Miss Power."

"I'm the man for the ladies," said Mr Browne, pursing his lips until his moustache bristled and smiling in all his wrinkles. "You know, Miss Morkan, the reason they are so fond of me is——"

He did not finish his sentence, but, seeing that Aunt Kate was out of earshot, at once led the three young ladies into the back room. The middle of the room was occupied by two square tables placed end to end, and on these Aunt Julia and the caretaker were straightening and smoothing a large cloth. On the sideboard were arrayed dishes and plates, and glasses and bundles of knives and forks and spoons. The top of the closed square piano served also as a sideboard for viands[6] and sweets. At a smaller sideboard in one corner two young men were standing, drinking hop-bitters.

Mr Browne led his charges thither and invited them all, in jest, to some ladies' punch, hot, strong and sweet. As they said they never took anything strong, he opened three bottles of lemonade for them. Then he asked one of the young men to move aside, and, taking hold of the decanter, filled out for himself a goodly measure of whisky. The young men eyed him respectfully while he took a trial sip.

"God help me," he said, smiling, "it's the doctor's orders."

His wizened face broke into a broader smile, and the three young ladies laughed in musical echo to his pleasantry, swaying their bodies to and fro, with nervous jerks of their shoulders. The boldest said:

"O, now, Mr Browne, I'm sure the doctor never ordered anything of the kind."

Mr Browne took another sip of his whisky and said, with sidling mimicry:

"Well, you see, I'm like the famous Mrs Cassidy, who is reported to have said: 'Now, Mary Grimes, if I don't take it, make me take it, for I feel I want it.'"

His hot face had leaned forward a little too confidentially and he had assumed a very low Dublin accent so that the young ladies, with one instinct, received his speech in silence. Miss Furlong, who was one of Mary Jane's pupils, asked Miss Daly what was the name of the pretty waltz she had played; and Mr Browne, seeing that he was ignored, turned promptly to the two young men who were more appreciative.

---

[6] Food.

A red-faced young woman, dressed in pansy, came into the room, excitedly clapping her hands and crying:

"Quadrilles! Quadrilles!"[7]

Close on her heels came Aunt Kate, crying:

"Two gentlemen and three ladies, Mary Jane!"

"O, here's Mr Bergin and Mr Kerrigan," said Mary Jane. "Mr Kerrigan, will you take Miss Power? Miss Furlong, may I get you a partner, Mr Bergin. O, that'll just do now."

"Three ladies, Mary Jane," said Aunt Kate.

The two young gentlemen asked the ladies if they might have the pleasure, and Mary Jane turned to Miss Daly.

"O, Miss Daly, you're really awfully good, after playing for the last two dances, but really we're so short of ladies tonight."

"I don't mind in the least, Miss Morkan."

"But I've a nice partner for you, Mr Bartell D'Arcy, the tenor. I'll get him to sing later on. All Dublin is raving about him."

"Lovely voice, lovely voice!" said Aunt Kate.

As the piano had twice begun the prelude to the first figure Mary Jane led her recruits quickly from the room. They had hardly gone when Aunt Julia wandered slowly into the room, looking behind her at something.

"What is the matter, Julia?" asked Aunt Kate anxiously. "Who is it?"

Julia, who was carrying in a column of table-napkins, turned to her sister and said, simply, as if the question had surprised her:

"It's only Freddy, Kate, and Gabriel with him."

In fact right behind her Gabriel could be seen piloting Freddy Malins across the landing. The latter, a young man of about forty, was of Gabriel's size and build, with very round shoulders. His face was fleshy and pallid, touched with colour only at the thick hanging lobes of his ears and at the wide wings of his nose. He had coarse features, a blunt nose, a convex and receding brow, tumid and protruded lips. His heavy-lidded eyes and the disorder of his scanty hair made him look sleepy. He was laughing heartily in a high key at a story which he had been telling Gabriel on the stairs and at the same time rubbing the knuckles of his left fist backwards and forwards into his left eye.

"Good-evening, Freddy," said Aunt Julia.

---

[7] Type of square dance.

Freddy Malins bade the Misses Morkan good-evening in what seemed an offhand fashion by reason of the habitual catch in his voice and then, seeing that Mr Browne was grinning at him from the sideboard, crossed the room on rather shaky legs and began to repeat in an undertone the story he had just told to Gabriel.

"He's not so bad, is he?" said Aunt Kate to Gabriel.

Gabriel's brows were dark but he raised them quickly and answered:

"O, no, hardly noticeable."

"Now, isn't he a terrible fellow!" she said. "And his poor mother made him take the pledge on New Year's Eve. But come on, Gabriel, into the drawing-room."

Before leaving the room with Gabriel she signalled to Mr Browne by frowning and shaking her forefinger in warning to and fro. Mr Browne nodded in answer and, when she had gone, said to Freddy Malins:

"Now, then, Teddy, I'm going to fill you out a good glass of lemonade just to buck you up."

Freddy Malins, who was nearing the climax of his story, waved the offer aside impatiently but Mr Browne, having first called Freddy Malins' attention to a disarray in his dress, filled out and handed him a full glass of lemonade. Freddy Malins' left hand accepted the glass mechanically, his right hand being engaged in the mechanical readjustment of his dress. Mr Browne, whose face was once more wrinkling with mirth, poured out for himself a glass of whisky while Freddy Malins exploded, before he had well reached the climax of his story, in a kink of high-pitched bronchitic laughter and, setting down his untasted and overflowing glass, began to rub the knuckles of his left fist backwards and forwards into his left eye, repeating words of his last phrase as well as his fit of laughter would allow him.

Gabriel could not listen while Mary Jane was playing her Academy piece, full of runs and difficult passages, to the hushed drawing-room. He liked music but the piece she was playing had no melody for him and he doubted whether it had any melody for the other listeners, though they had begged Mary Jane to play something. Four young men, who had come from the refreshment-room to stand in the doorway at the sound of the piano, had gone away quietly in couples after a few minutes. The only persons who seemed to follow the music were Mary Jane herself, her hands racing along the key-board or lifted from it at the pauses like those of a priestess in momentary imprecation, and Aunt Kate standing at her elbow to turn the page.

Gabriel's eyes, irritated by the floor, which glittered with beeswax under the heavy chandelier, wandered to the wall above the piano. A picture of the balcony scene in *Romeo and Juliet* hung there and beside it was a picture of the two murdered princes in the Tower which Aunt Julia had worked in red, blue and brown wools when she was a girl. Probably in the school they had gone to as girls that kind of work had been taught for one year. His mother had worked for him as a birthday present a waistcoat of purple tabinet,[8] with little foxes' heads upon it, lined with brown satin and having round mulberry buttons. It was strange that his mother had had no musical talent though Aunt Kate used to call her the brains carrier of the Morkan family. Both she and Julia had always seemed a little proud of their serious and matronly sister. Her photograph stood before the pierglass. She held an open book on her knees and was pointing out something in it to Constantine who, dressed in a man-o-war suit, lay at her feet. It was she who had chosen the name of her sons for she was very sensible of the dignity of family life. Thanks to her, Constantine was now senior curate in Balbrigan and, thanks to her, Gabriel himself had taken his degree in the Royal University. A shadow passed over his face as he remembered her sullen opposition to his marriage. Some slighting phrases she had used still rankled in his memory; she had once spoken of Gretta as being country cute and that was not true of Gretta at all. It was Gretta who had nursed her during all her last long illness in their house at Monkstown.

He knew that Mary Jane must be near the end of her piece for she was playing again the opening melody with runs of scales after every bar and while he waited for the end the resentment died down in his heart. The piece ended with a trill of octaves in the treble and a final deep octave in the bass. Great applause greeted Mary Jane as, blushing and rolling up her music nervously, she escaped from the room. The most vigorous clapping came from the four young men in the doorway who had gone away to the refreshment-room at the beginning of the piece but had come back when the piano had stopped.

---

[8] A type of fabric.

Lancers were arranged. Gabriel found himself partnered with Miss Ivors. She was a frank-mannered talkative young lady, with a freckled face and prominent brown eyes. She did not wear a low-cut bodice and the large brooch which was fixed in the front of her collar bore on it an Irish device and motto.

When they had taken their places she said abruptly:

"I have a crow to pluck[9] with you."

"With me?" said Gabriel.

She nodded her head gravely.

"What is it?" asked Gabriel, smiling at her solemn manner.

"Who is G. C.?" answered Miss Ivors, turning her eyes upon him.

Gabriel coloured and was about to knit his brows, as if he did not understand, when she said bluntly:

"O, innocent Amy! I have found out that you write for *The Daily Express*. Now, aren't you ashamed of yourself?"

"Why should I be ashamed of myself?" asked Gabriel, blinking his eyes and trying to smile.

"Well, I'm ashamed of you," said Miss Ivors frankly. "To say you'd write for a paper like that. I didn't think you were a West Briton."

A look of perplexity appeared on Gabriel's face. It was true that he wrote a literary column every Wednesday in *The Daily Express*, for which he was paid fifteen shillings. But that did not make him a West Briton surely. The books he received for review were almost more welcome than the paltry cheque. He loved to feel the covers and turn over the pages of newly printed books. Nearly every day when his teaching in the college was ended he used to wander down the quays to the second-hand booksellers, to Hickey's on Bachelor's Walk, to Web's or Massey's on Aston's Quay, or to O'Clohissey's in the bystreet. He did not know how to meet her charge. He wanted to say that literature was above politics. But they were friends of many years' standing and their careers had been parallel, first at the University and then as teachers: he could not risk a grandiose phrase with her. He continued blinking his eyes and trying to smile and murmured lamely that he saw nothing political in writing reviews of books.

---

[9] Bone to pick.

When their turn to cross had come he was still perplexed and inattentive. Miss Ivors promptly took his hand in a warm grasp and said in a soft friendly tone:

"Of course, I was only joking. Come, we cross now."

When they were together again she spoke of the University question and Gabriel felt more at ease. A friend of hers had shown her his review of Browning's poems. That was how she had found out the secret: but she liked the review immensely. Then she said suddenly:

"O, Mr Conroy, will you come for an excursion to the Aran Isles this summer? We're going to stay there a whole month. It will be splendid out in the Atlantic. You ought to come. Mr Clancy is coming, and Mr Kilkelly and Kathleen Kearney. It would be splendid for Gretta too if she'd come. She's from Connacht, isn't she?"

"Her people are," said Gabriel shortly.

"But you will come, won't you?" said Miss Ivors, laying her arm hand eagerly on his arm.

"The fact is," said Gabriel, "I have just arranged to go——"

"Go where?" asked Miss Ivors.

"Well, you know, every year I go for a cycling tour with some fellows and so——"

"But where?" asked Miss Ivors.

"Well, we usually go to France or Belgium or perhaps Germany," said Gabriel awkwardly.

"And why do you go to France and Belgium," said Miss Ivors, "instead of visiting your own land?"

"Well," said Gabriel, "it's partly to keep in touch with the languages and partly for a change."

"And haven't you your own language to keep in touch with—Irish?" asked Miss Ivors.

"Well," said Gabriel, "if it comes to that, you know, Irish is not my language."

Their neighbours had turned to listen to the cross-examination. Gabriel glanced right and left nervously and tried to keep his good humour under the ordeal which was making a blush invade his forehead.

"And haven't you your own land to visit," continued Miss Ivors, "that you know nothing of, your own people, and your own country?"

"O, to tell you the truth," retorted Gabriel suddenly, "I'm sick of my own country, sick of it!"

"Why?" asked Miss Ivors.

Gabriel did not answer for his retort had heated him.

"Why?" repeated Miss Ivors.

They had to go visiting together[10] and, as he had not answered her, Miss Ivors said warmly:

"Of course, you've no answer."

Gabriel tried to cover his agitation by taking part in the dance with great energy. He avoided her eyes for he had seen a sour expression on her face. But when they met in the long chain he was surprised to feel his hand firmly pressed. She looked at him from under her brows for a moment quizzically until he smiled. Then, just as the chain was about to start again, she stood on tiptoe and whispered into his ear:

"West Briton!"

When the lancers were over Gabriel went away to a remote corner of the room where Freddy Malins' mother was sitting. She was a stout feeble old woman with white hair. Her voice had a catch in it like her son's and she stuttered slightly. She had been told that Freddy had come and that he was nearly all right. Gabriel asked her whether she had had a good crossing. She lived with her married daughter in Glasgow and came to Dublin on a visit once a year. She answered placidly that she had had a beautiful crossing and that the captain had been most attentive to her. She spoke also of the beautiful house her daughter kept in Glasgow, and of all the friends they had there. While her tongue rambled on Gabriel tried to banish from his mind all memory of the unpleasant incident with Miss Ivors. Of course the girl or woman, or whatever she was, was an enthusiast but there was a time for all things. Perhaps he ought not to have answered her like that. But she had no right to call him a West Briton before people, even in joke. She had tried to make him ridiculous before people, heckling him and staring at him with her rabbit's eyes.

He saw his wife making her way towards him through the waltzing couples. When she reached him she said into his ear:

"Gabriel. Aunt Kate wants to know won't you carve the goose as usual. Miss Daly will carve the ham and I'll do the pudding."

"All right," said Gabriel.

---

[10] Separate.

"She's sending in the younger ones first as soon as this waltz is over so that we'll have the table to ourselves."

"Were you dancing?" asked Gabriel.

"Of course I was. Didn't you see me? What row had you with Molly Ivors?"

"No row. Why? Did she say so?"

"Something like that. I'm trying to get that Mr D'Arcy to sing. He's full of conceit, I think."

"There was no row," said Gabriel moodily, "only she wanted me to go for a trip to the west of Ireland and I said I wouldn't."

His wife clasped her hands excitedly and gave a little jump.

"O, do go, Gabriel," she cried. "I'd love to see Galway again."

"You can go if you like," said Gabriel coldly.

She looked at him for a moment, then turned to Mrs Malins and said:

"There's a nice husband for you, Mrs Malins."

While she was threading her way back across the room Mrs Malins, without adverting to the interruption, went on to tell Gabriel what beautiful places there were in Scotland and beautiful scenery. Her son-inlaw brought them every year to the lakes and they used to go fishing. Her son-in-law was a splendid fisher. One day he caught a beautiful big fish and the man in the hotel cooked it for their dinner.

Gabriel hardly heard what she said. Now that supper was coming near he began to think again about his speech and about the quotation. When he saw Freddy Malins coming across the room to visit his mother Gabriel left the chair free for him and retired into the embrasure of the window. The room had already cleared and from the back room came the clatter of plates and knives. Those who still remained in the drawing room seemed tired of dancing and were conversing quietly in little groups. Gabriel's warm trembling fingers tapped the cold pane of the window. How cool it must be outside! How pleasant it would be to walk out alone, first along by the river and then through the park! The snow would be lying on the branches of the trees and forming a bright cap on the top of the Wellington Monument. How much more pleasant it would be there than at the supper-table!

He ran over the headings of his speech: Irish hospitality, sad memories, the Three Graces, Paris, the quotation from Browning. He repeated to himself a phrase he had written in his review: *One feels that one is listening to a thought-tormented music.* Miss Ivors had praised the review. Was she sincere? Had she really any life of her own behind all her propagandism? There had never been any ill-feeling between them until that night. It unnerved him to think that she would be at the supper-table, looking up at him while he spoke with her critical quizzing eyes. Perhaps she would not be sorry to see him fail in his speech. An idea came into his mind and gave him courage. He would say, alluding to Aunt Kate and Aunt Julia: *Ladies and Gentlemen, the generation which is now on the wane among us may have had its faults but for my part I think it had certain qualities of hospitality, of humour, of humanity, which the new and very serious and hypereducated generation that is growing up around us seems to me to lack.* Very good: that was one for Miss Ivors. What did he care that his aunts were only two ignorant old women?

A murmur in the room attracted his attention. Mr Browne was advancing from the door, gallantly escorting Aunt Julia, who leaned upon his arm, smiling and hanging her head. An irregular musketry of applause escorted her also as far as the piano and then, as Mary Jane seated herself on the stool, and Aunt Julia, no longer smiling, half turned so as to pitch her voice fairly into the room, gradually ceased. Gabriel recognised the prelude. It was that of an old song of Aunt Julia's—*Arrayed for the Bridal*. Her voice, strong and clear in tone, attacked with great spirit the runs which embellish the air and though she sang very rapidly she did not miss even the smallest of the grace notes. To follow the voice, without looking at the singer's face, was to feel and share the excitement of swift and secure flight. Gabriel applauded loudly with all the others at the close of the song and loud applause was borne in from the invisible supper-table. It sounded so genuine that a little colour struggled into Aunt Julia's face as she bent to replace in the music-stand the old leather-bound songbook that had her initials on the cover. Freddy Malins, who had listened with his head perched sideways to hear her better, was still applauding when everyone else had ceased and talking animatedly to his mother who nodded her head gravely and slowly in acquiescence. At last, when he could clap no more, he stood up suddenly and hurried across the room to Aunt Julia whose hand he seized and held in both his hands, shaking it when words failed him or the catch in his voice proved too much for him.

"I was just telling my mother," he said, "I never heard you sing so well, never. No, I never heard your voice so good as it is to-night. Now! Would you believe that now? That's the truth. Upon my word and honour that's the truth. I never heard your voice sound so fresh and so… so clear and fresh, never."

Aunt Julia smiled broadly and murmured something about compliments as she released her hand from his grasp. Mr Browne extended his open hand towards her and said to those who were near him in the manner of a showman introducing a prodigy to an audience:

"Miss Julia Morkan, my latest discovery!"

He was laughing very heartily at this himself when Freddy Malins turned to him and said:

"Well, Browne, if you're serious you might make a worse discovery. All I can say is I never heard her sing half so well as long as I am coming here. And that's the honest truth."

"Neither did I," said Mr Browne. "I think her voice has greatly improved."

Aunt Julia shrugged her shoulders and said with meek pride:

"Thirty years ago I hadn't a bad voice as voices go."

"I often told Julia," said Aunt Kate emphatically, "that she was simply thrown away in that choir. But she never would be said by me."

She turned as if to appeal to the good sense of the others against a refractory child while Aunt Julia gazed in front of her, a vague smile of reminiscence playing on her face.

"No," continued Aunt Kate, "she wouldn't be said or led by anyone, slaving there in that choir night and day, night and day. Six o'clock on Christmas morning! And all for what?"

"Well, isn't it for the honour of God, Aunt Kate?" asked Mary Jane, twisting round on the piano-stool and smiling.

Aunt Kate turned fiercely on her niece and said:

"I know all about the honour of God, Mary Jane, but I think it's not at all honourable for the Pope to turn out the women out of the choirs that have slaved there all their lives and put little whipper-snappers of boys over their heads. I suppose it is for the good of the Church if the Pope does it. But it's not just, Mary Jane, and it's not right."

She had worked herself into a passion and would have continued in defence of her sister for it was a sore subject with her but Mary Jane, seeing that all the dancers had come back, intervened pacifically:

"Now, Aunt Kate, you're giving scandal to Mr Browne who is of the other persuasion."

Aunt Kate turned to Mr Browne, who was grinning at this allusion to his religion, and said hastily:

"O, I don't question the Pope's being right. I'm only a stupid old woman and I wouldn't presume to do such a thing. But there's such a thing as common everyday politeness and gratitude. And if I were in Julia's place I'd tell that Father Healey straight up to his face…"

"And besides, Aunt Kate," said Mary Jane, "we really are all hungry and when we are hungry we are all very quarrelsome."

"And when we are thirsty we are also quarrelsome," added Mr Browne.

"So that we had better go to supper," said Mary Jane, "and finish the discussion afterwards."

On the landing outside the drawing-room Gabriel found his wife and Mary Jane trying to persuade Miss Ivors to stay for supper. But Miss Ivors, who had put on her hat and was buttoning her cloak, would not stay. She did not feel in the least hungry and she had already overstayed her time.

"But only for ten minutes, Molly," said Mrs Conroy. "That won't delay you."

"To take a pick itself," said Mary Jane, "after all your dancing."

"I really couldn't," said Miss Ivors.

"I am afraid you didn't enjoy yourself at all," said Mary Jane hopelessly.

"Ever so much, I assure you," said Miss Ivors, "but you really must let me run off now."

"But how can you get home?" asked Mrs Conroy.

"O, it's only two steps up the quay."

Gabriel hesitated a moment and said:

"If you will allow me, Miss Ivors, I'll see you home if you are really obliged to go."

But Miss Ivors broke away from them.

"I won't hear of it," she cried. "For goodness' sake go in to your suppers and don't mind me. I'm quite well able to take care of myself."

"Well, you're the comical girl, Molly," said Mrs Conroy frankly.

"*Beannacht libh,*"[11] cried Miss Ivors, with a laugh, as she ran down the staircase.

Mary Jane gazed after her, a moody puzzled expression on her face, while Mrs Conroy leaned over the banisters to listen for the hall-door. Gabriel asked himself was he the cause of her abrupt departure. But she did not seem to be in ill humour: she had gone away laughing. He stared blankly down the staircase.

At the moment Aunt Kate came toddling out of the supper-room, almost wringing her hands in despair.

"Where is Gabriel?" she cried. "Where on earth is Gabriel? There's everyone waiting in there, stage to let, and nobody to carve the goose!"

"Here I am, Aunt Kate!" cried Gabriel, with sudden animation, "ready to carve a flock of geese, if necessary."

A fat brown goose lay at one end of the table and at the other end, on a bed of creased paper strewn with sprigs of parsley, lay a great ham, stripped of its outer skin and peppered over with crust crumbs, a neat paper frill round its shin and beside this was a round of spiced beef. Between these rival ends ran parallel lines of side-dishes: two little minsters of jelly, red and yellow; a shallow dish full of blocks of blancmange[12] and red jam, a large green leaf-shaped dish with a stalk-shaped handle, on which lay bunches of purple raisins and peeled almonds, a companion dish on which lay a solid rectangle of Smyrna figs, a dish of custard topped with grated nutmeg, a small bowl full of chocolates and sweets wrapped in gold and silver papers and a glass vase in which stood some tall celery stalks. In the centre of the table there stood, as sentries to a fruit-stand which upheld a pyramid of oranges and American apples, two squat old-fashioned decanters of cut glass, one containing port and the other dark sherry. On the closed square piano a pudding in a huge yellow dish lay in waiting and behind it were three squads of bottles of stout and ale and minerals, drawn up according to the colours of their uniforms, the first two black, with brown and red labels, the third and smallest squad white, with transverse green sashes.

Gabriel took his seat boldly at the head of the table and, having looked to the edge of the carver, plunged his fork firmly into the goose. He felt quite at ease now for he was an expert carver and

---

[11] Bless you.
[12] A sweet pudding.

liked nothing better than to find himself at the head of a well-laden table.

"Miss Furlong, what shall I send you?" he asked. "A wing or a slice of the breast?"

"Just a small slice of the breast."

"Miss Higgins, what for you?"

"O, anything at all, Mr Conroy."

While Gabriel and Miss Daly exchanged plates of goose and plates of ham and spiced beef Lily went from guest to guest with a dish of hot floury potatoes wrapped in a white napkin. This was Mary Jane's idea and she had also suggested apple sauce for the goose but Aunt Kate had said that plain roast goose without any apple sauce had always been good enough for her and she hoped she might never eat worse. Mary Jane waited on her pupils and saw that they got the best slices and Aunt Kate and Aunt Julia opened and carried across from the piano bottles of stout and ale for the gentlemen and bottles of minerals for the ladies. There was a great deal of confusion and laughter and noise, the noise of orders and counter-orders, of knives and forks, of corks and glass-stoppers. Gabriel began to carve second helpings as soon as he had finished the first round without serving himself. Everyone protested loudly so that he compromised by taking a long draught of stout for he had found the carving hot work. Mary Jane settled down quietly to her supper but Aunt Kate and Aunt Julia were still toddling round the table, walking on each other's heels, getting in each other's way and giving each other unheeded orders. Mr Browne begged of them to sit down and eat their suppers and so did Gabriel but they said there was time enough, so that, at last, Freddy Malins stood up and, capturing Aunt Kate, plumped her down on her chair amid general laughter.

When everyone had been well served Gabriel said, smiling:

"Now, if anyone wants a little more of what vulgar people call stuffing let him or her speak."

A chorus of voices invited him to begin his own supper and Lily came forward with three potatoes which she had reserved for him.

"Very well," said Gabriel amiably, as he took another preparatory draught, "kindly forget my existence, ladies and gentlemen, for a few minutes."

He set to his supper and took no part in the conversation with which the table covered Lily's removal of the plates. The subject of talk was the opera company which was then at the Theatre Royal. Mr Bartell D'Arcy, the tenor, a dark-complexioned young man with a smart moustache, praised very highly the leading contralto of the company but Miss Furlong thought she had a rather vulgar style of production. Freddy Malins said there was a Negro chieftain singing in the second part of the Gaiety pantomime who had one of the finest tenor voices he had ever heard.

"Have you heard him?" he asked Mr Bartell D'Arcy across the table.

"No," answered Mr Bartell D'Arcy carelessly.

"Because," Freddy Malins explained, "now I'd be curious to hear your opinion of him. I think he has a grand voice."

"It takes Teddy to find out the really good things," said Mr Browne familiarly to the table.

"And why couldn't he have a voice too?" asked Freddy Malins sharply. "Is it because he's only a black?"

Nobody answered this question and Mary Jane led the table back to the legitimate opera. One of her pupils had given her a pass for *Mignon*. Of course it was very fine, she said, but it made her think of poor Georgina Burns. Mr Browne could go back farther still, to the old Italian companies that used to come to Dublin—Tietjens, Ilma de Murzka, Campanini, the great Trebelli, Giuglini, Ravelli, Aramburo. Those were the days, he said, when there was something like singing to be heard in Dublin. He told too of how the top gallery of the old Royal used to be packed night after night, of how one night an Italian tenor had sung five encores to *Let me like a Soldier Fall*, introducing a high C every time, and of how the gallery boys would sometimes in their enthusiasm unyoke the horses from the carriage of some great *prima donna* and pull her themselves through the streets to her hotel. Why did they never play the grand old operas now, he asked, *Dinorah*, *Lucrezia Borgia*? Because they could not get the voices to sing them: that was why.

"Oh, well," said Mr Bartell D'Arcy, "I presume there are as good singers to-day as there were then."

"Where are they?" asked Mr Browne defiantly.

"In London, Paris, Milan," said Mr Bartell D'Arcy warmly. "I suppose Caruso, for example, is quite as good, if not better than any of the men you have mentioned."

"Maybe so," said Mr Browne. "But I may tell you I doubt it strongly."

"O, I'd give anything to hear Caruso sing," said Mary Jane.

"For me," said Aunt Kate, who had been picking a bone, "there was only one tenor. To please me, I mean. But I suppose none of you ever heard of him."

"Who was he, Miss Morkan?" asked Mr Bartell D'Arcy politely.

"His name," said Aunt Kate, "was Parkinson. I heard him when he was in his prime and I think he had then the purest tenor voice that was ever put into a man's throat."

"Strange," said Mr Bartell D'Arcy. "I never even heard of him."

"Yes, yes, Miss Morkan is right," said Mr Browne. "I remember hearing of old Parkinson but he's too far back for me."

"A beautiful, pure, sweet, mellow English tenor," said Aunt Kate with enthusiasm.

Gabriel having finished, the huge pudding was transferred to the table. The clatter of forks and spoons began again. Gabriel's wife served out spoonfuls of the pudding and passed the plates down the table. Midway down they were held up by Mary Jane, who replenished them with raspberry or orange jelly or with blancmange and jam. The pudding was of Aunt Julia's making and she received praises for it from all quarters. She herself said that it was not quite brown enough.

"Well, I hope, Miss Morkan," said Mr Browne, "that I'm brown enough for you because, you know, I'm all brown."

All the gentlemen, except Gabriel, ate some of the pudding out of compliment to Aunt Julia. As Gabriel never ate sweets the celery had been left for him. Freddy Malins also took a stalk of celery and ate it with his pudding. He had been told that celery was a capital thing for the blood and he was just then under doctor's care. Mrs Malins, who had been silent all through the supper, said that her son was going down to Mount Melleray in a week or so. The table then spoke of Mount Melleray, how bracing the air was down there, how hospitable the monks were and how they never asked for a penny-piece from their guests.

"And do you mean to say," asked Mr Browne incredulously, "that a chap can go down there and put up there as if it were a hotel and live on the fat of the land and then come away without paying anything?"

"O, most people give some donation to the monastery when they leave." said Mary Jane.

"I wish we had an institution like that in our Church," said Mr Browne candidly.

He was astonished to hear that the monks never spoke, got up at two in the morning and slept in their coffins. He asked what they did it for.

"That's the rule of the order," said Aunt Kate firmly.

"Yes, but why?" asked Mr Browne.

Aunt Kate repeated that it was the rule, that was all. Mr Browne still seemed not to understand. Freddy Malins explained to him, as best he could, that the monks were trying to make up for the sins committed by all the sinners in the outside world. The explanation was not very clear for Mr Browne grinned and said:

"I like that idea very much but wouldn't a comfortable spring bed do them as well as a coffin?"

"The coffin," said Mary Jane, "is to remind them of their last end."

As the subject had grown lugubrious it was buried in a silence of the table during which Mrs Malins could be heard saying to her neighbour in an indistinct undertone:

"They are very good men, the monks, very pious men."

The raisins and almonds and figs and apples and oranges and chocolates and sweets were now passed about the table and Aunt Julia invited all the guests to have either port or sherry. At first Mr Bartell D'Arcy refused to take either but one of his neighbours nudged him and whispered something to him upon which he allowed his glass to be filled. Gradually as the last glasses were being filled the conversation ceased. A pause followed, broken only by the noise of the wine and by unsettlings of chairs. The Misses Morkan, all three, looked down at the tablecloth. Someone coughed once or twice and then a few gentlemen patted the table gently as a signal for silence. The silence came and Gabriel pushed back his chair.

The patting at once grew louder in encouragement and then ceased altogether. Gabriel leaned his ten trembling fingers on the tablecloth and smiled nervously at the company. Meeting a row of upturned faces he raised his eyes to the chandelier. The piano was playing a waltz tune and he could hear the skirts sweeping against the drawing-room door. People, perhaps, were standing in the snow on the quay outside, gazing up at the lighted windows and listening to the waltz music. The air was pure there. In the distance lay the park where the trees were weighted with snow. The Wellington

Monument wore a gleaming cap of snow that flashed westward over the white field of Fifteen Acres.

He began:

"Ladies and Gentlemen,

"It has fallen to my lot this evening, as in years past, to perform a very pleasing task but a task for which I am afraid my poor powers as a speaker are all too inadequate."

"No, no!" said Mr Browne.

"But, however that may be, I can only ask you to-night to take the will for the deed and to lend me your attention for a few moments while I endeavour to express to you in words what my feelings are on this occasion.

"Ladies and Gentlemen, it is not the first time that we have gathered together under this hospitable roof, around this hospitable board. It is not the first time that we have been the recipients—or perhaps, I had better say, the victims—of the hospitality of certain good ladies."

He made a circle in the air with his arm and paused. Everyone laughed or smiled at Aunt Kate and Aunt Julia and Mary Jane who all turned crimson with pleasure. Gabriel went on more boldly:

"I feel more strongly with every recurring year that our country has no tradition which does it so much honour and which it should guard so jealously as that of its hospitality. It is a tradition that is unique as far as my experience goes (and I have visited not a few places abroad) among the modern nations. Some would say, perhaps, that with us it is rather a failing than anything to be boasted of. But granted even that, it is, to my mind, a princely failing, and one that I trust will long be cultivated among us. Of one thing, at least, I am sure. As long as this one roof shelters the good ladies aforesaid—and I wish from my heart it may do so for many and many a long year to come—the tradition of genuine warm-hearted courteous Irish hospitality, which our forefathers have handed down to us and which we in turn must hand down to our descendants, is still alive among us."

A hearty murmur of assent ran round the table. It shot through Gabriel's mind that Miss Ivors was not there and that she had gone away discourteously: and he said with confidence in himself:

"Ladies and Gentlemen,

"A new generation is growing up in our midst, a generation actuated by new ideas and new principles. It is serious and enthusiastic for these new ideas and its enthusiasm, even when it is misdirected, is, I believe, in the main sincere. But we are living in a sceptical and, if I may use the phrase, a thought-tormented age: and sometimes I fear that this new generation, educated or hypereducated as it is, will lack those qualities of humanity, of hospitality, of kindly humour which belonged to an older day. Listening tonight to the names of all those great singers of the past it seemed to me, I must confess, that we were living in a less spacious age. Those days might, without exaggeration, be called spacious days: and if they are gone beyond recall let us hope, at least, that in gatherings such as this we shall still speak of them with pride and affection, still cherish in our hearts the memory of those dead and gone great ones whose fame the world will not willingly let die."

"Hear, hear!" said Mr Browne loudly.

"But yet," continued Gabriel, his voice falling into a softer inflection, "there are always in gatherings such as this sadder thoughts that will recur to our minds: thoughts of the past, of youth, of changes, of absent faces that we miss here tonight. Our path through life is strewn with many such sad memories: and were we to brood upon them always we could not find the heart to go on bravely with our work among the living. We have all of us living duties and living affections which claim, and rightly claim, our strenuous endeavours.

"Therefore, I will not linger on the past. I will not let any gloomy moralising intrude upon us here to-night. Here we are gathered together for a brief moment from the bustle and rush of our everyday routine. We are met here as friends, in the spirit of good fellowship, as colleagues, also to a certain extent, in the true spirit of *camaraderie*, and as the guests of—what shall I call them?—the Three Graces of the Dublin musical world."

The table burst into applause and laughter at this allusion. Aunt Julia vainly asked each of her neighbours in turn to tell her what Gabriel had said.

"He says we are the Three Graces, Aunt Julia," said Mary Jane.

Aunt Julia did not understand but she looked up, smiling, at Gabriel, who continued in the same vein:

"Ladies and Gentlemen,

"I will not attempt to play to-night the part that Paris played on another occasion. I will not attempt to choose between them. The task would be an invidious one and one beyond my poor powers. For when I view them in turn, whether it be our chief hostess herself, whose good heart, whose too good heart, has become a byword with all who know her, or her sister, who seems to be gifted with perennial youth and whose singing must have been a surprise and a revelation to us all to-night, or, last but not least, when I consider our youngest hostess, talented, cheerful, hard-working and the best of nieces, I confess, Ladies and Gentlemen, that I do not know to which of them I should award the prize."

Gabriel glanced down at his aunts and, seeing the large smile on Aunt Julia's face and the tears which had risen to Aunt Kate's eyes, hastened to his close. He raised his glass of port gallantly, while every member of the company fingered a glass expectantly, and said loudly:

"Let us toast them all three together. Let us drink to their health, wealth, long life, happiness and prosperity and may they long continue to hold the proud and self-won position which they hold in their profession and the position of honour and affection which they hold in our hearts."

All the guests stood up, glass in hand, and turning towards the three seated ladies, sang in unison, with Mr Browne as leader:

> For they are jolly gay fellows,
> For they are jolly gay fellows,
> For they are jolly gay fellows,
> Which nobody can deny.

Aunt Kate was making frank use of her handkerchief and even Aunt Julia seemed moved. Freddy Malins beat time with his pudding-fork and the singers turned towards one another, as if in melodious conference, while they sang with emphasis:

> Unless he tells a lie,
> Unless he tells a lie.

Then, turning once more towards their hostesses, they sang:

> For they are jolly gay fellows,
> For they are jolly gay fellows,
> For they are jolly gay fellows,
> Which nobody can deny.

The acclamation which followed was taken up beyond the door of the supper-room by many of the other guests and renewed time after time, Freddy Malins acting as officer with his fork on high.

*****

The piercing morning air came into the hall where they were standing so that Aunt Kate said:

"Close the door, somebody. Mrs Malins will get her death of cold."

"Browne is out there, Aunt Kate," said Mary Jane.

"Browne is everywhere," said Aunt Kate, lowering her voice.

Mary Jane laughed at her tone.

"Really," she said archly, "he is very attentive."

"He has been laid on here like the gas," said Aunt Kate in the same tone, "all during the Christmas."

She laughed herself this time good-humouredly and then added quickly:

"But tell him to come in, Mary Jane, and close the door. I hope to goodness he didn't hear me."

At that moment the hall-door was opened and Mr Browne came in from the doorstep, laughing as if his heart would break. He was dressed in a long green overcoat with mock astrakhan cuffs and collar and wore on his head an oval fur cap. He pointed down the snow-covered quay from where the sound of shrill prolonged whistling was borne in.

"Teddy will have all the cabs in Dublin out," he said.

Gabriel advanced from the little pantry behind the office, struggling into his overcoat and, looking round the hall, said:

"Gretta not down yet?"

"She's getting on her things, Gabriel," said Aunt Kate.

"Who's playing up there?" asked Gabriel.

"Nobody. They're all gone."

"O no, Aunt Kate," said Mary Jane. "Bartell D'Arcy and Miss O'Callaghan aren't gone yet."

"Someone is fooling at the piano anyhow," said Gabriel.

Mary Jane glanced at Gabriel and Mr Browne and said with a shiver:

"It makes me feel cold to look at you two gentlemen muffled up like that. I wouldn't like to face your journey home at this hour."

"I'd like nothing better this minute," said Mr Browne stoutly, "than a rattling fine walk in the country or a fast drive with a good spanking goer between the shafts."[13]

"We used to have a very good horse and trap[14] at home," said Aunt Julia sadly.

"The never-to-be-forgotten Johnny," said Mary Jane, laughing.

Aunt Kate and Gabriel laughed too.

"Why, what was wonderful about Johnny?" asked Mr Browne.

"The late lamented Patrick Morkan, our grandfather, that is," explained Gabriel, "commonly known in his later years as the old gentleman, was a glue-boiler."

"O, now, Gabriel," said Aunt Kate, laughing, "he had a starch mill."

"Well, glue or starch," said Gabriel, "the old gentleman had a horse by the name of Johnny. And Johnny used to work in the old gentleman's mill, walking round and round in order to drive the mill. That was all very well; but now comes the tragic part about Johnny. One fine day the old gentleman thought he'd like to drive out with the quality to a military review in the park."

"The Lord have mercy on his soul," said Aunt Kate compassionately.

"Amen," said Gabriel. "So the old gentleman, as I said, harnessed Johnny and put on his very best tall hat and his very best stock collar and drove out in grand style from his ancestral mansion somewhere near Back Lane, I think."

Everyone laughed, even Mrs Malins, at Gabriel's manner and Aunt Kate said:

"O, now, Gabriel, he didn't live in Back Lane, really. Only the mill was there."

"Out from the mansion of his forefathers," continued Gabriel, "he drove with Johnny. And everything went on beautifully until Johnny came in sight of King Billy's statue: and whether he fell in love with the horse King Billy sits on or whether he thought he was back again in the mill, anyhow he began to walk round the statue."

---

[13] Fast horse connected to the carriage.
[14] Carriage.

Gabriel paced in a circle round the hall in his galoshes amid the laughter of the others.

"Round and round he went," said Gabriel, "and the old gentleman, who was a very pompous old gentleman, was highly indignant. 'Go on, sir! What do you mean, sir? Johnny! Johnny! Most extraordinary conduct! Can't understand the horse!'"

The peal of laughter which followed Gabriel's imitation of the incident was interrupted by a resounding knock at the hall-door. Mary Jane ran to open it and let in Freddy Malins. Freddy Malins, with his hat well back on his head and his shoulders humped with cold, was puffing and steaming after his exertions.

"I could only get one cab," he said.

"O, we'll find another along the quay," said Gabriel.

"Yes," said Aunt Kate. "Better not keep Mrs Malins standing in the draught."

Mrs Malins was helped down the front steps by her son and Mr Browne and, after many manoeuvres, hoisted into the cab. Freddy Malins clambered in after her and spent a long time settling her on the seat, Mr Browne helping him with advice. At last she was settled comfortably and Freddy Malins invited Mr Browne into the cab. There was a good deal of confused talk, and then Mr Browne got into the cab. The cabman settled his rug over his knees, and bent down for the address. The confusion grew greater and the cabman was directed differently by Freddy Malins and Mr Browne, each of whom had his head out through a window of the cab. The difficulty was to know where to drop Mr Browne along the route, and Aunt Kate, Aunt Julia and Mary Jane helped the discussion from the doorstep with cross-directions and contradictions and abundance of laughter. As for Freddy Malins he was speechless with laughter. He popped his head in and out of the window every moment to the great danger of his hat, and told his mother how the discussion was progressing, till at last Mr Browne shouted to the bewildered cabman above the din of everybody's laughter:

"Do you know Trinity College?"

"Yes, sir," said the cabman.

"Well, drive bang up against Trinity College gates," said Mr Browne, "and then we'll tell you where to go. You understand now?"

"Yes, sir," said the cabman.

"Make like a bird for Trinity College."

"Right, sir," said the cabman.

The horse was whipped up and the cab rattled off along the quay amid a chorus of laughter and adieus.

Gabriel had not gone to the door with the others. He was in a dark part of the hall gazing up the staircase. A woman was standing near the top of the first flight, in the shadow also. He could not see her face but he could see the terra-cotta and salmon-pink panels of her skirt which the shadow made appear black and white. It was his wife. She was leaning on the banisters, listening to something. Gabriel was surprised at her stillness and strained his ear to listen also. But he could hear little save the noise of laughter and dispute on the front steps, a few chords struck on the piano and a few notes of a man's voice singing.

He stood still in the gloom of the hall, trying to catch the air that the voice was singing and gazing up at his wife. There was grace and mystery in her attitude as if she were a symbol of something. He asked himself what is a woman standing on the stairs in the shadow, listening to distant music, a symbol of. If he were a painter he would paint her in that attitude. Her blue felt hat would show off the bronze of her hair against the darkness and the dark panels of her skirt would show off the light ones. *Distant Music* he would call the picture if he were a painter.

The hall-door was closed; and Aunt Kate, Aunt Julia and Mary Jane came down the hall, still laughing.

"Well, isn't Freddy terrible?" said Mary Jane. "He's really terrible."

Gabriel said nothing but pointed up the stairs towards where his wife was standing. Now that the hall-door was closed the voice and the piano could be heard more clearly. Gabriel held up his hand for them to be silent. The song seemed to be in the old Irish tonality and the singer seemed uncertain both of his words and of his voice. The voice, made plaintive by distance and by the singer's hoarseness, faintly illuminated the cadence of the air with words expressing grief:

> O, the rain falls on my heavy locks
> And the dew wets my skin,
> My babe lies cold...

"O," exclaimed Mary Jane. "It's Bartell D'Arcy singing and he wouldn't sing all the night. O, I'll get him to sing a song before he goes."

"O, do, Mary Jane," said Aunt Kate.

Mary Jane brushed past the others and ran to the staircase, but before she reached it the singing stopped and the piano was closed abruptly.

"O, what a pity!" she cried. "Is he coming down, Gretta?"

Gabriel heard his wife answer yes and saw her come down towards them. A few steps behind her were Mr Bartell D'Arcy and Miss O'Callaghan.

"O, Mr D'Arcy," cried Mary Jane, "it's downright mean of you to break off like that when we were all in raptures listening to you."

"I have been at him all the evening," said Miss O'Callaghan, "and Mrs Conroy, too, and he told us he had a dreadful cold and couldn't sing."

"O, Mr D'Arcy," said Aunt Kate, "now that was a great fib to tell."

"Can't you see that I'm as hoarse as a crow?" said Mr D'Arcy roughly.

He went into the pantry hastily and put on his overcoat. The others, taken aback by his rude speech, could find nothing to say. Aunt Kate wrinkled her brows and made signs to the others to drop the subject. Mr D'Arcy stood swathing his neck carefully and frowning.

"It's the weather," said Aunt Julia, after a pause.

"Yes, everybody has colds," said Aunt Kate readily, "everybody."

"They say," said Mary Jane, "we haven't had snow like it for thirty years; and I read this morning in the newspapers that the snow is general all over Ireland."

"I love the look of snow," said Aunt Julia sadly.

"So do I," said Miss O'Callaghan. "I think Christmas is never really Christmas unless we have the snow on the ground."

"But poor Mr D'Arcy doesn't like the snow," said Aunt Kate, smiling.

Mr D'Arcy came from the pantry, fully swathed and buttoned, and in a repentant tone told them the history of his cold. Everyone gave him advice and said it was a great pity and urged him to be very careful of his throat in the night air. Gabriel watched his wife, who did not join in the conversation. She was standing right under the dusty fanlight[15] and the flame of the gas lit up the rich bronze of her hair, which he had seen her drying at the fire a few days before. She was in the same attitude and seemed unaware of the talk about her. At last she turned towards them and Gabriel saw that there was colour on her cheeks and that her eyes were shining. A sudden tide of joy went leaping out of his heart.

"Mr D'Arcy," she said, "what is the name of that song you were singing?"

"It's called *The Lass of Aughrim*," said Mr D'Arcy, "but I couldn't remember it properly. Why? Do you know it?"

"*The Lass of Aughrim*," she repeated. "I couldn't think of the name."

"It's a very nice air," said Mary Jane. "I'm sorry you were not in voice tonight."

"Now, Mary Jane," said Aunt Kate, "don't annoy Mr D'Arcy. I won't have him annoyed."

Seeing that all were ready to start she shepherded them to the door, where good-night was said:

"Well, good-night, Aunt Kate, and thanks for the pleasant evening."

"Good-night, Gabriel. Good-night, Gretta!"

"Good-night, Aunt Kate, and thanks ever so much. Good-night, Aunt Julia."

"O, good-night, Gretta, I didn't see you."

"Good-night, Mr D'Arcy. Good-night, Miss O'Callaghan."

"Good-night, Miss Morkan."

"Good-night, again."

"Good-night, all. Safe home."

"Good-night. Good-night."

The morning was still dark. A dull, yellow light brooded over the houses and the river; and the sky seemed to be descending. It was slushy underfoot; and only streaks and patches of snow lay on the roofs, on the parapets of the quay and on the area railings. The lamps were still burning redly in the murky air and, across the river, the palace of the Four Courts stood out menacingly against the heavy sky.

She was walking on before him with Mr Bartell D'Arcy, her shoes in a brown parcel tucked under one arm and her hands holding

---

[15] A window in the door.

her skirt up from the slush. She had no longer any grace of attitude, but Gabriel's eyes were still bright with happiness. The blood went bounding along his veins; and the thoughts went rioting through his brain, proud, joyful, tender, valorous.

She was walking on before him so lightly and so erect that he longed to run after her noiselessly, catch her by the shoulders and say something foolish and affectionate into her ear. She seemed to him so frail that he longed to defend her against something and then to be alone with her. Moments of their secret life together burst like stars upon his memory. A heliotrope envelope was lying beside his breakfast-cup and he was caressing it with his hand. Birds were twittering in the ivy and the sunny web of the curtain was shimmering along the floor: he could not eat for happiness. They were standing on the crowded platform and he was placing a ticket inside the warm palm of her glove. He was standing with her in the cold, looking in through a grated window at a man making bottles in a roaring furnace. It was very cold. Her face, fragrant in the cold air, was quite close to his; and suddenly he called out to the man at the furnace:

"Is the fire hot, sir?"

But the man could not hear with the noise of the furnace. It was just as well. He might have answered rudely.

A wave of yet more tender joy escaped from his heart and went coursing in warm flood along his arteries. Like the tender fire of stars moments of their life together, that no one knew of or would ever know of, broke upon and illumined his memory. He longed to recall to her those moments, to make her forget the years of their dull existence together and remember only their moments of ecstasy. For the years, he felt, had not quenched his soul or hers. Their children, his writing, her household cares had not quenched all their souls' tender fire. In one letter that he had written to her then he had said: "Why is it that words like these seem to me so dull and cold? Is it because there is no word tender enough to be your name?"

Like distant music these words that he had written years before were borne towards him from the past. He longed to be alone with her. When the others had gone away, when he and she were in the room in the hotel, then they would be alone together. He would call her softly:

"Gretta!"

Perhaps she would not hear at once: she would be undressing. Then something in his voice would strike her. She would turn and look at him...

At the corner of Winetavern Street they met a cab. He was glad of its rattling noise as it saved him from conversation. She was looking out of the window and seemed tired. The others spoke only a few words, pointing out some building or street. The horse galloped along wearily under the murky morning sky, dragging his old rattling box after his heels, and Gabriel was again in a cab with her, galloping to catch the boat, galloping to their honeymoon.

As the cab drove across O'Connell Bridge Miss O'Callaghan said:

"They say you never cross O'Connell Bridge without seeing a white horse."

"I see a white man this time," said Gabriel.

"Where?" asked Mr Bartell D'Arcy.

Gabriel pointed to the statue, on which lay patches of snow. Then he nodded familiarly to it and waved his hand.

"Good-night, Dan," he said gaily.

When the cab drew up before the hotel, Gabriel jumped out and, in spite of Mr Bartell D'Arcy's protest, paid the driver. He gave the man a shilling over his fare. The man saluted and said:

"A prosperous New Year to you, sir."

"The same to you," said Gabriel cordially.

She leaned for a moment on his arm in getting out of the cab and while standing at the curbstone, bidding the others good-night. She leaned lightly on his arm, as lightly as when she had danced with him a few hours before. He had felt proud and happy then, happy that she was his, proud of her grace and wifely carriage. But now, after the kindling again of so many memories, the first touch of her body, musical and strange and perfumed, sent through him a keen pang of lust. Under cover of her silence he pressed her arm closely to his side; and, as they stood at the hotel door, he felt that they had escaped from their lives and duties, escaped from home and friends and run away together with wild and radiant hearts to a new adventure.

An old man was dozing in a great hooded chair in the hall. He lit a candle in the office and went before them to the stairs. They followed him in silence, their feet falling in soft thuds on the thickly carpeted stairs. She mounted the stairs behind the porter, her head bowed in the ascent, her frail shoulders curved as with a burden, her skirt girt tightly about her. He could have flung his arms about her hips and held her still, for his arms were trembling with desire to seize her and only the stress of his nails against the palms of his hands held the wild impulse of his body in check. The porter halted on the stairs to settle his guttering candle. They halted, too, on the steps below him. In the silence Gabriel could hear the falling of the molten wax into the tray and the thumping of his own heart against his ribs.

The porter led them along a corridor and opened a door. Then he set his unstable candle down on a toilet-table and asked at what hour they were to be called in the morning.

"Eight," said Gabriel.

The porter pointed to the tap[16] of the electric-light and began a muttered apology, but Gabriel cut him short.

"We don't want any light. We have light enough from the street. And I say," he added, pointing to the candle, "you might remove that handsome article, like a good man."

The porter took up his candle again, but slowly, for he was surprised by such a novel idea. Then he mumbled good-night and went out. Gabriel shot the lock to.

A ghastly light from the street lamp lay in a long shaft from one window to the door. Gabriel threw his overcoat and hat on a couch and crossed the room towards the window. He looked down into the street in order that his emotion might calm a little. Then he turned and leaned against a chest of drawers with his back to the light. She had taken off her hat and cloak and was standing before a large swinging mirror, unhooking her waist. Gabriel paused for a few moments, watching her, and then said:

"Gretta!"

She turned away from the mirror slowly and walked along the shaft of light towards him. Her face looked so serious and weary that the words would not pass Gabriel's lips. No, it was not the moment yet.

"You looked tired," he said.
"I am a little," she answered.
"You don't feel ill or weak?"
"No, tired: that's all."

---

[16] Switch.

She went on to the window and stood there, looking out. Gabriel waited again and then, fearing that diffidence was about to conquer him, he said abruptly:

"By the way, Gretta!"

"What is it?"

"You know that poor fellow Malins?" he said quickly.

"Yes. What about him?"

"Well, poor fellow, he's a decent sort of chap, after all," continued Gabriel in a false voice. "He gave me back that sovereign I lent him, and I didn't expect it, really. It's a pity he wouldn't keep away from that Browne, because he's not a bad fellow, really."

He was trembling now with annoyance. Why did she seem so abstracted? He did not know how he could begin. Was she annoyed, too, about something? If she would only turn to him or come to him of her own accord! To take her as she was would be brutal. No, he must see some ardour in her eyes first. He longed to be master of her strange mood.

"When did you lend him the pound?" she asked, after a pause.

Gabriel strove to restrain himself from breaking out into brutal language about the sottish[17] Malins and his pound. He longed to cry to her from his soul, to crush her body against his, to overmaster her. But he said:

"O, at Christmas, when he opened that little Christmas-card shop in Henry Street."

He was in such a fever of rage and desire that he did not hear her come from the window. She stood before him for an instant, looking at him strangely. Then, suddenly raising herself on tiptoe and resting her hands lightly on his shoulders, she kissed him.

"You are a very generous person, Gabriel," she said.

Gabriel, trembling with delight at her sudden kiss and at the quaintness of her phrase, put his hands on her hair and began smoothing it back, scarcely touching it with his fingers. The washing had made it fine and brilliant. His heart was brimming over with happiness. Just when he was wishing for it she had come to him of her own accord. Perhaps her thoughts had been running with his. Perhaps she had felt the impetuous desire that was in him, and then the yielding mood had come upon her. Now that she had fallen to him so easily, he wondered why he had been so diffident.

---

[17] Drunk.

He stood, holding her head between his hands. Then, slipping one arm swiftly about her body and drawing her towards him, he said softly:

"Gretta, dear, what are you thinking about?"

She did not answer nor yield wholly to his arm. He said again, softly:

"Tell me what it is, Gretta. I think I know what is the matter. Do I know?"

She did not answer at once. Then she said in an outburst of tears:

"O, I am thinking about that song, *The Lass of Aughrim*."

She broke loose from him and ran to the bed and, throwing her arms across the bed-rail, hid her face. Gabriel stood stock-still for a moment in astonishment and then followed her. As he passed in the way of the cheval-glass[18] he caught sight of himself in full length, his broad, well-filled shirtfront, the face whose expression always puzzled him when he saw it in a mirror, and his glimmering gilt-rimmed eyeglasses. He halted a few paces from her and said:

"What about the song? Why does that make you cry?"

She raised her head from her arms and dried her eyes with the back of her hand like a child. A kinder note than he had intended went into his voice.

"Why, Gretta?" he asked.

"I am thinking about a person long ago who used to sing that song."

"And who was the person long ago?" asked Gabriel, smiling.

"It was a person I used to know in Galway when I was living with my grandmother," she said.

The smile passed away from Gabriel's face. A dull anger began to gather again at the back of his mind and the dull fires of his lust began to glow angrily in his veins.

"Someone you were in love with?" he asked ironically.

"It was a young boy I used to know," she answered, "named Michael Furey. He used to sing that song, *The Lass of Aughrim*. He was very delicate."

Gabriel was silent. He did not wish her to think that he was interested in this delicate boy.

---

[18] Mirror.

"I can see him so plainly," she said, after a moment. "Such eyes as he had: big, dark eyes! And such an expression in them—an expression!"

"O, then, you are in love with him?" said Gabriel.

"I used to go out walking with him," she said, "when I was in Galway."

A thought flew across Gabriel's mind.

"Perhaps that was why you wanted to go to Galway with that Ivors girl?" he said coldly.

She looked at him and asked in surprise:

"What for?"

Her eyes made Gabriel feel awkward. He shrugged his shoulders and said:

"How do I know? To see him, perhaps."

She looked away from him along the shaft of light towards the window in silence.

"He is dead," she said at length. "He died when he was only seventeen. Isn't it a terrible thing to die so young as that?"

"What was he?" asked Gabriel, still ironically.

"He was in the gasworks," she said.

Gabriel felt humiliated by the failure of his irony and by the evocation of this figure from the dead, a boy in the gasworks. While he had been full of memories of their secret life together, full of tenderness and joy and desire, she had been comparing him in her mind with another. A shameful consciousness of his own person assailed him. He saw himself as a ludicrous figure, acting as a pennyboy[19] for his aunts, a nervous, well-meaning sentimentalist, orating to vulgarians and idealising his own clownish lusts, the pitiable fatuous fellow he had caught a glimpse of in the mirror. Instinctively he turned his back more to the light lest she might see the shame that burned upon his forehead.

He tried to keep up his tone of cold interrogation, but his voice when he spoke was humble and indifferent.

"I suppose you were in love with this Michael Furey, Gretta," he said.

"I was great[20] with him at that time," she said.

---

[19] Errand boy.
[20] Close.

Her voice was veiled and sad. Gabriel, feeling now how vain it would be to try to lead her whither he had purposed, caressed one of her hands and said, also sadly:

"And what did he die of so young, Gretta? Consumption, was it?"

"I think he died for me," she answered.

A vague terror seized Gabriel at this answer, as if, at that hour when he had hoped to triumph, some impalpable and vindictive being was coming against him, gathering forces against him in its vague world. But he shook himself free of it with an effort of reason and continued to caress her hand. He did not question her again, for he felt that she would tell him of herself. Her hand was warm and moist: it did not respond to his touch, but he continued to caress it just as he had caressed her first letter to him that spring morning.

"It was in the winter," she said, "about the beginning of the winter when I was going to leave my grandmother's and come up here to the convent. And he was ill at the time in his lodgings in Galway and wouldn't be let out, and his people in Oughterard were written to. He was in decline, they said, or something like that. I never knew rightly."

She paused for a moment and sighed.

"Poor fellow," she said. "He was very fond of me and he was such a gentle boy. We used to go out together, walking, you know, Gabriel, like the way they do in the country. He was going to study singing only for his health. He had a very good voice, poor Michael Furey."

"Well; and then?" asked Gabriel.

"And then when it came to the time for me to leave Galway and come up to the convent he was much worse and I wouldn't be let see him so I wrote him a letter saying I was going up to Dublin and would be back in the summer, and hoping he would be better then."

She paused for a moment to get her voice under control, and then went on:

"Then the night before I left, I was in my grandmother's house in Nuns' Island, packing up, and I heard gravel thrown up against the window. The window was so wet I couldn't see, so I ran downstairs as I was and slipped out the back into the garden and there was the poor fellow at the end of the garden, shivering."

"And did you not tell him to go back?" asked Gabriel.

"I implored of him to go home at once and told him he would get his death in the rain. But he said he did not want to live. I can see his eyes as well as well! He was standing at the end of the wall where there was a tree."

"And did he go home?" asked Gabriel.

"Yes, he went home. And when I was only a week in the convent he died and he was buried in Oughterard, where his people came from. O, the day I heard that, that he was dead!"

She stopped, choking with sobs, and, overcome by emotion, flung herself face downward on the bed, sobbing in the quilt. Gabriel held her hand for a moment longer, irresolutely, and then, shy of intruding on her grief, let it fall gently and walked quietly to the window.

She was fast asleep.

Gabriel, leaning on his elbow, looked for a few moments unresentfully on her tangled hair and half-open mouth, listening to her deep-drawn breath. So she had had that romance in her life: a man had died for her sake. It hardly pained him now to think how poor a part he, her husband, had played in her life. He watched her while she slept, as though he and she had never lived together as man and wife. His curious eyes rested long upon her face and on her hair: and, as he thought of what she must have been then, in that time of her first girlish beauty, a strange, friendly pity for her entered his soul. He did not like to say even to himself that her face was no longer beautiful, but he knew that it was no longer the face for which Michael Furey had braved death.

Perhaps she had not told him all the story. His eyes moved to the chair over which she had thrown some of her clothes. A petticoat string dangled to the floor. One boot stood upright, its limp upper fallen down: the fellow of it lay upon its side. He wondered at his riot of emotions of an hour before. From what had it proceeded? From his aunt's supper, from his own foolish speech, from the wine and dancing, the merry-making when saying good-night in the hall, the pleasure of the walk along the river in the snow. Poor Aunt Julia! She, too, would soon be a shade with the shade of Patrick Morkan and his horse. He had caught that haggard look upon her face for a moment when she was singing *Arrayed for the Bridal*. Soon, perhaps, he would be sitting in that same drawing-room, dressed in black, his silk hat on his knees. The blinds would be drawn down and Aunt Kate would be sitting beside him, crying and blowing her nose and telling him how

Julia had died. He would cast about in his mind for some words that might console her, and would find only lame and useless ones. Yes, yes: that would happen very soon.

The air of the room chilled his shoulders. He stretched himself cautiously along under the sheets and lay down beside his wife. One by one, they were all becoming shades. Better pass boldly into that other world, in the full glory of some passion, than fade and wither dismally with age. He thought of how she who lay beside him had locked in her heart for so many years that image of her lover's eyes when he had told her that he did not wish to live.

Generous tears filled Gabriel's eyes. He had never felt like that himself towards any woman, but he knew that such a feeling must be love. The tears gathered more thickly in his eyes and in the partial darkness he imagined he saw the form of a young man standing under a dripping tree. Other forms were near. His soul had approached that region where dwell the vast hosts of the dead. He was conscious of, but could not apprehend, their wayward and flickering existence. His own identity was fading out into a grey impalpable world: the solid world itself, which these dead had one time reared and lived in, was dissolving and dwindling.

A few light taps upon the pane made him turn to the window. It had begun to snow again. He watched sleepily the flakes, silver and dark, falling obliquely against the lamplight. The time had come for him to set out on his journey westward. Yes, the newspapers were right: snow was general all over Ireland. It was falling on every part of the dark central plain, on the treeless hills, falling softly upon the Bog of Allen and, farther westward, softly falling into the dark mutinous Shannon waves. It was falling, too, upon every part of the lonely churchyard on the hill where Michael Furey lay buried. It lay thickly drifted on the crooked crosses and headstones, on the spears of the little gate, on the barren thorns. His soul swooned slowly as he heard the snow falling faintly through the universe and faintly falling, like the descent of their last end, upon all the living and the dead.

CRAFT: THE DEAD

Reading as a Writer and Writing as a Reader

I read this story for the very first time in graduate school. I was overly resistant to clichés, and overly skeptical of the things others told me were great. Therefore, I had prepared myself to stubbornly dismiss "The Dead," perhaps because I feared—as I often do—being disappointed by something others predicted I would appreciate.

But the deeper I traveled into the story and the more I got to know Gabriel the happier I was that my instructor had not asked me to lead class discussion on this story. Every sentence seemed to trick or fool my critical eye. I was unable to analyze it. The story made me feel stupid. It made me feel less like a graduate student and more like just a fan.

When I reached the end, I had not one critical perspective. Okay, there was the snow. The snow was certainly a symbol—imagery. There was... Wait, what *was* there? I was desperate for an idea so that I could discuss "The Dead" and provide my peers and my instructor with insights they hadn't considered before. I even felt a little like Gabriel, mulling over the effect of his speech on Miss Ivors and trying to come up with something that would impress her.

Nothing struck me. I was paralyzed. It wasn't until I started reading others' critical perspectives that I understood why. Everything I read about "The Dead" seemed empty to me. It wasn't that any of it seemed wrong necessarily. It just seemed almost unnecessary or even cheap.

It took time and multiple readings of "The Dead" before I could penetrate the beauty to the nuts and bolts underneath. It was as if my mind wasn't ready to give up its suspension of disbelief. But finally, after some cajoling, it relented.

What follows in this section is a thorough analysis of the characterization techniques Joyce uses in representing Gabriel, and a series of questions to begin a conversation about the craft of "The Dead." I hope that readers, now armed with a vocabulary and understanding of the craft of *Dubliners*, won't feel as paralyzed as I did when addressing these questions. I also hope that readers will not skip the questions. Even if you read them with no intention of answering them, they will help to synthesize the craft elements we have discussed in this book. And once readers and writers can do that here, they can begin to unpack the craft of stories and novels everywhere.

Characterization

We have discussed **satirical** characters, **round** characters, **flat** characters and the ways in which writers embed characters in a **narrative structure**. But we haven't yet laid out the ways in which writers represent characters on the page—a craft technique called **characterization**.

There are two reasons I waited until "The Dead" to discuss characterization. First, Gabriel is the roundest and most fully developed character in *Dubliners*, and provides us with an excellent example of how a writer uses a variety of techniques to represent a character on the page. Second, characterization is hands down the most complex and difficult part of creating fiction. Arguably, it is also the most important, especially in contemporary literary fiction. Books with great characters can get by with poor or nonexistent **plots**, but books with great plots and poor or nonexistent characters just don't fly. J.D. Salinger masterfully characterizes Holden Caulfield in *Catcher in the Rye*, but the plot fails to create causality between narrative events, and the novel lacks a core **idea**. Salinger's *Franny and Zoey* suffers the same problem—great characterization, but lacking when it comes to plot. Jonathan Franzen's *Freedom* reads more like an extended character study he wrote for a novel he wanted to write someday.

Telling a story and creating a plot are relatively easy. Everybody can do it, and a lot of people can do it very well. When we sit around campfires and tell stories, we are creating plots. What very few campfire storytellers are able to do, however, is characterize the people in that plot. Think about it. Think of every story you've ever told or heard spontaneously. Did it include detailed physical descriptions of the characters? Did it include background information about their childhoods? Did it include **backstory**? How about inner thoughts? What about direct dialogue? Most likely, the answer to every one of these questions is no. And yet if I asked if the story had **conflict, crisis, tension, tone**, structure… you'd answer yes.

Because creating character is the most difficult thing for a writer to do well, it has created an unfortunate divide in contemporary fiction. Those who are good at creating plots are often pigeonholed into what is called genre fiction, which is considered by many as subpar literature. Those who are good at creating characters are often exalted as literary writers. They don't even have to be good at creating plot. In fact, many of them aren't. Nobody would say that Jane Austen did not write literary fiction, and yet she masterfully weaves characterization with plot. So does Dickens. And so does Joyce in "The Dead."

There are two main categories of characterization: **showing** and **telling**. We have discussed showing and telling previously in regards to **action**, scene and **dialogue**. The same applies to character. When a writer tells us about a character, he or she interprets the character for us through observations, exposition, backstory, and inner thoughts. When a writer shows us a character, he or she presents the character for the reader to visualize or interpret through appearance, action, and dialogue.

CHARACTERIZATION
Representing a character in writing

TELLING
The author interprets the character for the reader.

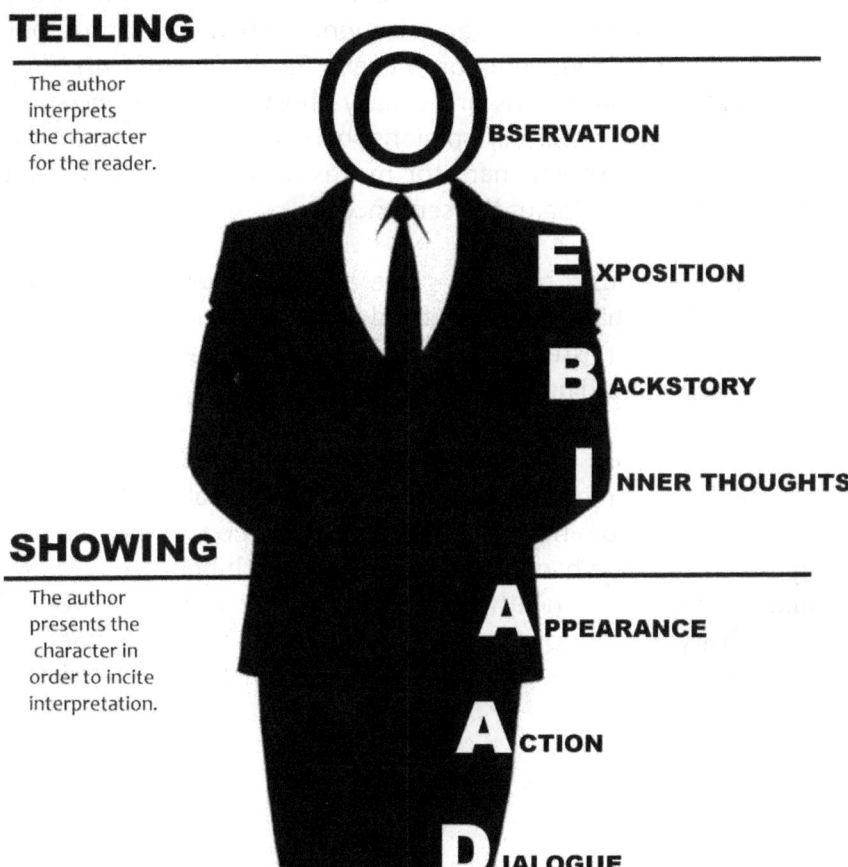

OBSERVATION

EXPOSITION

BACKSTORY

INNER THOUGHTS

SHOWING
The author presents the character in order to incite interpretation.

APPEARANCE

ACTION

DIALOGUE

Let's examine Gabriel's character piece by piece to see how Joyce uses each of these elements to characterize him.

Telling: **Observation**

Observations from the narrator are the most straightforward and least complex form of characterization. When a narrator points something out or comments on a character, he or she is making an observation. Observations are usually short and often include the character's likes or dislikes, opinions, habits, or psychological traits. Here, Joyce's omniscient narrator makes a brief observation about Gabriel at the beginning of the sentence:

> He liked music but the piece she was playing had no melody for him and he doubted whether it had any melody for the other listeners, though they had begged Mary Jane to play something.

The narrator does not show us Gabriel's fondness for music. Likewise, he doesn't note that Gabriel is thinking about his fondness for music. The comment is a simple observation. Other examples might include: "She had a tendency to play with her hair." "Nobody could penetrate beneath the surface because he wore his inscrutability like a stone suit." "Ryan hated all men named Bill." "She believed that people had no right to make any decisions for her."

Telling: **Exposition**

Exposition is background information that informs us about the character, usually about his or her past. Often, exposition can sound like observation. But observations about a character do not include background. "Because his nasty stepfather was named Bill, Ryan hated all men named Bill." That observation has been turned into exposition because it explains the background of Ryan's dislike.

Here, Joyce provides exposition about Gabriel's past as he considers his mother's role in his life:

> It was she who had chosen the name of her sons for she was very sensible of the dignity of family life. Thanks to her, Constantine was now senior curate in Balbrigan and, thanks to her, Gabriel himself had taken his degree in the Royal University.

This explains Gabriel's career and the importance of family in his life. He recognizes the impact his mother had on him, which tells us a lot about what's important to him. He's not so egotistical that he can't recognize the part his mother played in his own successes.

Exposition can often sound didactic. Because of that, it can also easily slip into sounding ridiculous, overly-psychological, or even illogical. At its worst, exposition tells us what the writer really should be showing us. Joyce would have a hard time showing us Gabriel's mother's role in his early life. However, imagine how different the story would be if Joyce provided significant exposition about Gabriel's and Gretta's past in the beginning of the narrative. One of the things that creates so much tension and tone in "The Dead" is the way in which Joyce slowly reveals how Gabriel and Gretta interact. He shows them to us first. He tells us more about them in the end.

Telling: **Backstory**

Now we're getting into murky water. Backstory differs from exposition in that it provides the reader with some context in the past, rather than just explaining background information. However, it doesn't "flash back" or put that past event in scene in the plot. The purpose of backstory is to contextualize past information in order to communicate something about the character.

As I indicated above, Joyce shows great restraint in telling us about Gabriel and Gretta. Finally, near the end of the narrative, he provides us with some backstory:

> A wave of yet more tender joy escaped from his heart and went coursing in warm flood along his arteries. Like the tender fire of stars moments of their life together, that no one knew of or would ever know of, broke upon and illumined his memory. He longed to recall to her those moments, to make her forget the years of their dull existence together and remember only their moments of ecstasy. For the years, he felt, had not quenched his soul or hers. Their children, his writing, her household cares had not quenched all their souls' tender fire. In one letter that he had written to her then he had said: "Why is it that words like these seem to me so dull and cold? Is it because there is no word tender enough to be your name?"

From this we get Gabriel's nostalgia, the longing for romance that he is unable to articulate to Gretta in words, his desire for her, the ecstasy of their early years, and the dullness of their later years. It summarizes the story (or history) of their lives quickly. That's backstory. It could be a novel of its own, but that's not its purpose. Joyce places it here to further characterize Gabriel by telling us about how his relationship with Gretta has changed over the years.

Telling: **Inner Thoughts**

It would be difficult to show Gabriel's self-doubt and even occasional pettiness without the narrator providing us his inner thoughts. Gabriel is exceedingly good at guarding his doubts and exhibiting the best part of himself. Often writers overuse inner thoughts to inform us of things we already know about a character. Obviously, a first person narrator more often relies on her own inner thoughts to tell the story because she has access only to her own perspective. An omniscient narrator, on the other hand, has access to all the characters' inner thoughts, and must control that freedom.

From the action and dialogue, we do not see the full extent of Gabriel's self-doubt and irritation when it comes to Miss Ivors's comments about his writing. Here, Joyce reveals Gabriel's inner thoughts as he mulls over his speech:

> He ran over the headings of his speech: Irish hospitality, sad memories, the Three Graces, Paris, the quotation from Browning. He repeated to himself a phrase he had written in his review: *One feels that one is listening to a thought-tormented music.* Miss Ivors had praised the review. Was she sincere? Had she really any life of her own behind all her propagandism? There had never been any ill-feeling between them until that night. It unnerved him to think that she would be at the supper-table, looking up at him while he spoke with her critical quizzing eyes. Perhaps she would not be sorry to see him fail in his speech. An idea came into his mind and gave him courage. He would say, alluding to Aunt Kate and Aunt Julia: *Ladies and Gentlemen, the generation which is now on the wane among us may have had its faults but for my part I think it had certain qualities of hospitality, of humour, of humanity, which the new and very serious and hypereducated generation that is growing up around us seems to me to lack.* Very good: that was one for Miss Ivors. What did he care that his aunts were only two ignorant old women?

We learn something new here about Gabriel. Despite his considerateness, he is not beyond pettiness. His confidence is easily shaken, and he is clearly nervous about the speech. In effect, these inner thoughts tell us about the vulnerabilities of his character, and create tension between what he says and what we understand he is thinking.

Showing: **Appearance**

Many think that describing a character's appearance seems like telling rather than showing, but the appearance of the character doesn't directly tell us anything about the character. We must interpret the character's appearance. For example, the description of a character's perfectly shined shoes might show us that he is fastidious. But what the writer tells us is that the character has shiny shoes.

As you read this example from "The Dead," pay close attention to what Joyce shows us about Gabriel:

> He was a stout, tallish young man. The high colour of his cheeks pushed upwards even to his forehead, where it scattered itself in a few formless patches of pale red; and on his hairless face there scintillated restlessly the polished lenses and the bright gilt rims of the glasses which screened his delicate and restless eyes. His glossy black hair was parted in the middle and brushed in a long curve behind his ears where it curled slightly beneath the groove left by his hat.

What do we have? We've got a blotchy-faced guy with hat hair, right? Sure. But we also have a tall guy with great eyes that never stop moving and very smart glasses. This tells us that Gabriel perhaps has lost a bit of control over his "stout" figure, but pays close attention to the details of his appearance—the polished glasses, the shaved face, the carefully brushed hair that is parted straight down the middle. The narrator shows that he has money, that he's vain, and that he's very observant and always aware of the details of his surroundings. By placing such importance on his glasses and his restless eyes, Joyce shows us that Gabriel has a discerning intensity and significant amount of ambition and social awareness.

When writers describe characters' appearances, they are showing us what the character looks like so that we can visualize him or her. But effective writers are also **characterizing**, carefully choosing the details of that character's appearance to show us parts of his or her personality.

Showing: **Action**

When we use the term **action** to talk about fiction, we can mean two things. First, we can use the term loosely to include the actions of characters. The second way we use the term describes dramatic events—events that have tension and all the ingredients necessary for a character change, discovery, or revelation. The distinction is important, but very straightforward. If Linda went to the zoo, that's an action. But it's not dramatic. If Linda went to the zoo to meet her fugitive ex-husband in the underground aquarium, we have the makings of dramatic action because there will be tension and very likely a change, discovery, or revelation.

Dramatic action is great at characterizing. You get to know someone very well very quickly when you put them in a tense situation. Of course, some dramatic action works better to characterize. If you throw a character immediately into some kind of extreme action—locked in a burning building with three others, for example—you might find subtlety difficult. This might establish whether your character handles extremely stressful situations well or poorly, but you'd be hard pressed to suggest that his divorce at the early age of nineteen from his high school sweetheart turned him into a misanthrope who uses his college classroom as a laboratory to see how fast and how efficiently he can inoculate young, impressionable minds with his own brand of cynicism.

We get to know the narrator and Mahony in "An Encounter" extremely well just by seeing how each of them reacts during the tense encounter with the stranger. It's at that moment we understand the narrator's imagination, his fear, his attempts to be polite, and his capricious feelings toward Mahony at the end that run in counterpoint to his relief—"in my heart I had always despised him a little." That action shows us an incredible amount about his character.

In "The Dead" we learn a lot about Gabriel during his exchange with Miss Ivors, who prods him about his literary column in *The Daily Express* and accuses him of being a "West Briton," which she uses pejoratively to suggest that he has no loyalty to Ireland and believes that Ireland is part of England.

> …He continued blinking his eyes and trying to smile and murmured lamely that he saw nothing political in writing reviews of books.
>
> When their turn to cross had come he was still perplexed and inattentive. Miss Ivors promptly took his hand in a warm grasp and said in a soft friendly tone:
>
> "Of course, I was only joking. Come, we cross now."
>
> When they were together again she spoke of the University question and Gabriel felt more at ease. A friend of hers had shown her his review of Browning's poems. That was how she had found out the secret: but she liked the review immensely.

What's magical about the action here is that Miss Ivors is in the lead. She has mastered Gabriel, who is feeling defensive and under attack. As they dance, it's Miss Ivors who promptly takes Gabriel's hand. Miss Ivors who tells him to cross. Miss Ivors who reassures him she was only joking. This reveals Gabriel's delicacy (remember his "delicate" eyes in Joyce's description of his appearance?), his paralysis in the face of aggression, and his emotional sensitivity that he guards behind his spectacles and his glossy black hair.

Showing: **Dialogue**

After they dance, Miss Ivors continues to lay into Gabriel as they speak with Mr. Conroy about visiting the Aran Islands in the summer. Gabriel declines Miss Ivors' invitation, telling her that he has arrangements to go to France, Belgium or Germany on a cycling tour:

"And haven't you your own land to visit," continued Miss Ivors, "that you know nothing of, your own people, and your own country?"

"O, to tell you the truth," retorted Gabriel suddenly, "I'm sick of my own country, sick of it!"

"Why?" asked Miss Ivors.

Gabriel did not answer for his retort had heated him.

"Why?" repeated Miss Ivors.

They had to go visiting together and, as he had not answered her, Miss Ivors said warmly:

"Of course, you've no answer."

When I read this scene, I want to tell Gabriel to just be cool, to ignore Miss Ivors' relentless jabs. Her "undoing" of him with her earlier jokes and sarcasm about his column has now turned more aggressive. She is questioning his patriotism. And Gabriel is anything but cool. First he's defensive, then he explodes. His dialogue reveals not only his exasperation with Miss Ivors, but the fact that she's also right in a way—Gabriel does harbor some frustrations with Ireland. Joyce has used Miss Ivors' dialogue carefully, slowly but surely carving deeply into Gabriel to expose his vulnerabilities and private beliefs.

Showing Versus Telling

It's easy to say that writers should never tell if they can show. But that's ridiculous. Certainly, Joyce could have managed to create a scene that showed us Gabriel's mother's effect on his life, but it's a detail that's only marginally important. It's a detail that belongs just where he put it: in exposition.

Showing is often difficult because it takes time, details, verisimilitude, increasing action and tension—all those things that make for effective fiction. When writers feel lazy or lack true authority and conviction over their narratives and characters, they often tend to tell more than show. How can you show us a character you don't really know yourself? If writers find themselves telling us who a character is more than showing us, it's often an indication that they need to do more work establishing the details of the character's personality.

The better rule when it comes to showing versus telling is to be deliberate. If you show us, show for a reason. If you tell us, tell for a reason. When we read a piece of fiction, perhaps the best indication of complex characters appears in the synthesis between telling and showing. The best characters in all of fiction are represented both ways. The things the narrator tell us about the character align with what the narrator shows us, and the relationship between what we're told and shown creates tension and a deeper understanding.

Questions

1. It takes approximately ninety minutes to read "The Dead" out loud, and depending on the speed one reads, approximately one hour to read it silently. The narrative, however, spans approximately six hours. We know that Gabriel and Gretta arrive just after 10 pm in the beginning of the story, and that it is morning and getting light at the end of the story (let's say 5 am). How do you experience **narrative time** in "The Dead"? Do certain moments seem longer than others, and if so, are they? Would you consider Joyce's use of narrative time in "The Dead" democratic, or does he vary the amount of attention he gives to certain moments?

2. Would we call the end of "The Dead" an instance of **epiphany** or **peripeteia**? How does Joyce construct Gabriel's realization, and do you find it believable? Why or why not?

3. Would you call Freddy Malins a **satirical** character? Similarly, what makes his character either **round** or **flat**?

4. Take a moment to think about the **symbolism** in "The Dead." As you think and investigate, what **images** stick out? What objects and **details**? Begin to classify them. What objects act as **objective correlatives**, and what emotions are they associated with? What **images** does Joyce use in "The Dead"? What **images** does Joyce return to again and again to create **imagery**? What is the **symbolic architecture** of "The Dead" and how do individual symbols fit in this symbolic design? Furthermore, how does that symbolic design reflect on the **idea** of this narrative?

5. How would you categorize the **point of view**? **First person**? **Second person**? **Third person**? **Close (limited)** or **omniscient**? **Subjective** or **objective**? After you come to a conclusion about the point of view, how does that **narrative mode** operate as a means to communicate the **plot**?

6. Let's examine the very first sentence under the lens of **narrative mode**. "Lily, the caretaker's daughter, was literally run off her feet." This mistaken use of "literally" to describe the figurative phrase "run off her feet" suggests what about the **point of view**? Would you

consider this the narrator's error? James Joyce's error? Lily's error? How does that affect your reading experience?

7. Does Joyce create realistic and believable characters and situations in the **plotting** of this story? Would you consider this story successful in terms of its **verisimilitude**? Why or why not?

8. Does this narrative follow the typical **narrative structure**? Does it have a **setup, conflict**, and **resolution**? Can you insert those elements into this illustration?

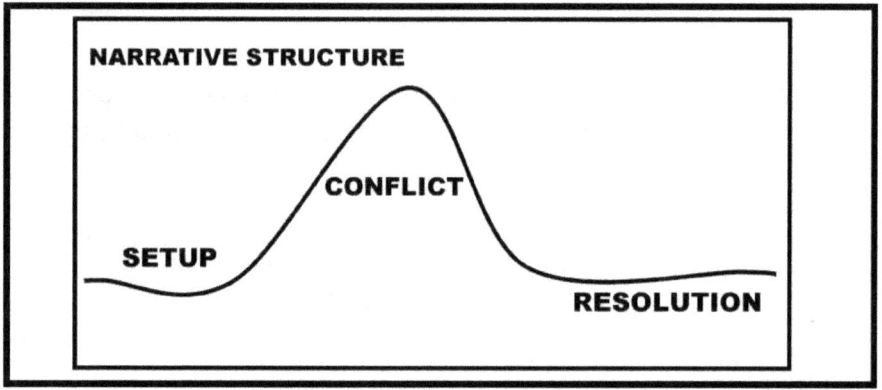

9. How does Joyce construct the **plot** of this **story**? For example, this plot is divided into two primary parts. The first part consists of the party at the Morkan's house. The second part focuses on Gabriel's and Gretta's return to their hotel, and the exchange they have there. First, why would Joyce craft this story by plotting these two events? Second, by plotting these two events, what is the causal relationship between them?

10. What would you say is the **premise** of this story, and how does Joyce follow through on the **contract** he sets up with this premise?

11. Examine the moments of high **tension** and **conflict** in the narrative. How does Joyce create them, and after he creates them, how does he **increase** the tension? Does that increasing tension lead to a clear **climax** or moment of **crisis**?

12. Does Joyce provide the reader with any **allusions** to other works of art, and do those allusions work to make comparisons to bigger ideas or contexts? If so, explain them.

13. Isolate the exchanges between Gretta and Gabriel. What are these characters doing to each other? How do these characters "undo" each other through **dialogue**? What makes these exchanges **dynamic** rather than **static**?

14. Can you pick a character in "The Dead" who acts as a **foil**? If so, how does that character reflect Gabriel? How does that reflection affect your understanding of Gabriel's character?

15. Are there any elements in "The Dead" that Joyce intentionally keeps in shadow? Joycean **gnomons**? How does such an element affect the reading experience?

16. Choose a page. If you have underlined or marked the text, choose a page with a lot of markings. Read it over and isolate the **tropes**—all the figurative words and expressions used in a symbolic or nonliteral way, especially **similes** and **metaphors**. Based on your findings, try to imagine that page without any of those tropes. Imagine it with only literal words and expressions. How would that change your reading experience? By crafting those tropes, what has Joyce added to "The Dead"?

Endnote: Transcendence

Perhaps one of the hardest lessons writers ever learn about crafting fiction is that there is something impossible to pinpoint, impossible to fully deconstruct, and impossible to teach about writing a great story. After centuries and centuries of telling, reading, writing and analyzing stories, something still mystifies us about them. For readers, this can be equally frustrating. Readers aren't out to imitate, equal, or even necessarily learn anything from stories. But they do often wonder this: *Why exactly do I like this so much?*

Of course, after all this hard work, all the analysis of the writer's craft, I'd like to be able to tell readers that they can now set forth and read other stories with a complete knowledge of how writers crafted them and how they operate as narratives to achieve catharsis or satire or new ideas, laughter or tears.  But the reading experience is much like the writing experience—it is individual and sacrosanct. It is an undertaking that never ends the exact same way for any two people. Both reading and writing are conversations that we carry out with the narrator, the characters, and ourselves.

As readers and writers, there are times when we have to say: *I don't know how exactly the author accomplished this.* And while we don't have to accept our ignorance, while we can consider it an invitation to inquire further, to investigate and unpack and analyze, the fact of the matter is that we may never find a satisfactory answer. The stealth of the author may be too great. The craft of the narrative too elusive, too complex, too original. The meanings too big and too sprawling to articulate. We love it and we don't know why. We want to find and read another story that great, but we don't know where. We want to write a story that cathartic, but we don't know how. We're paralyzed by the greatness of it, and confused as hell.

Isn't that wonderful?

Bibliography

Beck, Warren. *Joyce's* Dubliners: *Substance, Vision and Art.* Durham N.C.: Duke University Press, 1969.

Burroway, Janet. *Writing Fiction: A Guide to Narrative Craft, Fourth Edition.* New York: HarperCollinsCollegePublishers, 1996.

Eliot, T.S. *Selected Essay 1917 – 1932.* New York: Harcourt, Brace and Company, Inc., 1932.

Forster, E.M. *Aspects of the Novel.* Rosetta Books, 2010.

Gardner, John. *The Art of Fiction: Notes on Craft for Young Writers.* New York: Alfred A. Knopf, 1984.

Garret, Peter, ed. *Twentieth Century Interpretations of* Dubliners: *A Collection of Critical Essays.* Englewood Cliffs, New Jersey: Prentice-Hall, Inc., 1968.

Joyce, James. *Dubliners.* Edited by Sean Latham. Boston: Longman, 2011.

Joyce, James. *Dubliners.* New York: The Modern Library, 1926, 1954.

Lodge, David. *The Art of Fiction.* New York: Viking, 1992.

Lodge, David. *The Practice of Writing.* New York: Penguin Books, 1996

Norris, Margot. *Suspicious Readings of Joyce's* Dubliners. Philadelphia: University of Pennsylvania Press, 2003.

Pierce, David. *Reading Joyce.* Harlow, England: Pearson Longman, 2008.

Riquelme, John Paul. *Teller and Tale in Joyce's Fiction.* Baltimore and London: The Johns Hopkins University Press, 1983.

Roberts, Edgar, and Jacobs, Henry. *Literature: An Introduction to Reading and Writing*, 2nd ed. New Jersey: Prentice Hall, 2003.

San Juan, Jr., Epifanio. *James Joyce and the Craft of Fiction.* New Jersey: Associated University Presses, Inc., 1972.

Staley, Thomas F. ed. *James Joyce Today: Essays on the Major Works.* Bloomington and London: Indiana University Press, 1966.

Indexed Glossary

Action 155-156, 307-309
Either physical movement or dramatic activity that occurs at any particular moment in the narrative. Also see "Increasing Action."

Allegory 249-251
A literary device writers use to suggest connections between the characters and/or events in the narrative and abstract ideas.

Allusion 207-208
A reference to another work of art.

Antagonist 49-50
A character who comes into conflict with the protagonist.

Backstory 304
Narrative information or "background" that occurs chronologically earlier than the narrative's plotted scenes.

Caricature 222
A device in which a character's traits are exaggerated, oversimplified, or both. Caricatures are often **flat** characters.

Challenge 118
The obstacles a character faces in his or her attempt to achieve a **goal**.

Characterization 299-310
The way in which an author portrays a character in a narrative. Characterization occurs in one of two ways: **"showing"** or **"telling."**

Chiasmus 91, **252-256**
A reversal of grammatical structures, words, images, characters, or events in a narrative, usually following an ABBA or ABCCBA structure (as in the shape of an X).

Choice 80-81
A selection a character makes or must make—one that often creates a dilemma that adds tension to the narrative.

Climax 53
The highest point of tension and conflict in a narrative—the moment of crisis.

Close Third Person Point of View 78-80
A **narrative mode** in which the narrator limits his or her narration to the movements and actions and sometimes the thoughts of one character.

Conflict 155-156
Antagonistic or oppositional forces that a character faces that creates tension, increases the stakes, and often drives the action.

Contract 27-29
The "deal" an author makes with a reader when creating the premise of a narrative. If the premise establishes the narrator, narrative mode, and the beginning of a plot, the contract is the writer's agreement to follow through on that premise.

Craft 13
The skills and techniques a writer uses to "make" a narrative.

Denouement 53
See **Resolution**

Detail 120
A particular. When we speak about details in writing, we can mean anything from small, described objects to word choice to particularized scenes.

Dialogue 138, 308
The words characters speak in a narrative, usually indicated by quotation marks.

Discourse 80-81
The narrator's engagement of the reader in a "conversation" about a character's dilemma, often accomplished through the inner thoughts or inner conversation a character has with him- or herself.

Distance 79, 181
Often referred to as "narrative distance," this describes the degree of objectivity or subjectivity of a narrator. A third person narrator who remains **objective**, would be considered at a further distance from a character than a third person narrator who is **subjective**. Distance can also be applied to the amount of time between the narration and the **action** in the narrative. An elderly first person narrator telling a story about his or her youth is at a greater distance than a teenage narrator telling a story about yesterday.

Donnée 27-29
See **Premise**

Doppelganger 106
A double of a main character. Often a paranormal or ghostly double.

Dramatic Irony 167-169
A device in which the reader knows something that the character does not.

Dynamic 225-226
The movement or changes that occur in language, scene, or character. When applied to language, dynamic refers to the variety of vocabulary, sentence length, and sentence structure. When applied to a scene, dynamic refers to changes in action or the changes in dialogue between characters. When applied to characters, dynamic often means the character is "round," or shows a range of actions and reactions.

Epiphany 105, 184-185
A realization a character makes, motivated by previous events in the narrative.

Exposition 92, 303
Explanation of an idea or an event offered by the narrator out of scene. Often writers call instances of exposition **"telling,"** where the narrator tells

the reader what happens as opposed to **showing** the reader what happens in scene.

Figurative Language 90-92
Words or expressions used in a nonliteral way. Often called **trope**.

First Person Point of View 31-34
A **narrative mode** in which the narrator refers to him- or herself in the story using "I."
Note: First Person Plural would use "we."

Flat 225-226
A two-dimensional character who fails to change in the narrative.

Foil 105-107
A character who contrasts or "reflects" another character for the effect of shedding light on that character's personality or situation.

Foreshadowing 56-57
An implicit indication or implication of things to come.

Gnomon 47-48
An element of the narrative that the writer intentionally conceals or keeps in shadow.

Hyperbole
Exaggeration.

Idea 29-31
The abstract and often implicit concept that informs and drives the narrative.

Idiom 107
An expression that is particular to a certain group, and part of that group's vernacular—often an expression that cannot be understood with language alone.

Image 67-68
A visual representation a writer creates for readers, usually with descriptive language.

Imagery 67-68
A recurring visual representation, and often one that has symbolic meaning in the narrative.

Increasing Action 155-156
An increase in the activity in a moment or series of moments, often building to conflict, crisis, and climax.

Increasing Conflict 155-156
An increase in the antagonistic or oppositional forces a character faces, often building to crisis and climax.

Increasing Tension 155-156
An increase in the activity between conflicting elements in a narrative, often building to crisis and climax.

Individual
See **type**

Irony 77-78, 167-169
Expressing something different from the obvious or literal interpretation.

Jargon 183-184
Terminology or language that is specific to a particular group or profession.

Limited Third Person Point of View 78
See **Close Third Person Point of View**

Metafiction 181-182
A self-conscious device in which the author exposes the fictional artifice in order to comment on the fiction itself.

Metaphor 90-92
A **trope** in which a word or phrase represents something other than its intended meaning for the purpose of making a comparison without indicating that a comparison is being made.

Motif 119-120, **140-141**
A recurring element that holds symbolic significance in the story.

Narrative
A narrated account. See also **plot**.

Narrative Mode 117
The mode or set of craft methods the writer employs as a means to communicate a plot to a reader. Most often used in reference to **point of view**.

Narrative Structure 52-56
The framework or "architecture" of a plot on which all characters and events are placed. Typical narrative structure starts with setup, rises to conflict, and falls to resolution.

Narrative Time 311
The sequence of events as they occur in the narrative. We would describe the narrative time of a photograph as frozen. We would describe the narrative time of a story as something often in flux—slowed down with copious descriptions or sped up with summary, for example. Narrative time refers both to the "speed" of singular moments, and the sequence by which moments are strung together.

Narrator
The person who tells the story to the reader.

Objective Correlative 205-207
A type of symbol in which an object represents or incites an emotion.

Objective Point of View 78-80
A narrator who describes the events, but does not have access to any character's inner thoughts.

Omniscient Point of View 117-118
A third person narrator who has complete knowledge of all the events that happen in the story and the inner thoughts and actions of all the characters, and can navigate freely between characters, time, and space.

Pace (Pacing)
The speed at which a moment or a sequence of moments occur in a narrative.

Parody 249-251
An imitation of another work of art.

Pathos 168-169
Feelings of pity and/or sympathy. The term is often used in reference to a character or moment in the narrative that provokes those feelings in the reader.

Peripeteia 184-185
A reversal or a shift in the world of the narrative that causes or parallels a character's realization or epiphany.

Personification 68
The act of assigning inanimate objects with human characteristics.

Plot 50-52
The causal sequence of events that an author chooses to include on the page in the order he or she chooses to place them.

Point of View 31-34
In the broadest sense, point of view in fiction describes two things: Who tells the story (narrator) and the perspective from which the narrator tells the story (time).

Point of View Inflection 78-80
An instance in which the character's voice invades the third person narrator's voice.

Premise (or *Donnée*) 27-29
The proposition or "contract" the writer establishes in a narrative, usually in the setup.

Protagonist 49-50
The main character.

Pun 48-49
A play on words.

Reference 207-208
See **Allusion**

Resolution 52-56
In typical narrative structure, the effect of the conflict on the plot.

Rhetorical Motif 119-120
A recurring word or phrase that holds some symbolic meaning in the narrative.

Round 225-226
A character who changes in a story and shows a range of actions and reactions to events and characters.

Satire 222-224
An instance of an author who holds characters or events up for ridicule, usually for the purpose of social criticism and/or humor.

Second Person Point of View 31-34
A **narrative mode** in which the narrator uses the pronoun "you" to refer to the **protagonist**.

Sentimentality 251
The exaggeration of emotions in a narrative without indicative or logical motivations for those emotions.

Setting 137, 157-158
The place where the narrative occurs.

Setup 52-56
The first part in typical narrative structure in which the characters, setting, and premise are established.

Show (Showing) 92-93, 299-310
An instance in which an author chooses to put a narrative event "in scene," as opposed to **telling** the reader what happened.

Simile 90
A trope in which a word or phrase represents something other than its intended meaning for the purpose of making a comparison, indicated with the words "like" or "as."

Situational Irony
A device in which the end result(s) differs greatly from the expected result(s).

Static 225-226
A scene, or sometimes a character, that has little to no movement or activity. In terms of dialogue, static indicates speech that fails to increase our knowledge, understanding, or sense of tension about a character or characters.

Story 50-52
The sequence of consequential events an author works with when constructing a plot. The things that happened when they happened and in the order they happened.

Structure 52-56
See **Narrative Structure**

Style
A broad term used to describe the ways in which an author expresses him- or herself through a narrator.

Subjective Point of View 78-80
A narrator who accesses one or more characters' inner thoughts.

Suspension of Disbelief 182
The reader's ability to suspend his or her judgment or knowledge about the artifice of the story and temporarily "believe it" as though it were true.

Symbol 34-35
Something, like an object, that represents something else, like an idea.

Symbolic Architecture 35
The larger, figurative and representational design an author establishes to connect his or her tropes and symbols to an idea.

Tell (Telling) 92-93, 299-310
An instance in which an author chooses to summarize or narrate an event as opposed to putting it "in scene" or **showing** it.

Tension 155-156
A dynamic state of suspense and/or fear created by the activity between conflicting elements in a narrative.

Theme 27-28
A vague, blanket term often used to mean anything from the **premise**, an **idea, imagery, symbolism,** or the narrative's message.

Third Person Point of View 31-34
A **narrative mode** in which the narrator uses the pronouns "he" or "she" to refer to characters.

Tone 167-169
The "sound," color, and feeling expressed by the language and pace of a narrative.

Trope 90-92
Figurative word or expressions used in a symbolic or nonliteral way.

Type 156-157
A character whose personality traits are largely similar to characteristics observable in a group or cultural milieu. The term is often used in opposition to "individual."

Understatement 251-252
An instance where information is implied but not explicitly stated.

Verbal Irony 77-78, 252
An instance in which what a character or narrator says is drastically different or opposite from what he or she means.

Verisimilitude 182-184
The quality of appearing plausible and believable. Narrative persuasiveness.

Acknowledgements

I actually went to school for this—this *writing* thing. In school I learned all about the craft of fiction from writer/teachers who made it their mission to make young, big-headed writers like me as good as we thought we were. Lysley Tenorio taught me how to read others' work. Rosemary Graham taught me how to read my own work. Ann Cummins taught me how to see what was working. Julie Orringer taught me how to see and re-craft what wasn't. Barry Horwitz taught me how to teach. And Chris Sindt gave me a chance that changed my life. Thank you.

But it was my mother and the illustrator of this book, Dede Leither, who first taught me how to see. Not just the surface. Beyond it.

My biggest thanks goes out to Rosa del Duca, whose feedback was instrumental—who *is* instrumental.

-Nicholas Leither

www.ingramcontent.com/pod-product-compliance
Lightning Source LLC
Chambersburg PA
CBHW070622160426
43194CB00009B/1345